THE YEAR
AMERICA DISCOVERED TEXAS

CENTENNIAL
'36

Number Twenty-three:
THE CENTENNIAL SERIES
of the Association of Former Students,
Texas A&M University

The Year
America Discovered Texas
CENTENNIAL
'36

Kenneth B. Ragsdale

FOREWORD BY STANLEY MARCUS

TEXAS A&M UNIVERSITY PRESS
College Station

Library of Congress Cataloging-in-Publication Data

Ragsdale, Kenneth Baxter, 1917–
    The year America discovered Texas.

    (The Centennial series of the Association of Former
Students, Texas A&M ; no. 23)
    Bibliography: p.
    1. Texas — Centennial celebrations, etc.   2. Texas
Centennial (1936 : Dallas, Tex.)   I. Title.   II. Series.
F391.R14   1987   976.4'062   86-30041
ISBN 0-89096-299-5

FOR
KEITH AND JEFFREY
whom I missed while traveling

I have frequently said that modern Texas history started with the celebration of the Texas Centennial, because it was in 1936 . . . that the rest of America discovered Texas.

— STANLEY MARCUS

CONTENTS

LIST OF ILLUSTRATIONS

FOREWORD

When I visited the ninety-year-old Bernard Berenson at his Florentine villa "I Tatti" in the late fifties, he greeted me with a question: "You're from Texas, I understand? It's been so long since I have been to America, I'm a bit confused. As I recall, Texas is located somewhere between Chicago and the Pacific Ocean. Is that correct?" I assured him that he wasn't far off.

Much the same state of ignorance characterized most Americans in the second decade of this century. I remember only too well that when I went east to college in 1921, my classmates had only the most vague idea where Texas was located and what life was like on the frontier. If they didn't know much about Texas, they knew even less about Dallas. They were extremely disappointed when I told them my family was transported by automobile and not horses, that I had never been on a ranch and had never seen a genuine cowboy or an Indian.

My business career with Neiman-Marcus began in 1926, in time to get a little experience before the stock market break of 1929 and the subsequent Great Depression. The customer base of the business was essentially located in Texas and the neighboring states, with only an occasional stray Yankee. In an effort to broaden the business, I persuaded my father to permit me to place advertisements in national fashion magazines like *Vogue* and *Harper's Bazaar* on the theory that sooner or later people from the East Coast and Midwest would be passing through Dallas and could become customers if only they knew about us. The idea did lure a few stray winter vacationers on their way to Phoenix or Mexico (like Tom Watson of I.B.M.), but the greatest result of the advertising was the pride that local customers felt when they saw their hometown store's messages in a national magazine.

Consequently, when I first heard the discussions about the possibility of a centennial celebration in Dallas, I was delighted with the prospect of an attraction that would reinforce my business strategy. When the decision to locate the major event in Dallas was finally confirmed, I was able to justify an enlarged national advertising budget for 1935 and 1936.

Neiman-Marcus not only participated in the original underwriting, but, along with other local business enterprises, it coughed up at every weekly meeting in the spring and summer months when Bob Thornton issued a call for additional funds to open the Fair and to keep it running. Thornton realized very quickly that he had to have executives at these meetings who had the ability to commit their companies on the spot. "Don't send any vice-presidents; send me *yes* men." So successful were these early morning money-raising sessions that they were the genesis of what later developed as the Dallas Citizens Council.

For the opening of the Centennial Fair, we decided to produce a fashion-show extravaganza of such scope that it would attract fashion-conscious customers from all over Texas and the rest of the country as well. To that end we developed original merchandise based on native Southwestern Indian designs and colors inspired by the indigenous colors of Texas products, such as cactus, grapefruit, and oil. These fashions were reported in the June issue of *Vogue* magazine in full color, with appropriate editorials about the store and the Centennial celebration.

As an honored guest for the occasion, we invited the dean of American fashion authorities, Edna Woolman Chase, editor of *Vogue*, who was encouraged by her boss, Conde Nast, the magazine's publisher, to make this historic trip, her first west of the Hudson River. She was reluctant to travel alone and consented on the condition that I accompany her as a protector against any marauding Indians. Along with us were editorial assistants, photographers, and a number of New York socialites.

They and other "foreign" visitors were amazed by our presentation, by the homes of the Dallasites who entertained them, by the Centennial show, despite the heat which almost overwhelmed them. They marvelled at home air-conditioning, with which many of them were previously unfamiliar.

They came, they looked, they liked it. They returned to New York and Chicago and New Jersey with a clear understanding where Texas was located and what it was all about. They've been sending their friends back ever since. It was fun to be present at a turning point in history.

July 28, 1986   STANLEY MARCUS
Santa Fe, New Mexico

PREFACE

lthough Sam Houston's official report stated it lasted only eigh- teen minutes, historians describe the Battle of San Jacinto as one of the decisive battles of the world. It legitimized the con- cept of a Texas republic and set in motion a complex of forces that led to the annexation of almost one-third of the present area of the American nation. Such is the stuff from which great myths grow. By the time the sun set on the afternoon of April 21, 1836, it was inevitable that this event would be properly celebrated with one heck-of-a-big party. The one most Texans attended, however, came a century later, during the 1936 Texas Centennial celebrations. Just as the Battle of San Jacinto produced its residual shock waves, so did the centennial.

Various proposals for a statewide centennial celebration were ad- vanced early in the twentieth century but failed to gain widespread support. The idea lay dormant until November 6, 1923. On that date the keynote speaker addressing a district meeting of the Associated Advertising Clubs of America in Corsicana, Texas, proposed holding a centennial exposition primarily to introduce Texas' unrecognized economic resources to the nation. Theodore H. Price, a New York publisher and economist, believed an advertising campaign based on the state's "gloriously romantic history . . . [would] attract the atten- tion and presence of the world." He envisioned a new wave of outside investment capital to expand the state's economic base. Media repre- sentatives, joined by the state's business leaders, grasped the idea and single-handedly launched the centennial movement based on a dual theme, patriotism and commercialism. For the next thirteen years this credo remained intact. Texas celebrated its centennial and at the same time developed a nationwide campaign to merchandise the state. A half-century later, the nation is still buying.

The story of the Texas centennial is a study in bad timing. By the time the movement's leaders began soliciting legislative support, the state and the nation were locked in the throes of the Great Depression. And in addition to the economic strictures, the state constitution forbade the use of state funds for fairs and expositions. Despite a well-organized opposition, the constitution was subsequently amended, but that opposition remained intact throughout the ensuing legislative process. Their arguments were valid; feeding the hungry and destitute was more important than holding a birthday party. By 1934, however, the support for a major celebration had grown too strong to be denied. In September the Texas Centennial Commission selected Dallas over Houston and San Antonio to host the central exposition, and shortly thereafter the state legislature and the federal government each appropriated $3 million as their participation in the celebration.

When the legislature passed the appropriation bill on April 23, 1935, less than fourteen months remained before the central exposition was scheduled to open. Yet the seemingly impossible was accomplished. In September, 1935, Dallas embarked on one of the largest peacetime construction programs in the state's history. In approximately ten months a 185-acre site, encompassing the State Fair of Texas complex, was transformed into a $25 million world's fair. This was a tremendous economic boon to the host city. By mid-February, $20 million was being spent on construction, including $15 million at the exposition site. The fair opened on schedule. By June 6, 1936, Texas was attracting "the attention and the presence of the world."

The state legislature enacted into law the celebration's dual theme, patriotism and commercialism. The Advisory Board of Texas Historians outlined a statewide program for permanent memorials, markers, museums, and restorations, while the Advisory Board for Advertising developed a $500,000 publicity and advertising campaign (one-sixth of the total state appropriation) to promote Texas' century of progress and to lure visitors (and investors) to the state. Both programs were eminently successful.

Throughout the thirteen-year period from 1923 to 1936, public information became the dominant force in the centennial movement. Through news releases, historical publications, writing contests, a Texas history study week, an organized pledge to "think, talk, and write . . . the Texas Centennial in 1936," pageants, and lectures, the state received a thoroughly concentrated historical brainwashing. Statewide, the centennial celebration evolved as a truly grassroots movement. Each of the 254 counties organized a Texas Centennial Committee to develop local centennial observances in addition to those mandated by the legislature. Excepting national tragedies, probably no event in the state's history touched the lives of so many people, both children and adults, as did the Texas centennial celebrations. Ethnocentrism reached high tide in 1936.

The national advertising campaign was equally effective. More than 60 percent of the state's $500,000 advertising budget, plus the resources of the Central Exposition Corporation and the Fort Worth Frontier Centennial Exposition, were invested to promote out-of-state travel to Texas. This well-planned, well-coordinated, and professionally executed state publicity program stands today without parallel. The investment paid huge dividends: 6,354,385 people paid admission to the Central Exposition in Dallas, and 986,125 visited the Fort Worth exposition. Many of these were from out-of-state; they discovered Texas as a modern reality and not the never-never-land of myth.

In retrospect, 1936 marked a historical milestone in the Texas experience. The discovery syndrome, however, remains paramount in any historical evaluation of the centennial era. As one astute observer of the Texas scene for some six decades explained: "Modern Texas history started with the celebration of the Texas Centennial, because it was in 1936 . . . that *the rest of America discovered Texas.*" But of even greater importance, Texans were also participants in the discovery process. Thus, the residual shockwaves of 1936 endure a half-century later.

Any author whose research activities span a nine-year period creates a large personal indebtedness to those who aided in the endeavor. To employ all the data collected and recognize everyone who patiently responded to my calls for help would require several additional volumes, which this publisher maintains are out of the question. So in order to do justice to some and injustice to others, I will abide by the publisher's admonition and keep this tribute to a minimum.

First, I must confess my enduring literary love affair with librarians and archivists, figuratively speaking, of course. How can I place one before the other? So geographically we proceed, south to north. Sharon Crutchfield and the Daughters of the Republic of Texas Library staff were professionally efficient in organizing the centennial files for my perusal. During the months spent at the Texas State Archives (Mike Green is a great coffee companion) and at the Barker

Texas History Center (where parking is no problem), both staffs honored me with "part-time employee" status. Their help was always beneficial and the friendships endure. And a special word of thanks for Bonnie Grobar, at the Texas State Library, who could always locate those obscure volumes through interlibrary loan. Staff personnel at the Fort Worth *Star-Telegram* library, Amon G. Carter Archives, University of Texas at Arlington special collections library, and the Dallas Public Library also aided me enormously in this research. Linda Sellers, librarian for public services at Southern Methodist University, was extremely helpful to me.

Much of the data collected from some eighty interviews would have remained temporarily unusable without the cooperation of the Baylor University Program for Oral History. Through the consideration of Tom Charlton, Rebecca Sharpless Jimenez, and Kent Keeth, and a grant from Mr. and Mrs. Von E. McReynolds, these oral recollections were transcribed well in advance of the writing phase of the project. For that I am deeply grateful. John Crain, my longtime friend and colleague, and his staff at the Dallas Historical Society aided me in this undertaking from the outset. And a special word of thanks is due John's former business manager, Jan Upton, who through persistence and diplomacy was able to organize a highly productive interview schedule in the Dallas area. Jan served the project well.

And following Jan's schedule, I discovered that historical research can be as filling, entertaining, and mildly intoxicating as it can be informative. Food was ever abundant. I recall a delightful breakfast with Donald Nelson at the Dallas Athletic Club, hotcakes and jalapeño peppers with Dale Miller at Austin's Villa Capri, and shrimp gumbo with Dick West at a noisy Greenville Avenue restaurant (Dick's is the only taped interview with a country-and-western music background). Breakfast was a prerequisite for L. B. Houston's interview, and when the discussions ran longer than anticipated, he also served lunch. Internationally known folksinger Belen Ortega prepared dinner for us (she rejected my offer to go out) and after the interview serenaded me with Spanish folk songs. Sculptor José Martin placed a bottle of vintage French wine between us as he described his centennial work, while orchestra leader Ligon Smith favored the more domestic Bloody Marys. And there was a country club luncheon with Wayne Gallagher, executive vice-president and general manager of the State Fair of Texas, who supported and encouraged the project

from the outset. Interviews with four ex–Casa Mañana showgirls —
Dorothy Litrel, Evelyn Barkow, Janice Holmes, and Virginia Martinez
— evolved in a gala party atmosphere.

There were those who extended special favors. Joe Frantz, Jerry
Bywaters, Blake Alexander, and David Horton each made helpful and
informed suggestions, while Bill Jary's continuous stream of centennial memorabilia was deeply appreciated. And Barry Bishop's careful reading of the manuscript and entertaining marginalia were both
a help and a pleasure. A special note of thanks is reserved for Mrs.
O. K. Stephenson, who typed both this manuscript and *Wings Over
the Mexican Border*. Mrs. Stephenson is O.K. So is the effervescent
Vicki Bell, who always found time among her many other duties to
transcribe my dictation tapes, always accurately and always on time.
You all helped make it enjoyable.

A special word of recognition is reserved for that creative, imagi-
native, and inspiring history teacher, Gail Riley, who originally suggested that I embark on this project. Neither Gail nor I could foresee
the obstacles, the opportunities, and the personal rewards this undertaking has yielded. To the above, and to all of the other thoughtful
and generous people listed in the bibliography, you made researching the Texas Centennial a great personal adventure. Thanks for the
memories.

My last and most heartfelt words of appreciation are reserved for
my wife, Janet, who makes writing possible and living a pleasure.

THE YEAR
AMERICA DISCOVERED TEXAS
CENTENNIAL
'36

1

GENESIS:
A CONVENTION AT CORSICANA

The weather had been nice all week, typical Indian summer with bright cloudless days and cool brisk nights. Those who staffed the *Corsicana Daily Sun* saw this as a good omen; big things were in the offing. Come Monday, November 5, 1923, that small-town daily newspaper, in conjunction with the Texas Press Association, would host the Tenth District Convention of the Associated Advertising Clubs of America.

The community recognized the importance of the occasion and moved to fulfill its role as convention host. When guests began arriving on Sunday, a welcoming committee met them at the Corsicana railroad station, escorted them to the Elks Club for registration, and took them on to the Corsicana Country Club for an afternoon golf tournament. More than a half-century later Ethel Wortham, wife of the *Daily Sun* editor, remembered the excitement of the preparations. She had purchased a new taupe-colored suit with hat, fur, and shoes to match from the J. M. Dyer Dry Goods Company especially for the occasion. And she still recalled her anticipation as she entered the Elks Club auditorium that November morning to hear Theodore H. Price of New York City address the convention. She sensed something important was about to happen. Indeed it was.

Price was an appropriate choice to address the meeting of newspaper and advertising executives. He was an international authority on industrial and financial matters, whose exploits as the head of the cotton brokerage firm, Price, McCormick and Company, had earned him the title "Cotton King." In 1910, however, he turned from cotton brokerage to become editor and publisher of the business weekly *Commerce and Finance,* in which capacity he appeared at the Corsicana conference.

While not a Texan by birth, he was one in spirit. He visited the state frequently and possessed an enormous knowledge of the state's history and an optimistic view of its unrealized economic potential.[1] In his prepared address, "What Texas Has to Advertise and How to Advertise It," Price encouraged his audience to explore new fields of industrial and agricultural endeavor and through advertising, to attract millions of visitors and billions of dollars to a state noticeably lacking in national prestige.

This, however, marked Price's point of departure. "But you have something else," he challenged, "whose value and whose appeal I doubt whether you yourselves appreciate. It is your gloriously romantic history."[2] Price saw in the state's history an advertising campaign theme sufficiently strong to turn the nation's attention toward Texas. He suggested celebrating "a centenary so important and so auspicious by an exposition that will attract the attention and presence of the world." The mere thought of such an undertaking "inflames my imagination as I hope it may yours." He concluded that in magnitude a Texas exposition "could and should be made to exceed anything else of the kind ever attempted and I am sure you will agree with me as to its transcendent value as an advertisement."[3]

In an extemporaneous addendum to his prepared speech, Price allowed his imagination to expand further on the centennial theme. He proposed building an exposition city somewhere out on the broad prairies of Texas "to utilize 100,000 or 200,000 acres of land—a city not now in existence, that could be adapted to the uses of an agricultural exposition of proportions never before attempted, where the world might come and see Texas in miniature living and working 365 days in the year and watch the panorama of Texas agriculture from the first green shoots of borning spring to the stubble after the harvest."[4]

If the thought of a centennial inflamed Price's imagination, his message also found a sympathetic audience in the some four hundred members of the advertising and newspaper fraternity assembled at Corsicana. Among them was Harry Benge Crozier, who reported

[1] The day prior to his Corsicana address, Price spoke to the Dallas Chamber of Commerce, predicting that "Texas is destined to be the textile milling center of the United States." *Dallas Morning News*, November 5, 1923.

[2] Theodore H. Price, "What Texas Has to Advertise and How to Advertise It," *Commerce and Finance*, November 14, 1923, p. 2107.

[3] Ibid., p. 2109. The exposition date Price suggested was 1924, the hundredth anniversary of the first issuance of land titles to Anglo settlers in Mexican Texas. Members of the Texas Press Association chose instead the 1936 centennial date.

[4] *Dallas Morning News*, November 7, 1923.

the event for the *Dallas Morning News.* "Six million Texans used to thinking in superlative and acting accordingly," he wrote, "were invited to heroic superlatives Tuesday [when Price] . . . sketched in words of romantic quality . . . a vision of a Texas centennial exposition gigantic in its proportions."[5]

Had Price been addressing an assemblage of less articulate individuals, this state's centennial history probably would have developed along vastly different lines. But such was not the case. His listeners were the perpetuators of the Texas myth of bigness and magnitude, and a less pretentious proposal might have failed to rally their creative imaginations. In addition, the timing was right; the delegates had previously expressed interest in identifying some agency to promote the interests of the state for future growth. Price's message clearly found its mark. At that very moment on a November morning in Corsicana the Texas centennial movement was conceived.[6] Before the convention adjourned on November 7, the delegates decided by unanimous vote that "Texas should hold a great celebration at the close of the century in order that the state might properly honor the heroes of the past and simultaneously advertise the wonders of the Texas of the present and the future."[7]

To launch the program, the advertising club members, aided by the Texas Press Association, formed the Texas Centennial Survey Committee to sample the statewide sentiment for such an undertaking. Lowry Martin, advertising manager of the *Corsicana Daily Sun* who made the motion for the program's adoption, was selected to chair the eight-man committee of newspaper and advertising executives. According to Ethel Wortham, the "live-wire advertising man that Lowry Martin was, he took the ball and ran with it, promoting the idea all over Texas."[8]

[5]Ibid.

[6]There were earlier suggestions for a commemorative celebration. The San Jacinto veterans meeting in Dallas on August 21, 1886, made some reference to an appropriate celebration, and Gov. James Stephen Hogg also referred to the forthcoming event in a 1903 public address. Some local centennial clubs were formed prior to the entry of the United States into World War I, but the movement failed to gain momentum.

[7]Lowry Martin, "First Authentic Memoirs of Texas Centennial Celebration History," *Texas Press Messenger* 12 (January, 1937): 24–29. In this article Martin described a proposed five-unit history of the centennial to be compiled and published by the Educational Bureau of the Texas Press Association. No record of that publication has been found.

[8]Mrs. Ethel Wortham, Corsicana, Texas, to Kenneth B. Ragsdale, March 16, 1980, in possession of author.

From the *Daily Sun* office in Corsicana, Martin mailed out 10,000 questionnaires to all areas of the state, soliciting public sentiment on the centennial matter. More than 6,000 were returned; the responses were overwhelmingly positive. Fearing the movement might lose its momentum, Martin moved quickly to crystallize this surge of public interest. He called for a meeting of his committee in Austin on January 8, 1924. When Martin arrived at the Driskill Hotel that morning, he carried a large suitcase (one source reported "two large grips") filled with the returned questionnaires, telegrams, and letters of encouragement. Anticipating the need for an organizational structure to produce a major exposition, Martin presented the committee with a two-volume report covering the organization, financing, and administration of the 1904 Louisiana Purchase Exposition held in Saint Louis, Missouri. Thereupon the committee revamped its organization, added eighteen new members to the original eight, and elected Cato Sells of Fort Worth as temporary chairman, Lowry Martin as temporary secretary, and journalist Harry Benge Crozier as chairman of the publicity committee. To ensure the continuation of the committee's work, J. K. Hughes of Mexia offered a motion that those present pledge a total of $2,000 for interim funding. The motion carried, and Oscar Holcombe of Houston was elected treasurer.[9]

Before the morning adjournment, Sells made an appointment to see Gov. Pat M. Neff that afternoon and solicit his endorsement of the centennial movement. Neff agreed to support the movement and asked the committee to draft a resolution which he would sign and release to the public. The proclamation, drafted by Harry Benge Crozier, was a masterpiece of emotional and patriotic fervor, which the future president of Baylor University could cherish as his very own. The focus was on the "pioneer fathers of Texas," who "with their blood [had] traced on the glorious canopy of the new republic, the pattern of a great empire." And to commemorate the heroic deeds of those "who laid the corner stone of the Texas Empire," Crozier—or rather the governor—called for "great centennial feats of art, history and industry, not only to show Texas to Texans, but invite the world to

---

[9]Minutes of a Called Meeting, Texas Centennial Survey Committee, January 8, 1924, in the Jesse Holman Jones Papers, Barker Texas History Center, University of Texas at Austin, cited hereafter as Minutes, Jones Papers. Cato Sells had served as Woodrow Wilson's Indian commissioner.

be our guests, that people everywhere may know that Texas is as great in achievement as in area." In conclusion the governor invited "a great assembly of loyal Texans" to meet in Austin on February 12, 1924, "to determine what action may be best to insure the fullest measure of success of this great undertaking."[10]

Governor Neff's endorsement gave the centennial movement the stamp of officialdom and ensured its continued momentum. Sells, Martin, and Crozier, however, were careful not to allow the enthusiasm to wane. Through the cooperation of the Texas Press Association, practically every newspaper and magazine in Texas reproduced the governor's proclamation with editorial support for full attendance at the forthcoming centennial convention. In addition, with Crozier manning the typewriter (he was the committee's only paid staff member), direct mail appeals, accompanied by copies of the governor's proclamation, were sent to civic, business, and professional organizations throughout the state. Again the committee's efforts — and especially the governor's proclamation — yielded positive results. By ten o'clock on the morning of February 12, 1924, more than two thousand patriotic citizens jammed the senate chamber to demonstrate their support for the proposed celebration.

The cavernous chamber resounded with the spoken word. This was an age of eloquence, when oratory was limited largely by the speaker's endurance; the relative importance of his message bore slight resemblance to the amount of time he — or she — consumed. And while the day became punctuated with seemingly interminable addresses, there were some major achievements; the February meeting remains an important milestone in Texas centennial history.

Although the patriotic impulse lured the delegates to the Austin convention, it was the boosterism drive to promote the state's assets that gave the movement an ongoing countertheme. This duality of purpose, sincere in its multiple objectives, continued to dominate the Austin meeting. Collins Thompson, former executive secretary of the Saint Louis World's Fair Board, appeared as the convention's keynote speaker. He urged the committee to establish a solid organizational structure upon which to develop an exposition. From this business-like approach Thompson envisioned a "centennial celebration on a

[10]Governor's Proclamation, Jones Papers.

huge scale sufficient to attract the entire world to our gates." In addition, he believed the timing was right; twenty years had elapsed since an exposition of world magnitude had been held in mid-America.[11]

Clara Driscoll Sevier of Austin and B. J. Woodward of San Antonio both responded to Thompson's address, encouraging the convention to move forward with plans for the celebration. A resolution followed, declaring that "there shall be held somewhere within the State of Texas, at a date as early as may be consistent with the magnitude of the task, a Texas Centennial Exposition, bold enough to please the still hearts of Austin, Travis, and Houston, and big enough to mirror the accomplishments of Texas to all the sons and daughters of earth, to all of which we pledge our support."[12]

The resolution called for the creation of a board of directors with powers sufficient to fulfill the objectives of the convention, including the selection of a time and place for the centennial celebration and the definition of its scope and character. They would ultimately settle on 1936, the hundredth anniversary of Texas' independence from Mexico, as the proper date to celebrate. The focus of the celebration, however, was not so easily determined. From the ensuing debate, patriotism and commercialism would emerge as the dual themes of the celebration. Within the context of the times, each seemed compatible with the purpose of the undertaking.

Following the adoption of the resolution, Oscar Holcombe, chairman of the finance committee, stated it was necessary to raise $7,500 to fund the activities. A thousand dollars was needed immediately to defray obligations created prior to the Austin meeting. Subscriptions were made from the floor and the fund was quickly subscribed. Following adjournment, the executive committee instructed Cato Sells and Lowry Martin to open a Texas centennial headquarters office in Dallas and begin immediately to perfect the agency's governing board.

Establishing an administrative structure for orderly development of the centennial concept was the convention's major achievement. Although unwieldly in size and complex in its formation, it nevertheless fulfilled the founders' democratic expectations of sectional representation. The resolution called for one hundred directors, with two district directors to be elected from each of the thirty-one sena-

[11]Minutes, Jones Papers.
[12]Resolution, Jones Papers.

torial districts and twenty-nine directors-at-large selected by the elected directors. In addition, the governor would appoint five directors-at-large, and the lieutenant governor and the speaker of the House of Representatives would appoint two each. Each of the directors possessed equal rights and rank. Combined, they would form the Centennial Governing Board of One Hundred which would keep alive the idea of a Texas centennial for more than a decade.[13] On April 12, 1924, county elections were held throughout the state, and one week later two directors were chosen in district elections to represent that senatorial district on the Centennial Governing Board.

The sixty-two elected district directors, together with the nine directors appointed by the governor, lieutenant governor, and speaker of the House of Representatives, met in Austin on May 21, 1924, to appoint the remaining twenty-nine directors-at-large. Cato Sells presided at the meeting and submitted the following five-point program, which the board approved: (1) launch a publicity campaign, (2) select a name for the centennial celebration, (3) conduct an industrial survey of Texas, (4) launch an educational campaign to "Texanize Texans," and (5) "teach the youth the significance of the historical value of Texas and her industrial worth."[14]

Sells obviously was attempting to chart a well-planned course for the new governing board to follow. And while he recognized the multiple problems facing that body, he obviously was overly optimistic about what the enlarged board could yield. Time was against him; the target date remained more than a decade in the future, and with that time-lag enthusiasm was destined to wane. And in 1924, who could foresee the destructive impact of 1929, still a half-decade in the future? Sells, however, continued to look to the future, ever holding before the board a vision of a great patriotic celebration that would produce equally rewarding economic spin-offs for the state.

The Centennial Governing Board of One Hundred held its first full meeting in Austin on January 19, 1925. Secretary Lowry Martin

---

[13]The district board members were selected as follows: each county could nominate one delegate per each 10,000 population. Local business, civic, labor, and farm organizations had one vote each in selecting the delegates. The county nominees then met at a designated point within the senatorial district for the final election of two board members to represent that district.

[14]Minutes of the Meeting of the Seventy-One Permanent Directors, April 19, 1924, Jones Papers.

opened the session by reading the membership roll, a prestigious list of the state's business, civic, and political leaders. The mandated election process had indeed elevated to the new board those who represented wealth, power, and business acumen, necessary ingredients to keep the movement alive until state and federal funding was forthcoming. Only six members of the board were female, and I. G. Fernandez of Brownsville was the board's only Hispanic member.

Other than two committee reports, this meeting was largely organizational, dealing with routine procedural matters. Will H. Mayes of Austin, one of Governor Neff's appointees, gave a report on the finance and plans and organization committees. He emphasized that while the board members were thoroughly in accord with the idea of a celebration, "the masses may not be prepared to give their endorsement to such an undertaking until they are better informed on the huge project." For this reason the plans committee recommended moving ahead with an educational program to "Texanize Texans." Mayes saw this program as a prelude to the board's ultimate request for state and federal funding for the celebration and predicted that when "the people become thoroughly aroused as to the purpose of the undertaking . . . no member of the legislature would dare pass an opposing vote to any kind of reasonable suggestion we might make for the success of the centennial."[15] Mayes's predictions were essentially correct; his projections about the ease and timing hit wide of their mark.

Scheduling the first meeting of the centennial governing board in Austin during the opening sessions of the Thirty-Ninth Legislature seemed more than a coincidence. Since the beginning of the centennial movement, legislative support was assumed, yet other than Governor Neff's proclamation, the matter had received no official recognition. This was destined to change. House Concurrent Resolution No. 11, introduced by C. E. Dinkle of Greenville and approved on February 2, 1925, recommended that "we give our endorsement to this Centennial Exposition movement as being a most worthy and beneficial undertaking to all Texas, and that we commend to all our

[15] Ibid. William Harding Mayes, who served as lieutenant governor of Texas in 1913 and 1914, founded the school of journalism at the University of Texas and served as its dean for twelve years. Mayes was a victim of Gov. James E. Ferguson's conflict with the university; he and seven other professors were dismissed by the board of regents, on the governor's orders, for personal reasons.

citizens, for their most earnest consideration, the proposed Texas Centennial."[16]

Thus, the soon-to-become magic words—Texas centennial—had at last been introduced into the legislative vocabulary, sans appropriation riders. (The term also appeared in Governor Neff's proclamation.) During the following decade these words would be articulated repeatedly within wide-ranging frames of reference, but ultimately its duality of purpose—patriotism and commercialism—would help fulfill Will H. Mayes's optimistic prediction.

The centennial leadership, understandably, remained ever cognizant of its heritage. Since the genesis of the movement sprang from the district convention of the Associated Advertising Clubs of America, that organization continued to monitor the governing board's activities with professional interest. Carl Hunt, the club's international manager based in New York City, sent the following telegram to the governing board on January 17, 1925: "Heartiest congratulations upon progress centennial celebration project. Texas has marvelous story to tell, both to her own people and to the world outside. No plan you make could be too big. We wish you every success."[17]

The early history of the Texas centennial is documented by meetings of various boards and organizations interested in the movement. While some yielded positive results, others were perfunctory gatherings seemingly held largely for the purpose of interminable oratory.[18] The second meeting of the new governing board, held in Dallas on April 30, 1925, appears to have had elements of both. At this meeting Chairman Cato Sells announced that, because of other interests, he could no longer serve as chairman and recommended that the board initiate an immediate search for his successor. Although Sells's leadership in the movement was sufficient to assure him a small niche in centennial history, he appears also to have attempted to erect an enduring verbal monument to his tenure as chairman. His farewell address, high Gothic in its verbal decorations and oral repetitions, seemed endless.

Sells finally turned to the business at hand. He recommended that the committee select a leader financially able to devote unlimited time

[16]*General Laws of the State of Texas, Thirty-Ninth Legislature, Regular Session*, p. 688.
[17]Minutes, Jones Papers (punctuation added).
[18]The resolution on the death of board member William Robert Jones of Brownsville, delivered at a board meeting, encompassed two-and-one-half pages, typed single spaced.

to the undertaking, one free of personal interests in when and where the celebration would be held, and most importantly, a man of national stature capable of making a "most forceful presentation to the Congress at Washington to secure the necessary many million dollar government appropriation" (Sells suggested $20 million). He also warned that the project could "require an amendment to the Texas Constitution preliminary to a considerable state appropriation."[19] Sells was indeed prophetic in his appraisal of the job that lay ahead. Before the meeting adjourned, the board selected Louis Lipsitz, a Dallas lumberman, to chair a search committee to receive suggestions for a director general. Lipsitz's group, in reality, became a chase committee; their objective was Jesse Holman Jones of Houston.

Jones's qualifications as financier, builder, publisher, and philanthropist fulfilled Sells's highest expectations; he was indeed a person of national stature. During World War I President Woodrow Wilson appointed Jones director general of the Department of Military Relief of the American Red Cross. In recognition of his philanthropic and humanitarian service, Southwestern University at Georgetown, Texas, and Southern Methodist University at Dallas conferred on him honorary Doctor of Laws degrees. The Democratic National Committee appointed Jones director of finance in 1924, and four years later he was largely responsible for securing the National Democratic Convention for Houston. His fellow Texans honored him at the convention with a favorite-son nomination for the presidency. In addition, Jones was recognized nationally in elite social and civic circles, holding memberships in some of the nation's most prestigious clubs. Jones's qualifications for the director generalship may have been his greatest weakness; he was a very busy man.

Jones rejected Lipsitz's initial entreaty, explaining that, because of prior commitments, he was "extremely reluctant" to accept the assignment. "Naturally I would not say 'No,'" he continued, "and this does not mean that I want to be unanimously invited: it does mean that I have not got the time and I doubt if I have the mental and physical endurance for so prolonged a thing." Jones concluded that there was "time for us all to think about the matter and talk about

[19]Minutes, Executive Meeting, Board of Directors, Texas Centennial Celebration, Dallas, Texas, April 30, 1935, Jones Papers.

it."[20] Lipsitz was not easily dissuaded. He persisted while Jones hedged, and after canceling several scheduled meetings, Jones finally met with Lipsitz and his committee on April 14, 1926, at the Rice Hotel in Houston. After a lengthy discussion, Jones accepted the assignment, ending the six-month search for a director general. There were, of course, conditions; it would be several months before he could get his affairs in shape to give the centennial movement the attention he felt it merited.

Jones had obviously viewed the tendered responsibility with ambivalence. Weighing his patriotic persuasion against his ongoing commitments was certainly a factor in his prolonged indecision. And while there may have been a touch of vanity in the protracted negotiations, his belief that he could contribute to the biggest civic enterprise ever launched in Texas was undoubtedly an overriding factor in his decision.

Jones's acceptance of the director generalship drew a flood of favorable correspondence. The state press also gave the event wide coverage. The *Austin American* headlined its report "Centennial on Big Scale Assured with Jesse Jones Its Head" and quoted board member Sam Sparks as saying: "The election of Jesse Jones . . . as director general of the Texas Centennial exposition is a long step forward, and an assurance of a vigorous, state-wide campaign leading up to a successful centennial."[21]

When Jones accepted the leadership role for the Texas centennial celebration, the movement had been gaining momentum for more than two years. No top executive ever entered a more favorable environment for success. He had inherited a dynamic executive committee, a dedicated governing board, and an enthusiastic body of state leaders eager to move forward with the project. They expected leadership and action. Unfortunately, they received little of either.

As the person most sought after as director general (lumberman John Kirby and attorney Will Hogg were also suggested), Jones found himself at a marked disadvantage. His identification with the movement, for example, had been limited by his prolonged absence from the state. Although he was a member-at-large elected by the governing board at the meeting in May, 1924, he had never attended a board

[20] Jones to Lipsitz, November 3, 1925, Jones Papers.
[21] *Austin American*, April 16, 1926.

meeting. In addition, his business and political responsibilities, combined with his unfamiliarity with the recent history of the movement, greatly restricted his effectiveness as director general.

Jones the businessman did understand the necessity of establishing a sound financial footing for the forthcoming celebration. A few days after accepting the position, he requested a legal opinion to determine if the state government, as well as the various city governments, possessed the power to render financial aid to a centennial exposition. He was advised that both were limited by terms of the Texas constitution; that condition could be altered, however, by an amendment.[22] Jones also considered visiting the Sesqui-Centennial International Exposition then in progress in Philadelphia, ostensibly to gather ideas for the Texas celebration. Although Mayor W. Freeland Kendrick offered him his fullest cooperation, Jones apparently never visited the exposition. On November 20 he wrote to one Charles M. Marsh in Philadelphia: "I was unexpectedly called home and do not expect to return East any time soon. We will probably make no active start at our Centennial for quite some time."[23]

From the outset as director, Jones established a performance pattern that would persist throughout his tenure — hesitancy and procrastination. This ran counter to the governing board's enthusiasm, especially that of dynamic Lowry Martin. In response to Martin's suggestion that he call a meeting of the board, Jones explained that while he had given much consideration to the matter, he was "of the opinion that we cannot at this time outline the form it [the centennial] should take. In fact, I have not developed ideas enough to think it advisable to put the members of the Governing Board to the trouble of having a meeting."[24] Martin, like his fellow board member Louis Lipsitz, did not accept Jones's rejection as final. The following day Martin protested that since the board had not met in a year, a meeting would tend "to keep the Governing Board interested so that when we do need them they will be in line with the movement." Seeing that little initiative was emanating from the new director general,

[22]On learning that the state constitution forbade the appropriation of state funds for official representation in the World's Columbian Exposition in Chicago in 1893, Gov. James Stephen Hogg encouraged the use of private funds for that purpose. Donations collected statewide financed the $300,000 Texas pavilion.

[23]Jones to Charles M. Marsh, November 20, 1926, Jones Papers.

[24]Jones to Martin, March 18, 1927, Jones Papers.

Martin further devised a method to open the lines of communication with the governing board. He suggested that Jones call a meeting of the board so that he, Jones, could "solicit suggestions for future plans in putting the Centennial over, and out of which would be created news for the many Texas citizens who are very much interested in the Centennial." There is no record of Jones's response, nor was the projected meeting ever held.[25]

On January 14, 1928, Martin wrote Jones congratulating him on his role in securing the Democratic National Convention for Houston. Martin also drew a parallel between the publicity the convention brought to the state and the comparable benefits a world exposition would yield. A prompt response was not forthcoming. On February 18, Jones dictated a five-sentence note to Martin, in which he agreed that he too recognized the parallel between the two events, "but in the meantime, I think we should do nothing about the Centennial this year. Let me know your views."[26] For the sake of recorded history, Martin kept his views to himself.

Jones finally broke his silence in a dinner address he delivered in Fort Worth on March 31, 1928. Ironically, his views were not directed to the centennial governing board, but to 265 members and guests of the Exchange Club honoring him as Fort Worth's greatest benefactor during 1927. (Jones's interests financed the Worth Hotel, Worth Theater, Medical Arts Building, and the Electric Building then under construction.) In outlining his plan for the coming celebration, he broke ranks with the movement's earlier leaders by deleting a world-class exposition from his proposal. "It seems to me the day of the world's fair is past," he explained. To him the "hoochy-koochy and Midway Plaisance" of former expositions were now passé, and even the more recent Philadelphia Sesqui-Centennial Exposition was "a comparative failure . . . and a great financial loss, notwithstanding much effort was put forth."[27] Jones also regarded Texas' enormity as the greatest deterrent to a single major exposition. He pointed out that "it is not possible to hold an exposition or centennial in Dallas County that the people of Harris County will take enough interest in, and that may be reversed and applied to any other section of the state."

[25] Jones to Martin, March 19, 1927, Jones Papers.
[26] Jones to Martin, February 18, 1928, Jones Papers.
[27] "The Texas Centennial," reprint of address delivered to Fort Worth Exchange Club, March 31, 1928, Jones Papers.

He believed that it would be impossible to enlist the support of all the people of Texas should a single activity be adopted.[28]

Turning from the exposition format, Jones viewed the state's history as the dominant factor in planning the coming celebration. He proposed transforming all of Texas into a great center of historical parks, shrines, pageants, and battle reenactments. He recommended specifically establishing permanent state parks at San Antonio and near Houston, where the tragedy of the Alamo and the victory at San Jacinto would be reenacted in great historical pageants.

Jones did not abandon the exposition concept entirely. He envisioned an expanded State Fair of Texas at Dallas during the celebration, and if Fort Worth was "willing to appropriate $10,000,000 for a great industrial, agricultural, and livestock park, a world's fair in itself . . . and the State of Texas and the congress of the United States matches dollars with you, you will have $30,000,000 for that part of our centennial." Jones added that his proposal was merely a suggestion that he wanted the people of Texas to consider for a least a year; after that he would call a statewide mass meeting to discuss the subject further. "I should like to add," he concluded, "that I am ready and anxious to pass the leadership of this movement to other hands at the very first opportunity."[29]

The address received front-page coverage in the *Fort Worth Star-Telegram* on Sunday, April 1, and the following day the *Dallas Morning News* carried Jones's complete centennial proposal. In spite of the wide interest generated by the address, no one came forward to accept Jones's offer of the directorship. He remained director general, and during the next three years plans for the Texas centennial celebration lay virtually dormant.

If Jones's inactivity annoyed some members of the governing board, he, no doubt, was equally vexed by the steady stream of job-seekers, promoters, politicians, and opportunists who flooded his Houston office with inquiries. These ran the gamut from fireworks salesmen to producers of historical pageants and motion pictures, all spurred on by the prospects of a world exposition. John A. Jackson, a Fort Worth realtor, proposed to Jones that the commission produce a motion picture depicting the history of Texas. He explained that since the proj-

[28] Ibid.
[29] Ibid.

ect "is too big for us . . . we are passing it on to you." Jackson believed that a motion picture of the "proper magnitude might take
the place of the Centennial."[30] Jones's response was typical in its brev-
ity: "I doubt if I will be able this year to give much time to the Centennial. . . . I want to . . . but other things are crowding in."[31] Betty
Blount Strong of Dallas, whose letterhead read, "Scenarist and Dramatic Plays," presented Jones with a more comprehensive project that
carried with it specific financial obligations. Mrs. Strong, in collabo-
ration with a "Mrs. Bringhurst, daughter of Sam Houston," had written
"The Birth of Texas," a motion picture script which she offered Jones
as "the official Scenario of the Centennial Exposition." For $600,000
the commission could acquire 51 percent of the capital stock in the
Texas Scenario Company.[32] These and other proposals were politely
rejected.

Politicians found it easier than dramatists and job-seekers to attract Jones's attention. His more comprehensive responses to their inquiries reflect his awareness of the political process and the inherent
sensitivities that frequently emerge from controversial issues. Jones
also knew that introducing funding legislation for an exposition, however patriotic, not to mention locating the celebration site in one area
of the state at the expense of another, did indeed contain the seeds
of controversy. State Representative Sam E. Bateman, chairman of
the Committee on Agriculture, wrote Jones on February 14, 1930, that
he planned to prepare a resolution endorsing his suggestions, urging
continuation of all the efforts to finance such an undertaking, and
pledging the state to do its part. Jones responded immediately. He
dictated a lengthy letter to Bateman on February 14, suggesting that
it might "be best to withhold your proposed resolution. . . . I feel
that at the proper time the legislature must discuss it in a very serious way because it cannot be financed except in a public way."[33]

In early 1930 Jones, probably more than most Texans, took daily
soundings of the nation's growing economic instability and foresaw
its negative impact on Texas. The changing economy undoubtedly
prompted him to dictate another letter to Bateman a few days later:
"It seems to me that it is advisable to keep the Centennial question

---

[30] Jackson to Jones, November 22 and 23, 1928, Jones Papers.

[31] Jones to Jackson, January 24, 1929, Jones Papers.

[32] Strong to Jones, June 6, 1928, Jones Papers.

[33] Jones to Bateman, February 14, 1930, Jones Papers.

out of this year's politics. While five or six years seems short enough to prepare for a centennial, conditions are changing so rapidly that what would be appropriate today may not be appropriate a few years hence, and this phase of the question is giving me a great deal of concern."[34]

By the time the decade of the twenties vanished into the thirties, Jones had been director general of the Texas centennial organization almost four years. The high expectations expressed by his many supporters when he accepted the position were never fulfilled. In retrospect it appears to have been a case of mutual misunderstanding. While the governing board anticipated an acceleration of the activity set in motion by Jones's predecessors, Jones obviously viewed his responsibilities in an entirely different light. Bascom Timmons, Jones's biographer, explained this recurring dilemma throughout his career in public service. He wrote: "On at least four occasions he was called to tasks that he fondly expected would require his attention only at policy-making board meetings. These were the development of the Houston port, his Red Cross services under President Wilson, the Texas Centennial, and . . . the RFC [Reconstruction Finance Corporation]. In every case he soon found himself carrying a tremendous load of administration. What seemed like part-time diversions turned out to be full-time jobs. In the course of such operations he made his own policies."[35]

Timmons was only partially correct. The centennial was never a full-time job for Jones, nor did he establish any substantial policies while in that position. If there was a policy at all, it was procrastination. However, Jones's posture in this instance was not entirely indefensible. He was essentially correct in assuring Representative Bateman that "five or six years seemed short enough to prepare for a Centennial." But he also, possibly unknowingly, pointed out to the legislator the fallacy of allowing the matter to drag on until 1930; conditions were changing rapidly. In ignoring Lowry Martin's earlier protestations to do something — anything — Jones had passed up a golden opportunity to launch a public information campaign that would have generated widespread interest in the centennial at a time

---

[34]Jones to Bateman, February 26, 1930, Jones Papers.
[35]Bascom N. Timmons, *Jesse H. Jones: The Man and the Statesman* (New York: Holt, 1956), p. 394.

when the state legislature would have been more disposed to provide a financial base for the celebration.

Jones also exhibited a lack of sensitivity to both the issues and the people he proposed to serve. This was evident in the program he outlined in his Fort Worth address; the history of the celebration would ultimately confirm two flaws in his reasoning. In recommending that the major focus of the centennial be on local celebrations (termed by journalist Harry Benge Crozier "a decentralized system of pageantry unfolding on all the stage of Texas"), Jones clearly misunderstood the objectives of the event as outlined by his predecessors. The dual purposes — patriotism and commercialism — were somewhere lost in the change of leadership. In addition, Jones obviously overestimated the nationwide fascination with the local events of Texas history. The belief that Americans in general were interested in the gamut of Texas history would be debated by Jones's successors and ultimately modified or abandoned entirely. Within this context, he further misread the attitude of the people of Texas when he stated that locating the central exposition in one area would alienate the remainder of the state. The number of people attending the Texas Centennial Central Exposition in Dallas in 1936 would exceed the number living in the state at the time Jones made that statement.

When Jones dictated his last letter to Representative Bateman on February 26, 1930, the nation was already feeling the first grips of the Great Depression, a term not yet entered into the popular vernacular. The free-wheeling spirit of the postwar twenties had about run its course, and in its place would emerge the somber tone of the 1930s as the Lone Star State faced an economic stagnation unprecedented in the twentieth century. In the middle of this troubled decade Texas was scheduled to celebrate its centenary. With no organized plan and no confirmed financing, the prospects were not too promising.

2

OPPORTUNITY OF THE CENTURY

ecords of the centennial movement's social history during 1930 and 1931 are noticeably sparse. And while there was little activity that gained public notice, the centennial stalwarts, Lowry Martin and Will Mayes, kept the spirit alive. During this period all the committee members gave of their time and talent with no compensation, even paying their own expenses at the meetings. Through their combined efforts — and with the gradual approach of the centennial year — the centennial spotlight ultimately switched from the public forum to the state legislature, where things begin to happen with accelerated speed. Fortunately for the historian, because of the mandated process, politicians leave good records.

The Forty-Second Legislature convened in regular session on January 13, 1931, one week before the inauguration of Ross S. Sterling as governor of Texas. (Sterling, who had run second to Mrs. Miriam A. Ferguson in the Democratic primary, had defeated her in a runoff election by 88,969 votes.) Governor Sterling, with the support of the Texas legislature, ushered in a new era of centennial activity. Senate Bill 106, introduced by Sen. Margie Neal and first read on January 26, marks the first major piece of legislation that would lead ultimately to the statewide celebration in 1936. Senator Neal, a newspaper publisher from Carthage, Texas, possessed a more-than-casual interest in the centennial movement; she was also a member of the Centennial Governing Board of One Hundred.

The bill created a temporary nine-member Texas Centennial Committee; a subsequent amendment increased the membership to twenty-one. Their responsibilities were enormous. They were to conduct a general survey of all major United States expositions since the 1876 Philadelphia centennial celebration. Specifically, they were to gather all available data relating to the cost, scope, construction, promotion, advertisement, character, and management of each exposition. The committee was then to make a full report to the Forty-Third Legislature in a printed pamphlet with at least one thousand copies. This would enable the lawmakers to "determine whether a Texas Centennial Exposition shall be held, and if so, the character of such Exposition." The bill's sponsors, cognizant of the lead time required for such an undertaking, moved with a sense of urgency as they ushered the bill through the legislature. The upper chamber passed the measure by voice vote, while the House voted 101 to 7, giving the bill final approval on May 18, 1931.[1]

Although the charge to the temporary committee was to compile data for the next legislature to consider, the Forty-Second Legislature moved with the assumption that the celebration was a foregone conclusion. To the centennial advocates, however, there remained one major stumbling block in the path to 1936 — the state constitution. Jesse Jones had first explored this problem in 1928, discovering that the constitution made no provision for funding expositions of the magnitude being considered. In addition, it restricted the issuance of state bonds in excess of $200,000. Recognizing that such an undertaking would indeed require legislative appropriation, Senator Neal again led the charge to save the centennial. A special committee from the Centennial Governing Board of One Hundred was appointed to draft a resolution which, if adopted, would authorize the legislature to issue bonds or otherwise provide funding for a major commemorative celebration. In addition to Senator Neal, the resolutions committee consisted of Jesse Jones, Jacob Wolters, Lowry Martin, and Rice Tilley, the Senate attorney. Senator Neal introduced Senate Joint Resolution No. 28 on March 28, 1931. It provided that the Constitution be amended to authorize the Texas legislature to make the necessary appropriations to fund the celebration.[2]

This resolution, limited in its scope, received final approval on May 20, 1931. It merely provided for a referendum to decide first if Texans wanted to celebrate its centennial anniversary and then whether the legislature, in the exercise of its judgment, should at some future date provide the necessary appropriation. Significantly, a specific date for the celebration, an appropriation, a bond issue, and new taxes are omitted from the amendment, according the legislature total dis-

[1]Senate Bill No. 106, *General Laws of the State of Texas, Forty-Second Legislature, Regular Session*, pp. 220–22, cited hereafter as *General Laws*.
[2]*General Laws*, pp. 944–45.

cretion when and if the measure became law. In addition, these proposed legislative powers were limited to a centennial celebration. With passage of the resolution, all that remained was voter approval. With the state and nation locked in the throes of an economic depression, this would not be an easy task.

The wheels of the centennial movement continued to turn, but now with increased regularity. On December 28, 1931, Secretary of State Jane Y. McCallum called the temporary Texas Centennial Committee together for its first work session in Austin.[3] In retrospect, this committee served as an interim body providing a continuity of leadership between the old Governing Board of One Hundred and a permanent commission that the legislature subsequently created. In addition to its fact-finding mission, this committee would also play an important role in the upcoming campaign to pass the constitutional amendment.

The Austin meeting was important primarily for two reasons. First, there occurred a switch in leadership. Jesse Jones, who had served as director general of the old governing board, announced that his appointment to the board of the Reconstruction Finance Corporation necessitated his retirement from the movement. Upon Jones's motion, Dallas attorney Cullen F. Thomas was named chairman of the new committee, which was to serve until the adjournment of the Forty-Third Legislature in 1933. Will H. Mayes of Austin was named secretary. In a second important decision, the new organization requested that the original governing board be held intact to serve in an advisory capacity to the temporary committee. This ensured a continuity of policy goals while keeping the organization in readiness for the forthcoming campaign.

With the approach of the 1932 general election, the Texas centennial faced its most crucial test. Voter rejection of the constitutional amendment was tantamount to rejecting the entire concept of an official celebration. (During the ensuing campaign the two terms — the amendment and the centennial — became synonymous.) Without state and federal funds, a major exposition of national and international scope would be out of the question. Passage of the amendment, on the other hand, would convey a positive message. If the people of Texas supported the amendment, it could be interpreted as a man-

[3]During her tenure as secretary of state, Mrs. McCallum found and rescued from decay the original Texas Declaration of Independence.

date to the Forty-Third Legislature to enact the measure into law. To those who had nurtured the centennial idea for almost a decade, the coming election represented a great political gamble. The stakes were high, but for many of the movement's leaders, political persuasion was their business. So as spring gave way to summer, the Texas Press Association and the Associated Advertising Clubs of Texas, in close cooperation with the centennial committee, began rallying their forces for the campaign that lay ahead.

The Texas Press Association appointed a campaign committee to spearhead the drive and established its base of operations in the *Daily Sun* offices in Corsicana. The committee consisted of Lowry Martin, chairman, Corsicana; Sam P. Harben, Richardson-Dallas; S. W. Papert, Dallas; W. C. Edwards, Austin; Will H. Mayes, secretary, Texas Centennial Committee, Austin; Peter Molyneaux, Fort Worth, all newspapermen; and Earl Racey, governor of the Advertising Clubs of Texas, who represented organized advertising. In addition to the advertising clubs and the press association, this membership also included representatives of the Texas Daily Press League and Progressive Texans, Incorporated. The Associated Railroads Organization of Texas, headed by Gen. John A. Hulen, J. L. Lancaster, and E. H. McReynolds, further added its resources to the committee's campaign arsenal. In order to facilitate the operation, the Texas Press Association created an auxiliary structure, the Texas Press Centennial Education Bureau, which cooperated with the state and centennial organizations to promote the amendment's passage.

From the press association's educational bureau in Corsicana, and the centennial committee's office in Austin, came a flood of reader information and campaign guidelines. Mayes structured the press releases to inform the voters of the fundamental issues in the campaign. "There are some who may vote against the Amendment," Mayes warned, "unless they understand its terms. These are plain." After explaining the provisions of the amendment, he was forced to come to terms with the economic depression of the period. The date for the celebration was flexible, he explained, and might be held later "if conditions do not seem to justify the Centennial in 1936." Mayes added, however, that most Texans thought postponement unnecessary, believing that long before 1936, "Texas will be in better financial condition than at any time in history, and others assert that a creditable Centennial celebration would do more than anything else to bring about economic and business rehabilitation." To counter the argument that private capital should finance the centennial, Mayes pronounced that view impractical. In the first place, he argued, private funding could not be secured, and even if it could, "the Centennial would be a private exploitation of the public rather than a prideful official State celebration." Mayes challenged the newspaper readers to "vote for the Amendment and make the Centennial possible. It is the opportunity of a Century."[4]

Activities of the various county committees were also coordinated through Mayes's office, which became a clearinghouse for ideas to stimulate local interest in the amendment's passage. He reported that the Bastrop County Federation of Women's Clubs had established a speakers' bureau to schedule addresses at every school and every civic and social club in the county. (The Austin office also provided pertinent information for prospective speakers.) That organization also sponsored a school essay contest entitled "Why Vote for the Texas Centennial?" and published the essays in local newspapers before October 25. Mayes also reported that several county committees had scheduled mid-October school pageants depicting early Texas history and Texas progress, at which centennial addresses would be made. He urged the county chairmen "to use every favorable opportunity for PUBLICITY. We are depending upon your continued, persistent activity and capable leadership for an overwhelming majority in your community for the Centennial Amendment."[5]

While the Austin and Corsicana publicity offices were distributing campaign information through the mails and newspapers, Earl Racey and members of the advertising clubs carried the centennial message to the highways and byways of Texas. The Outdoor Poster Association of Texas designed, printed, and distributed without cost more than five hundred outdoor posters throughout the state. The units bore a recurring message for passing motorists: "Texas is About to Have a Birthday," "Shall the Noble Deeds of Valor of Texas Heroes Go Unnoticed?" and "VOTE, Tuesday Nov. 8th to Authorize the Texas Centennial, 1936."[6]

---

[4]News release, Centennial Files, Daughters of the Republic of Texas Library at the Alamo, cited hereafter as DRT Library.

[5]Ibid.

[6]*Commemorating a Hundred Years of Texas History*, Texas Centennial Commission, undated, p. 13.

The campaign for voter approval of the constitutional amendment pitted the patriotic impulse against the state's economic well-being, with a large measure of latent regionalism thrown in to cloud the issue. This polarization of views ultimately shifted the electorate into opposing camps, articulating their different philosophical, economic, and regional views of the state and how it should commemorate its hundredth anniversary. And while the issue was sometimes overshadowed — and overshouted — by other political battles, the debate left little margin for the undecided voter.

The state's press became the public forum for the debate, with each publication expressing the views of its constituency, either for or against the amendment. But of all the state's newspapers and magazines, probably none embraced the centennial issue with greater emotional fervor than did the *Texas Weekly*. This Dallas-based magazine, edited and published by Peter Molyneaux, served primarily as a voice of Texas opinion on economics and politics and editorially espoused those positions it felt best reflected the state's interests. The centennial celebration, Molyneaux believed, fell well within that scope. On July 23, 1932, he launched his pro-amendment campaign with an editorial, "Do Texans Really Revere Their Past?" Molyneaux pointed out that during the last eleven years Texas had passed through a centennial period of which no formal public notice had been taken, and "we are beginning to wonder whether ever the centennial will be fittingly observed." He based his pessimistic view on the reluctance of political candidates to address the amendment issue. Their reason was economic; the amendment contained an appropriation provision likely to be rejected by the voters. Molyneaux warned: "It is being freely predicted by Texas political leaders that this proposed amendment will be defeated. If it is defeated, there will be no fitting centennial celebration. Members of the Legislature, standing for reelection, have told the editor of *The Texas Weekly* that they would not dare advocate . . . the adoption of this amendment. And we do not doubt that they are good judges of what is likely to be popular with the people."[7]

The candidates had every reason to view the amendment as po-

---

[7] *Texas Weekly*, July 23, 1932, p. 4. Some outsiders were more optimistic than some Texas politicos. The *New York Evening Post* reproduced much of this editorial with the conclusion: "We cannot believe, however, that the State will fail to celebrate the centennial battle of San Jacinto in 1936 with fitting ceremonies."

litical poison. During a period of economic gloom, advocating a non-emergency appropriation measure would not win many friends at the polls. The signs of the times were tragically apparent. During the first six months of 1932, 532 Texas firms went into bankruptcy; business failures were occurring at the rate of fifteen a week. Bank failures nationally conveyed an even more ominous impression. Bank suspensions in June, 1932, totaled 131, added to 80 in May, 75 in April, 53 in March, 128 in February, and 362 in January.[8]

The amendment issue clearly pitted latent patriotism against the state's pocketbook. And compared with the economic issues of the time, patriotism appeared to be an unpopular issue. Newspaper editors, however, live with the knowledge that unpopular positions do not go unchallenged. During the lull that followed the June primary election, the opposing sides of the amendment issue began taking up positions for the coming conflict. It is doubtful that Molyneaux anticipated such a well-organized and well-defined opponent, but the West Texas Chamber of Commerce quickly identified itself as a force to be dealt with. Molyneaux was ready; he gave it his best shot.

On September 19, 1932, Molyneaux received a letter from the West Texas Chamber of Commerce stating its firm position on the matter. Also enclosed was a copy of an address by Van Zandt Jarvis, chairman of the chamber's Central Committee on Public Expenditures (and later mayor of Fort Worth), in which he recommended to the ninety-nine local committees that they oppose the passage of the proposed constitutional amendment. The prospect of a legislative appropriation to fund the celebration sparked the chamber's opposition. Wilbur C. Hawk of Amarillo, the organization's president, favored a private undertaking, a self-supporting, self-liquidating celebration similar to the State Fair of Texas or the Fort Worth Fat Stock Show. To the chamber, the financing, and not the end result, was the only consideration. Molyneaux's response was predictable: the mere thought of equating taxes with patriotism was both unthinkable and unpatriotic. Molyneaux acknowledged that he had not contemplated this organized opposition. He believed, however, that "the gentlemen of the West Texas Chamber of Commerce have made a colossal blunder. . . . With the opposition of the West Texas body its defeat is practically certain. . . . And . . . if [the Chamber] wins and succeeds in

[8] *Texas Business Review*, July 28, 1932, pp. 2–3.

defeating the amendment, its youngest member will not live to see
the day that it will cease to regret that victory."[9]

The verbal battle for the centennial had begun. Opponents and
proponents of the issue began voicing their opinions on the editorial
pages of the state's newspapers, many of which the *Texas Weekly* reproduced, judiciously representing both causes. In the immediate wake
of the *Weekly* editorial, most newspapers appeared to support the
amendment. The *Austin American, Houston Post,* and even the West
Texas–oriented *Fort Worth Star-Telegram* rejected the West Texas
Chamber's position, explaining "the Amendment does not require the
Legislature to make any appropriation, nor does it specify the amount.
It merely, if voted, will remove the constitutional prohibition against
which and will open the way for an appropriation when the time
arrives, if such then be desirable." In Dumas, the *Moore County News,*
which served the central Panhandle area, also rejected the chamber's
advice, explaining that its action "was by no means indicative of the
feeling of West Texas generally. In my opinion the mistake of the committee was an honest but hasty one. It is not representative!"[10]

By the time editor Molyneaux surveyed the state's newspapers in
preparation for the October 8 issue, he discovered the opposition was
gaining a following that, significantly, did not follow a geographic
alignment. The Williamson County *Sun,* serving a Central Texas community, vehemently opposed the amendment as "a dangerous piece
of legislation and will cause trouble in the future." In like manner,
the Clarksville *Times,* the *McKinney Examiner,* the *Abilene News,*
the *Wills Point Chronicle,* and the McLean *News* also declared against
the amendment. The Clarksville *Times* stated: "The rest of you can
do as you please, but we expect to scratch the 'waddin' out of the
proposed amendment. . . . Not that we are against centennial celebrations, but because we quit ordering things until we get some idea
about what they cost." The *Brownwood Banner-Bulletin* viewed the
unexpected position of the West Texas chamber as a simple case of
short-sighted regional paranoia. It reported: "This action, which will
cause thousands of voters to oppose the Constitutional amendment,
was so unexpected that one is at a loss to understand the reasoning
which prompted it. [Opposition to the amendment] not only is pre-

[9] *Texas Weekly,* September 24, 1932, pp. 4–6.
[10] Quoted in *Texas Weekly,* October 1, 1932, p. 11.

sumptuous, but it is extremely short-sighted economy of a type which would not be countenanced in West Texas for a moment if the Centennial project were to be located in that section of the State."[11]

In late October Molyneaux engaged Dale Miller as associate editor, a move calculated to further invigorate the *Weekly's* crusading staff. Miller, a recent graduate from the University of Texas school of journalism, had caught the editor's attention with his pro-amendment columns in the *Corpus Christi Caller*. Miller was considered one of the state's bright young journalists; Harry Benge Crozier described him as "that dynamic young apostle of the printed word."[12] Miller lived up to his advance billing. He recalled years later: "We took it [the centennial] on as a crusade. Nobody thought that in the Depression years of 1932 and 1933 that Texas would ever approve a constitutional amendment to permit that state to provide funds [for such an undertaking]."[13]

Miller could not have joined the *Weekly* staff at a more propitious time. In addition to the organized opposition to the amendment issue, other volatile factors were clouding the political picture, forcing the amendment into the background. Miriam A. Ferguson, who had defeated Ross A. Sterling in the 1932 primary for the Democratic gubernatorial nomination, was being abandoned by the mainline Texas Democrats in favor of Republican Orville Bullington. Sterling announced on October 8 that he would not support Mrs. Ferguson. To further confuse the issue, former Centennial Committee Chairman Cato Sells was appointed chairman of the Democrats for Bullington's campaign. (He had supported Republican Herbert C. Hoover for president four years earlier.) Amid this specter of political disorder, Molyneaux and Miller continued their crusade to win voter approval of the amendment. With the approach of the general election they were obviously heartened by the editorial trend in Texas newspapers. Of the forty-four editorial samplings quoted in the *Weekly*, thirty-three supported the amendment. In the November 5 issue, published four days before the election, Miller gave his last and best shot. He claimed that "approval of the amendment would accelerate rather than jeopardize recovery. It would rejuvenate business, restore confidence. It

[11]Ibid., October 8, 1932.

[12]Mrs. Ethel Wortham, Corsicana, Texas, to Kenneth B. Ragsdale, March 16, 1980, in possession of author.

[13]Interview with Dale Miller, Austin, Texas, July 21, 1978.

would lift us from the sluggish lethargy of these troubled years and face us directly toward the new era which lies ahead. . . . Vote the Centennial. The faith of those who bequeathed this heritage must be justified and the confidence of our children merited."[14]

On November 8, 1932, Texas did indeed vote the centennial, but to Molyneaux and Miller it was a bittersweet victory. The final tabulation: 277,147 votes for and 217,964 against the amendment; 849,538 votes were cast in the governor's race as Mrs. Ferguson defeated Bullington by more than 200,000 votes.[15] Only one of every four voters had registered approval or disapproval of the constitutional amendment. Preparing the November 12 issue of the *Weekly*, Miller reported that the centennial amendment had been adopted "though the vote was so small, relatively, as to leave little room for much exulting over the patriotism that put it over." Molyneaux likewise did not gloat over the victory. Instead he revealed uncommon restraint. "We feel impelled to send a public word of greeting to the West Texas Chamber of Commerce and to assure it of our continued cooperation in furthering its work," he wrote. "We are almost tempted to congratulate it on the success of the amendment, for had the amendment been defeated, the West Texas body, whether justly or not, would have had to bear the onus of this defeat."[16]

The passage of the constitutional amendment failed, however, to accelerate the committee's plan for a centennial celebration. As many opponents of the measure had warned, the Depression was no time to plan a birthday party. By 1933, unemployment in Texas had become widespread. Retail sales had dropped 53 percent since 1929, leaving some 50,000 former members of the sales force out of work. During that same period, 1,550 manufacturing firms had terminated operations, reducing that work force by more than 43,000 people. Faced with these sobering facts, the Forty-Third Legislature, convening in Austin on January 10, 1933, turned its attention to far more critical issues than the centennial. The somber tone of this session was darkened further on March 6, when President Franklin D. Roosevelt closed

---

[14] *Texas Weekly*, November 5, 1932, p. 7.

[15] Orville Bullington's defeat did not remove him from the political scene. Bullington publicly accused University of Texas President Homer Price Rainey of coddling a "nest of homosexuals" on the faculty, an accusation which accelerated the controversy that led to Rainey's dismissal in 1944.

[16] *Texas Weekly*, November 12, 1932, p. 6.

the nation's commercial banks in an attempt to end a money panic. This was no time to consider nonessential legislation. The session adjourned on June 1 without the introduction of a single centennial measure.

On September 14, 1933, the legislature returned in special session to deal with unfinished fiscal matters, specifically, the issuance of $20 million in relief bonds. This time the centennial issue did gain considerable attention; six different centennial items were considered during the month-long session. None, however, can be considered milestones in the progress to 1936. On September 26, the Texas Centennial Committee, created by the Forty-Second Legislature, submitted its final report. This much-anticipated study, authorized in part to determine "the character of such Exposition," is notable mainly for its length (almost seven pages in the *Senate Journal*) and its lack of conclusive recommendations. Considering the committee's business and civic orientation, a far more substantive report had been expected.

The committee obviously did its homework well, surveying eleven United States expositions held since 1876. As none of the expositions studied had been held subsequent to World War I — Chicago's Century of Progress exposition had just opened at the time the study was conducted — most of the data were obsolete by 1933. The committee did focus on three topics that would have some future relevance in the centennial matter. First, although major expositions seldom returned a profit, there were residual benefits to consider. The committee found that expositions, regardless of their financial outcomes, yielded positive benefits: "immediate increase in business and noticeable growth to the cities and states in which they have been held, as well as a quickening on the part of the locality to all matters cultural and educational."[17]

The committee addressed the matter of sales tax revenues, a topic nonexistent when the previous expositions were held. The committee estimated that out-of-state motorists would pay $25,000,000 in sales tax revenue on gasoline and oil. This proved to be a valid but overly optimistic projection. The one aspect of the report that needed a conclusive recommendation — the type and general location of the proposed celebration — was purposely omitted. As justification for this

[17]*Journal of the Senate of Texas, First Called Session, Forty-Third Legislature,* p. 73.

obvious shortcoming, the committee pointed out that "plans of today may be rendered obsolete by the progress of tomorrow."[18] The three options offered were: (1) a major centralized exposition that would exemplify both the history and the progress of the state, (2) one principal exposition with satellite units located throughout the state at points of historic and developmental interest, and (3) several state-wide expositions or exhibitions of equal significance and importance. The report concluded that passage of the constitutional amendment gave the legislature a mandate to act. Time was of the essence, "for delay until the next regular session would leave insufficient time for preparing for and building a creditable celebration."[19]

Although subsequently two concurrent and identical centennial resolutions were tabled subject to call, Senator Neal was determined to keep the centennial matter before the legislature. On October 6, with Senators Gus Russeck, Nat Patton, and Archer (Archie) Parr, she introduced Senate Bill 89, which provided for a centennial celebration in 1936, and called on the legislature to create a Texas Centennial Commission and make a suitable appropriation to carry out provisions of the act. Because of the short time remaining, Senator Neal declared the act an emergency measure. The bill was read and referred to the committee on finance. Sam P. Harben, secretary of the Texas Press Association, made a final effort to spur the finance committee into action. On October 9, four days before adjournment, he petitioned Lieut. Gov. Edgar E. Witt to call the bill out of committee for a vote. To delay any longer, Harben warned, would imperil the movement. Witt refused to act, and all the effort expended by so many came to no avail. The first called session adjourned on October 13, having taken no positive action on the centennial.

The year ended on a mild economic upbeat; according to some indicators the Depression was gradually bottoming out. During November and December retail sales showed a greater increase than the average of the preceding seven years. Some areas of the state reported gains as high as 22 percent. During 1933 new car registrations were 63 percent greater than in 1932, while commercial failures were about half those of the previous year. There was, however, a darker side of

---

[18] Ibid.
[19] Ibid., p. 78. This written report was presented to the legislature in lieu of the requested 1,000 printed pamphlets. The reason: no funds.

the economic picture. The ranks of the unemployed continued to grow as the rural economy gradually deteriorated. With both cotton production and prices on a seemingly endless downslide, rural foreclosures became the tragedy of the decade. It was into this bleak setting that Gov. Miriam A. Ferguson reconvened the Forty-Third Legislature in a second called session on January 29, 1934. The governor's message to the lawmakers focused on two emergency matters: issuing $5 million in state bonds to fund unemployment relief and enacting the necessary legislation to protect citizens from inequitable foreclosures on real estate mortgages.

Faced with these priority issues, the centennial faithful gave slight hope for favorable action during that session. Time was indeed running out; less than two years remained to prepare for the most important anniversary in the state's history. Should the measure fail in this session, no time would remain to legislate, fund, and produce a fitting celebration. Again Senator Neal began marshaling her forces for a final assault on the legislative opposition. If the centennial had a patron saint, it was indeed Senator Neal. On February 14, 1934, some two weeks into the session, she introduced Senate Bill No. 22, creating a public corporation to hold the Texas Centennial, administered by a board of governors to be known as the Texas Centennial Commission. This was essentially the same bill Senator Neal introduced during the previous session. In its final form that bill provided for:

(1) holding a centennial celebration in 1936;

(2) locating the central exposition and principal celebration in the city offering the largest financial inducement and support;

(3) holding other appropriate celebrations under the auspices and direction of the Texas Centennial Commision at San Antonio on or about March 2nd; at Houston, on or about April 21; and on appropriate historical dates at Goliad, Brenham, Nacogdoches, Huntsville, and other places identified with Texas' early history;

(4) establishing a governing board of not less than thirty members, possessing broad powers to plan and conduct the centennial celebrations and including the governor, lieutenant governor, and speaker of the house as ex-officio commission members;

(5) creating a Texas Centennial Advisory Board of not less than one hundred men and women, made up in part of the old Centennial Governing Board of One Hundred;

(6) establishing an executive board of not more than fifteen members to be selected at the first commission meeting; and

(7) appropriating $100,000 to finance the commission's interim activities.

As might be expected, the bill was not granted easy passage. The Senate, however, accorded Senator Neal almost unanimous support. Sen. Grady Woodruff of Decatur cast the lone dissenting vote attempting to reduce the amount of the appropriation, originally set at $250,000. In the House of Representatives the bill encountered its heaviest opposition. Two issues came under attack: the amount of the appropriation and the number of members in the commission. While a conference committee compromised the appropriation matter at $100,000, the membership issue, surprisingly, was not so easily adjusted. This provision, probably more than the appropriation, reflected the House members' negative attitude toward the centennial. They blasted the bill with some twenty-nine amendments, most adding names to the commission membership list. One nine-page amendment contained 233 names. Describing the temporary pandemonium that raged in the House, centennial historian and artifact collector Wallace O. Chariton wrote: "First, there was the attempt to have all the names in the Houston telephone book included as Commission members. Then another Representative wanted the names of every notary public in the state added to the list. . . . The supreme insult came when the names of Clyde Barrow and Bonnie Parker were offered for consideration for Commission membership."[20] Eventually the carnival atmosphere subsided, and on February 27, 1934, the last day of the session, the House finally voted eighty-three to forty for the bill.

The legislature had, at last, spoken; Texas would officially celebrate its centennial. The shouts of joy—and there were some—were restrained by the knowledge that many lawmakers felt no commitment to celebrate the most important anniversary in the state's history. Eighty-three to forty was no vote of confidence, but it was a victory. Ten years of persistent effort had finally produced Senate Bill No. 22. The struggle was destined to continue; much work was left to be done. The $100,000 legislative appropriation was a mere pit-

[20]Wallace O. Chariton, *Texas Centennial: The Parade of an Empire* (Plano: Privately printed, 1969), p. 6.

tance compared to the cost of producing a major exposition. The multimillion-dollar price tag was certain to polarize legislative detractors already grappling with the problems of unemployment, old age pensions, and the declining farm economy. In addition, the quest for a federal appropriation still lay somewhere in the future. But the immediate challenges for the new commission were determining the specific nature of the celebration, generating statewide interest in the undertaking, and selecting a site for the central exposition. Probably none sharing these responsibilities could foresee the emotional upheavals these decisions would ignite. During the battles that lay ahead, the struggle to pass Senate Bill No. 22 would be remembered as only a preliminary skirmish.

3

PRIDE, PATRIOTISM,
AND ECONOMIC SELF-INTEREST

he newly formed Texas Centennial Commission lost little time in swinging into action. Although House Bill No. 22 did not become law until June 16, 1934, Secretary of State W. W. Heath, at the insistence of several commission members, called an emergency meeting at the Driskill Hotel in Austin at 11:00 A.M. on March 24. Twenty members attended, as did ex-officio members Gov. Miriam A. Ferguson, Lieut. Gov. Edgar E. Witt, and Speaker of the House Coke Stevenson. Although this meeting was largely organizational — Cullen F. Thomas was elected temporary chairman and Will H. Mayes temporary secretary — one potentially volatile issue did emerge. When Houston representatives Clarence R. Wharton and Thomas Flaxman asked the commission for clarification of the process for selecting the central exposition site, they were referred to the law obligating the commission to choose the city "offering the largest financial inducement and support" and were told that "the law would likely be interpreted liberally by the Commission."[1] This policy of selecting the exposition site solely on a monetary basis would plague the commission throughout its existence.

Subsequent to this meeting Secretary Mayes secured the appointment of a Texas Centennial Advisory Board with additional boards representing each county in the state. With this membership established, a joint meeting with the commission was scheduled in Austin for June 6, 1934. Some six hundred members, representing every section of Texas, convened at 10:00 A.M. in the Driskill Hotel to hear former governor James E. Ferguson speak on behalf of Gov. Miriam A. Ferguson. He pledged the continued cooperation of that administration "in putting on 'a celebration that will make all posterity proud

[1] Report of the Secretary of Texas Centennial Commission, March 24, 1934, to January 7, 1935, Centennial Collection, Texas State Archives, p. 1, cited hereafter as Secretary's Report.

of us and of Texas.'"[2] This meeting too was largely organizational. The members elected Mrs. Volney W. Taylor of Brownsville temporary chairman, adopted resolutions asking for state and federal support for the celebration, and voted to create an executive committee composed of State Advisory Board officers plus thirty-one additional members chosen from each of the state's senatorial districts. This broad-based representation became a major factor in developing statewide support for the movement. Centennial historian Margaret Whitten explained: "This advisory board consisted of approximately twelve hundred leading citizens of the State, each Senator and Representative having been authorized to nominate for membership two persons from each county in his district. While this board functioned in a purely advisory capacity, its large membership provided a nucleus for Centennial activity in every county. Its activities stimulated and sustained state-wide interest in the movement, without hampering the work of the Centennial Commission."[3]

The twenty-six commission members attending the joint meeting withdrew to the Senate Chamber in the afternoon to proceed with their duties. At that session the commission voted to establish headquarters in Austin until the site for the central celebration was chosen. They also set September 1, 1934, as the deadline for receiving proposals for the central celebration and November 1, 1934, for receiving proposals for local historical celebrations. The commission also elected a permanent slate of officers: Cullen F. Thomas, Dallas, president; Lowry Martin, Corsicana, vice-president; Gus F. Taylor, Tyler, treasurer; and Will H. Mayes, Austin, secretary. In another important move, the commission established an executive committee which became that organization's primary decision-making body. In addition to the four officers, this nine-member board consisted of Walter D. Cline, Wichita Falls, chairman; J. K. Hughes, Mexia; John D. Middleton, Greenville; Cliff Caldwell, Abilene; and Herman H. Ochs, San Antonio. Mayes, the only salaried officer (he resigned his commission membership), received $300 monthly.[4]

[2] Ibid., p. 2.

[3] Margaret Whitten, "Certain Aspects of the Texas Centennial Celebration," Master's thesis, Southern Methodist University, 1937, p. 42.

[4] Commission members were compensated only for actual charges for room and meals, which were estimated at $5.00 a day, and $0.04 a mile for use of personal cars in traveling on commission business.

After the meeting adjourned, Lowry Martin addressed the executive committee about organizing a Centennial Educational Press Bureau to assist the commission, through the Texas Press Association, in publicizing the centennial. The bureau would function, according to Martin, as a cooperative rather than as an independent organization. Martin's success in generating interest in the celebration led to the executive committee creating a three-member publicity committee chaired by Martin and staffed with J. E. Josey, chairman of the board of the *Houston Post*, and Wilbur C. Hawk, general manager of the Amarillo Globe-News Publishing Company. At the June 27 meeting in San Antonio, the executive committee approved Martin's proposal for a $15,000 statewide publicity campaign during July and August. Martin's effort, in cooperation with the press association, would carry the centennial message to thousands of people who had not the slightest understanding of what a commemorative celebration should entail. Through the interest generated by this organization, the drive to celebrate Texas' centennial became truly a grassroots movement.

The formation of the commission and the advisory board, as well as the horde of unofficial volunteers that would ultimately join the movement, represented an unprecedented groundswell of public opinion driven by a twofold desire to honor the heroes who helped establish Texas and to exhibit to the world the achievements of one hundred years of independence. Thus pride and patriotism became a dominant theme of the 1930s. The enthusiastic leadership exhibited by members of the centennial organizations revealed a facet of a regional character probably incident only to this specific time in the state's history. In this period Texans openly professed a deep sense of pride in their heritage, while at the same time, consciously or otherwise, they harbored an inferiority complex when compared with the older settled regions of the nation. The forthcoming centennial offered an opportunity to celebrate the one while attempting to remove the onus of the other. As the state was destined to grow and prosper, this regional dichotomy—pride with shame—would ultimately dissipate with the surge of new populations. But that was a half-century into the future. For the time being, Texas had an anniversary to commemorate, and for those responsible for the celebration, time was of the essence. Between March 24, 1934, and January 7, 1935, either the full commission or the executive committee met sixteen times at various locations to transact commission business. (This does not include full meetings and subcommittee meetings of the Texas Centennial Advisory Board or the county and district boards.) The problems the commission grappled with revealed much about the temper of the time and how Texans viewed themselves, and others, during the mid-1930s.

Martin's publicity campaign remains one of the major milestones in centennial history, undertaken at a most inopportune time. The Depression and its attendant woes, combined with the worst drought in the nation's history, created an unlikely if not a virtually impossible setting for raising $15 million, the amount the finance committee considered a minimum for the celebration.[5] Yet it appears these obstacles were not considered insurmountable; the movement's leaders, mostly successful businessmen, seemed oblivious to the potential for failure. But Lowry Martin was a unique personality, even for Texas in the 1930s. With a measure of frontier optimism and with a small-town newspaperman's crusading fervor, Martin proceeded on his self-chosen mission. Failure was a word omitted from his journalistic vocabulary; in his opinion, a man created his own opportunities. Publicity and public awareness, he believed, would clear the path to his ultimate goal, the 1936 Texas centennial celebrations.

The objectives of Martin's publicity campaign were three-fold: (1) to apprise Texans of the historical justification for the celebration; (2) to convince the state's major cities of the economic benefits of sponsoring the central exposition; and (3) to create citizen interest and support that would lead inevitably to favorable action by the state legislature—he hoped, with a multimillion-dollar appropriation to stage the celebrations. It appears in retrospect that Martin was attempting the impossible. And to make his task even more difficult, he was hemmed in by two highly restrictive factors, time and money. The finance committee had allocated Martin only $15,000 of the $100,000 appropriation to conduct the publicity campaign, while the planning committee, in setting September 1 as the target date for central exposition bids, allowed Martin only two months to create a favorable psychological climate for requesting the largest nonessential appropriation in the state's history. As June, 1934, drew to a close,

[5]Members of the Finance Committee were Gen. John A. Hulen, Fort Worth, chairman; Mrs. Fannie Campbell Womack, Palestine; and Roy Miller, Corpus Christi.

he began assembling a star-studded cast of newspaper and advertising men in the temporary quarters provided by the Corsicana Chamber of Commerce. Again the centennial spotlight switched to that
small central Texas town; Texans were about to be subjected to the
greatest historical brainwashing in the state's history.

Martin's publicity staff consisted of Harry Howard, chief of staff;
Harry Benge Crozier, publicity executive; Earl Racey, advertising executive; Louise Wood, general assistant; Bobbie Lee Staten, researcher;
two secretaries; and another general assistant. Staff operations began on July 5, 1934; results appeared almost immediately. Distribution of the first issue of the *Texas Centennial News* began on July 10.
This eight-page tabloid-size newspaper, published each Tuesday, was
directed to newspapers, periodicals, chambers of commerce, and other
club organizations throughout the state, and it served as the official
voice of the publicity committee. The usual press run was 15,000 copies;
reprints were ordered for some issues. The first issue focused primarily on the purposes of the forthcoming celebration and urged statewide support for the event. *Commemorating a Hundred Years of Texas
History*, an illustrated forty-page booklet, represented the committee's most comprehensive and enduring publication. It contained a
history of the centennial movement until 1934, a listing of all major
boards and committees, the patriotic and historical perspective of the
centennial movement, and an appeal to "every Texan to Think-Talk-
Write Centennial in 1936. . . . This is the biggest job that will con-
front this generation. . . . Every Texan now is expected to do his duty."[6]
This booklet was conceived as the complete handbook of the centennial movement.

Martin's publicity campaign utilized every service of the communications media, extended gratis to the centennial cause. In addition
to distributing copies of the weekly newspaper and the pamphlet,
the publicity staff serviced eight hundred Texas newspapers and three
hundred periodicals with a steady stream of illustrated (with newspaper mats) news stories and special features. The Outdoor Poster
Association again came to the aid of the centennial cause. Racey
reported in late July that outdoor advertising companies in Houston,
Galveston, San Antonio, San Benito, Dallas, Waco, and Austin had
received 325 posters for display in the areas they served. Each poster

[6]*Commemorating a Hundred Years of Texas History*, p. 31.

carried the centennial slogan, "Think, talk, and write centennial in 1936. It is your state. It is your celebration."

The entertainment media, radio and motion pictures, also pledged support of the centennial movement. The publicity office contacted every radio station in Texas, and most agreed to supply lists of their advertisers who were, in turn, asked to tie in centennial messages with their regular radio commercials. In addition to these spot announcements, various centennial officials were given free air time to speak in behalf of the movement. The Paramount Publix Theater chain (later Interstate Circuit, Inc.) offered to run centennial trailers in their 174 motion picture theaters in Texas.

Personal contact accounted for much of the publicity work. Copies of the publicity program were directed to every member of the Centennial Advisory Board, in each of the state's 254 counties, with a request that they act as the executive committee in their respective counties to direct the centennial publicity campaign. The committee also contacted all chambers of commerce and various civic, labor, and women's organizations, requesting that they help in disseminating centennial information. This effort bore immediate results. During July and August, Martin's office was flooded with requests from throughout the state for club and organization speakers. Responding to this interest, the Corsicana office began functioning as a speakers' bureau, either sending out members of the commission to fill the engagements or enlisting the support of local people who volunteered their services in this effort. Publicity field work fell mainly to staff members Earl Racey and Louise Wood, who visited every major city in the state on behalf of the centennial.

In mid-August the publicity effort received a mammoth boost when Governor Ferguson issued an official proclamation designating the week beginning August 13 as Texas Centennial Week. This event merited a special edition of the *Texas Centennial News*. Volume 1, Number 6, dated August 14, carried a front-page photograph of the granite-faced chief executive, along with a reprint of the official proclamation. This was accompanied by a plea for all editors, mayors, county judges, chambers of commerce, "and other patriotic citizens [to] act together immediately in getting [this proclamation reproduced] . . . in their cities, towns, and counties."[7]

---

[7] *Texas Centennial News*, August 14, 1934, p. 1.

The publicity committee's pleas for centennial support did not go unheeded; the incoming mail soon confirmed the success of its efforts. The flood of information emanating from the Corsicana office had indeed stirred the emotions of many Texans, setting loose a wellspring of latent patriotic zeal, tinged at times with measures of local booster-ism and economic self-interest. But by any measure, thousands of Tex-ans now knew the whys and wherefores of the forthcoming celebra-tion, and many wanted to share the responsibility in making it an unqualified success. Mrs. Richard J. Turrentine, president of the Texas Federation of Women's Clubs, pledged her support for a "celebration that will win the praise and commendation of Continental America and even the world."[8] Paul V. Johnson, assistant secretary of the Cham-ber of Commerce in Commerce, Texas, promised positive action. "Commerce wants to have a part in this great movement," he wrote Martin. "Our plan [is] to arouse our citizenship from their lethargy and to appeal to their patriotism, so that definite action, not mere discussion, will result."[9] R. N. "Bud" Price, secretary of the Overton, Texas, Chamber of Commerce, reported that his organization had printed some five thousand brochures which he planned to distrib-ute at a baseball tournament in Colorado. The one-page folder, type-written and mimeographed on both sides, promoted Overton ("Gate-way to the Golden Stream"), the Humble Oilers baseball club, and the centennial.

Various business enterprises recognized the commercial benefits of forming an alliance with the movement. The St. Louis Button Company requested any centennial-related material to use as inserts in the company's outgoing mail, and Edward T. Harrison, president of Trinity Universal Insurance Company of Dallas, ordered a sup-ply of centennial windshield stickers (this was before the age of bumper stickers) to use on his salesmen's automobiles. Jack Litton, president of the Jack Litton Drug Company in Abilene, Texas, wrote Martin that until he read the *Texas Centennial News* he had some misgivings about the proposed celebration, "but before I got to the last page I was so enthusiastic over it that it will take me until after the Centennial to get rid of my steam. I have been talking about it

[8] Mrs. Richard J. Turrentine to Lowry Martin, August 10, 1934, Centennial Collection, Texas State Archives; collection hereafter cited as State Archives.

[9] Paul V. Johnson to Lowry Martin, July 13, 1934, State Archives.

all day. . . . The boys up in Chicago will be wondering how Texas did it."[10]

The Texas press, for the most part, supported the movement. The *Dallas Morning News*, the *Dallas Journal*, and the *Fort Worth Star-Telegram* were all generous in their coverage of centennial activities, while E. P. Holland, Jr., vice-president of *Holland's* and *Farm and Ranch* magazines, and Eugene Butler, editor of *Progressive Farmer and Southern Ruralist*, both pledged wholehearted editorial support of the movement. Martin also discovered that while people might differ on some issues, supporting the centennial seemed to transcend all personal barriers. S. W. Papert, president of the Texas Daily Press League, wrote Martin on July 5 (the envelope was marked *personal*), that "you and I don't always see eye to eye on matters, but the Centennial proposition is one deal that I am for one thousand percent and if I can be of service to you in any capacity, I hope you will call on me."[11]

The provision that the publicity committee could expend no funds for advertising space in newspapers and magazines produced the only dissenting responses. Martin, defending this rule, explained to C. H. Odom, manager of *The East Texas Optimist* in Woodville, that "not one single line of this advertising has been paid for. . . . The press of the state has already given us . . . more than one-half million dollars worth of space had it been paid at regular space rate."[12] Fortunately for the centennial, Joseph B. Cross, editor of the *San Saba Star*, represented the minority viewpoint among Texas newspaper editors. He obviously was not moved by the patriotic impulse. He wrote Martin that "I am only interested in the Centennial on a business proposition and if I can increase the revenue of The Star through its inception, I am in favor of it. Otherwise, publicity received by this office unless tied up with an advertising campaign hastily finds itself in the wastebasket."[13]

As more people became aware of the centennial movement, Martin was besieged with a flood of bizarre suggestions, promotional opportunities, and blatantly self-serving solicitations. For example, Martin's attention was directed to the unrecognized opportunities both on the ground and in the air for publicizing the centennial. For

[10]Jack Litton to Lowry Martin, July 26, 1934, State Archives.
[11]S. W. Papert to Lowry Martin, July 5, 1934, State Archives.
[12]Lowry Martin to C. H. Odom, August 29, 1934, State Archives.
[13]Joseph B. Cross to Lowry Martin, July 26, 1934, State Archives.

$100 a week he could have the use of a GMC truck that was built like a locomotive and tender, entirely outlined with neon tubing, even to the tire rims. With a red neon star on the front of the engine (with 1936 in blue) and *Texas Centennial* emblazoned on the sides of the vehicle, this would create a sensation at the "Century of Progress" in Chicago, the owner believed. Another well-meaning citizen explained to Martin the ease with which a Ford trimotor aircraft could be purchased in Detroit for a nationwide aerial tour.

William Ort of Wichita Falls submitted an unsolicited centennial logo design that incorporated all the familiar Texas icons: the Texas longhorn, the Alamo, and the lone star, all pictured against a background of industry and commerce. Miss Glennie Vale Patterson of Medina, Texas, suggested to Martin that her original songs be used to advertise the centennial. Her patriotism, however, came at a price: "I will trade this song ["My Sweet Baby Girl"] for a new Chrysler Airflow sedan."[14] In addition to a proposed centennial edition of *The Cardinal Speller* textbook and the omnipresent destitute film producer who envisioned an epic production of the history of Texas, there was the ubiquitous Peggy Anne Sheffield's mother. Following Peggy Anne's tap dancing appearance at a Corsicana Lion's Club luncheon, her mother quickly recognized that the circuitous road to Hollywood began at the centennial publicity office. She urged Martin to speak to Fort Worth publisher Amon Carter, who might be persuaded to intercede with his friend actor Will Rogers, who in turn would introduce Peggy Anne to a Hollywood movie director. On the other hand, Mrs. Sheffield concluded, "Rogers [himself] might as well star a Texas child [in one of his movies] as any other."[15]

Despite this daily onslaught of absurd verbiage, Martin responded to each communication with calm recognition and appreciation. None, fortunately, received the harsh rejection or disregard they may have deserved. Martin, however, appeared never to be discouraged by the sometimes negative and often self-serving suggestions, remaining ever optimistic throughout the campaign. Near the end of August he wrote Sidney Kring, manager of the Corpus Christi Chamber of Commerce, that "every day the movement is gaining strength and by the first of September, we sincerely hope that there will not be a true Texan who

[14]Glennie Vale Patterson to Lowry Martin, August 9, 1934, State Archives.
[15]Mrs. J. E. Sheffield to Lowry Martin, August 8, 1934, State Archives.

is not thoroughly imbued with the spirit of the Centennial."[16] Within a few weeks Martin and his publicity staff had emerged as the ultimate change-makers. But this had come at a great personal sacrifice to Martin. In addition to his normal duties at the *Sun-Times* and the chairmanship of the publicity committee, Martin assumed the additional responsibility of temporary commission chairman during Cullen F. Thomas's unexpected two-month absence from the state. In a letter to J. E. Josey, dated August 15, Martin explained that he could not continue his responsibilities after September 1, because "I have now given practically all of my time for more than two months to this cause."[17]

In addition to Martin's publicity work, his role as temporary commission chairman necessitated his attending committee meetings and maintaining communication with commission members. He handled the latter primarily through correspondence, much of which was unnecessarily verbose. One communication to Josey covered six pages, typed single space, full of his unbounded enthusiasm and emotional outpourings: "In all my years of experience in advertising and publicity work, I have never seen any campaign develop in intensity and to the proportion the Centennial plan has developed in so short a time." Beyond the emotionalism, this letter contained two key points. Martin suggested that there be no letup in the publicity campaign after September 1, and he recommended that in addition to the central exposition, there should be a secondary local celebration of some type, somewhere, every day during 1936.[18]

This proposal reignited the ongoing conflict between those who saw patriotism and commercialism as best served by a single celebration and those who believed that the central exposition should not totally dominate the local events. Commission member John H. Shary of Mission, Texas, a businessman and land developer in the lower Rio Grande Valley took marked exception to Martin's recommendation of a year-long series of daily celebrations. Commercialism was the name of Shary's game, and he wrote:

> I am afraid that your enthusiasm has caused you to lose sight of the biggest thing that can happen to Texas, and that is that we make

[16]Lowry Martin to Sidney Kring, August 21, 1934, State Archives.
[17]Lowry Martin to J. E. Josey, August 15, 1934, State Archives.
[18]Ibid.

it [the centennial] such an outstanding success that we bring millions of new people into our State to visit.

If you want to make this just a family affair . . . that is just fine and dandy. You will have just what you are looking for, but people from the north . . . are not coming down to see a little one or two days celebration at some little point in Texas. . . . Please remember they don't possess the love of our traditions like the people who live here. They will only come to see big things, and that is to see the big exposition. . . . The great question and the great advantage to us is how best to get the people from outside of our State to come and look us over.[19]

Shary, not Martin, was articulating the commission's economic philosophy of the celebration. This had been blatantly spelled out in the booklet, *Commemorating a Hundred Years of Texas History*, which stated: "While it has been emphasized that the historical, the social, the cultural, the artistic, and the religious advancement of Texas for the last hundred years is, and must continue to be, the dominant thought in all Centennial ideas and plans, yet there is yet an economic side. The business and professional interests of the State which in the final analysis must foot the bill are entitled to know what the returns on the investment in a Centennial are likely to be."[20]

The commission had spoken; Shary's position would ultimately prevail. Texas would indeed stage a big exposition (in fact, two) of sufficient magnitude to induce many outsiders "to come and look us over."

[19]John H. Shary to Lowry Martin, August 18, 1934, State Archives.
[20]*Commemorating a Hundred Years of Texas History*, p. 29.

4

MIGHTY BIG TALK
IN SOME MIGHTY BIG CITIES

The next hurdle in the race toward 1936 was to induce a major Texas city to assume the financial responsibility for hosting the central exposition. This was one purpose of the publicity campaign, and by mid-August it appeared that objective had been reached. Martin reported to the commission that two, or possibly three, cities would submit proposals to host the exposition. These were Dallas, Houston, and San Antonio. Originally, Fort Worth was considered a contender, but with the approach of the September 1 deadline, that city quietly withdrew from the competition. The reasons remain unclear. Although Fort Worth publisher and premier civic booster Amon Carter was a member of the commission, he never attended a meeting or served on any of the working committees. Cullen Thomas had previously solicited his "dynamic, Texanic, aid in the great enterprise in behalf of all Texas," but to no avail.[1] Carter's departure in late August on an aerial tour of South American capitals with his friend Juan Trippe, president of Pan American Airways, further dramatized Carter's disinterest in the centennial movement. This, however, was destined to change.

The stringent financial requirements set forth by the planning committee were undoubtedly factors in Fort Worth's abstention from the competition. These, too, would be reconsidered in the near future. However, in 1934, Fort Worth, with the smallest population and resource base of the state's four major municipalities, had good reason not to compete.

The Central Exposition Proposal Forms contained the following requirements:

(1) Must have approximately 200 acres of land suitable for development as the exposition site.

---

[1]Cullen Thomas to Amon G. Carter, January 5, 1934, Amon G. Carter Archives, Amon Carter Museum of Western Art, Fort Worth, cited hereafter as Carter Archives.

(2) Must provide all utility services — electricity, gas, water, fire protection, sewage, and drainage — to the exposition site.

(3) Must state the city's maximum monetary offer, with a complete inventory of all property offered together with current value appraisals of all acreage and facilities.

(4) Upon receipt of the award, shall have sixty days to demonstrate to the Commission that all commitments are being fulfilled, and shall be prepared to deposit all funds required under the agreement.

(5) Shall agree that the Centennial Commission has the right to accept or reject any or all bids.

(6) Shall present the proposal in a sealed envelope to the chairman of the Commission on or before 12:00 o'clock noon, September 1, 1934.[2]

On July 18, 1934, Will H. Mayes, secretary of the commission, mailed copies of the proposal form to Mayor C. K. Quinn, San Antonio; Mayor Van Zandt Jarvis, Fort Worth; Mayor Oscar Holcombe, Houston; and Mayor C. E. Turner, Dallas. And the race was on. The ensuing developments cast in sharp relief the differing urban personalities of the state's leading cities, the quality of leadership each demonstrated, and the citizens' response to what many regarded as the opportunity of the century. The anticipated economic windfall and national prestige which the exposition would bring to the successful bidder gave the contest momentum but also provided some divisiveness. Marked disagreement over placing monetary consideration above historical importance in the selection process, debates between those who wanted primarily a historical celebration and those who advocated a commercial exposition, and the problematic attitude of the state legislature toward providing supplementary funding caused some hesitancy and indecision. The enthusiasm being generated by the publicity campaign, however, was sufficient to carry the contest to the September 1 deadline, creating along the way some moments of high drama and demonstrations of oral athletics. As might be expected, there was some mighty big talk in some mighty big towns.

San Antonio, the city with the most to offer historically, appeared the least aggressive in the contest to host the central exposition. Rely-

---

[2]Chariton, *Texas Centennial*, p. 9.

ing solely on its historical and geographic assets — the Alamo, Brackenridge Park, the Spanish missions, and close proximity to Mexico —
that city appeared either unable or uninterested in mounting a viable
campaign to compete with other Texas cities. Leadership appears to
have been a key factor. This posture was visible even before Lowry
Martin launched the publicity campaign. On March 28, Jack White,
manager of the Plaza Hotel, wrote San Antonio commission member
Mrs. O. M. Farnsworth: "I have just had two long distance telephone
calls from Austin asking why San Antonio was not busy trying to get
the Centennial for San Antonio. There was a meeting in Austin last
Saturday [March 24], as you probably know. It seems that we showed
very little interest in this meeting."[3]

The San Antonio Centennial Committee did, however, submit a
proposal to the commission. Drafted by Chamber of Commerce General Manager Porter A. Whaley and signed by Morris Stern, the local
centennial committee chairman, and Mayor C. K. Quinn, the document exuded an aura of negative self-righteousness while tendering
a financial proposal that was minimal, if not ludicrous, in view of
the nature of the celebration. Again the old tension between patriotism and commercialism became a paramount issue. The San Antonio
committee took the position that the centennial celebration "should
be [developed] strictly along patriotic and pageantry lines." A commercial celebration, they believed, would be "sordid . . . inappropri-
ate and unsatisfactory, and in fact likely to be very damaging to the
interests of the state." They took further exception to the provision
of Senate Bill 22, assigning the central exposition to the city offering
the largest financial inducement. Since the law did not specify a commercial exposition, they argued that in the forthcoming special session, the Texas Legislature could be induced to amend the law so
that it would "guarantee the holding of the exposition at a proper
place in Texas, meeting the historical requirements of the occasion."
And furthermore, they argued, the centennial should be considered
a strictly Texas affair. In view of the billions of dollars being spent
for emergency relief throughout the nation, "it is hardly to be ex-

[3]Jack White to Mrs. O. M. Farnsworth, March 28, 1934, Sara Roach Farnsworth Collection, Library of the Daughters of the Republic of Texas a, the Alamo, San Antonio,
cited hereafter as Farnsworth Collection.

pected that the Federal government would make an appropriation for a commercial exposition in Texas of measurable size."[4]

Mrs. Elinor Goldbeck Wilkes, a patriotic San Antonio citizen, appeared in total agreement with the committee's disdain for the financial consideration. She submitted the following statement to the *San Antonio Evening News* on the eve of the site selection. "That there is even a discussion over the location of the Texas Centennial celebration," she wrote, "is a tremendous indictment of the real patriotism of Texans. Is the location to be made at the sign of the dollar mark, or is it to be held where our millions of visitors can see for themselves the glorious past that is Texas?"[5] Yet, despite the negative views expressed in this matter, the San Antonio committee still considered their proposal valid and awaited the offers submitted by the other competing cities.

While Houston's approach to the issue was more positive than San Antonio's, that city's campaign to win the exposition lacked the determined leadership and positive outlook that might be expected from the state's major metropolis. Unlike the people of San Antonio, Houston citizens became involved. At a luncheon meeting held on July 18 in the main ballroom of the Rice Hotel, 300 luncheon and service club representatives "roared their approval" of a proposed $3 million bond issue as part of that city's monetary offer. This enthusiasm, however, was not reflected in Judge Clarence R. Wharton's address. "The question is, shall we try for it?" the local centennial committee chairman asked. "I don't want to appeal to emotions of the people in an effort to get the voters to do something they don't want." Wharton explained further that while he was opposed to bond issues, he could be persuaded to reverse his position; "if the majority wants it, we'll get it; if the majority is opposed, we'll drop it."[6]

As a civic leader, Wharton had abdicated his role. Apparently lacking the conviction to assume a firm posture on the issue, he was awaiting the will of the people in order to act. Strangely enough, other members of the civic establishment were equally uncommitted and

[4] City of San Antonio's proposal to host the Texas Centennial central exposition, Farnsworth Collection.

[5] Mrs. Elinor Goldbeck Wilkes to the *San Antonio Evening News*, August 13, 1934, Farnsworth Collection.

[6] *Houston Post*, July 19, 1934.

indecisive on the centennial matter. Judge W. O. Huggins, editor of the *Houston Chronicle*, stated that while his newspaper would support bringing the exposition to Houston, he was doubtful how the people stood on the issue. M. E. Foster, editor of the *Houston Press*, questioned the possibility of passing a bond issue unless the committee assured the voters that the bonds would be retired from the profits of the centennial. E. M. Biggers, organizer of the local taxpayers association, assumed a somewhat more positive stance. "I doubt if the people realize what the Centennial means to Houston," he explained. "To bring the Centennial here probably would be the greatest step Houston has taken since the ship channel was constructed."[7]

The centennial committee elected to move ahead with the bond drive. On August 2, Judge Wharton appointed Chester H. Bryan, a former Harris County judge, to head the campaign to gather 30,000 signatures on a petition urging approval of a $3 million bond issue. The cause appeared to be gaining momentum. The Houston Retail Merchants Association expressed unanimous approval of the bond issue, as did the newspapers, radio stations, and various civic and luncheon clubs. Judge Bryan also created a separate organization of black voters headed by John L. Blount, which planned to solicit every eligible black voter in the city. By this time Judge Wharton should have realized that the majority of Houston citizens would favor hosting the central exposition. He, nevertheless, remained virtually neutral on the issue. He warned that during the forthcoming canvass no high-pressure tactics would be tolerated in securing the signatures. "We want the true sentiment of the voters," he explained. "We want to know just how the people feel about the matter — whether Houston wants the centennial celebration."[8]

By early August Judge Wharton realized his centennial campaign lacked unified backing. While awaiting a mandate from the property owners, he had failed to gain the support of that segment of the urban community most critical in determining civic policy — the business community. There is a feeling of quiet desperation in his letter to George A. Hill, Jr., president of the Houston Oil Company. Dated August 8, 1934, Judge Wharton explained, "We have only two weeks to determine what Houston shall do to obtain this Centennial. We

[7]Ibid.
[8]Ibid., August 5, 1934.

are fearful that a tremendous lack of understanding exists on the part of our business leadership as to the possibilities of the Centennial. . . . We believe after investigation and study of this matter that Houston's leadership in this state hangs in the balance."[9]

In a final, and obviously hastily planned effort to rally support, Judge Wharton invited Hill to join one hundred of Houston's outstanding citizens two days later to discuss the matter. Even this attempt to salvage the cause lacked singleness of purpose. To discuss the "merits or demerits" of any issue is to acknowledge the potential for failure, especially for a $3 million bond issue during the Depression years. The reactions to Judge Wharton's appeal were, as might be expected, mixed. R. L. Blaffer, president of the Humble Oil and Refining Company, supported the issue. "I don't think that the first city of Texas can afford to step back and let the second and third city get the Centennial," he argued. "It would be a backward step that would take the city 25 years to overcome." W. P. Hobby, former governor of Texas and president of the *Houston Post*; Gus Wortham, president of the Houston Chamber of Commerce; and attorney James Elkins also expressed their accord. When he invited Mayor Oscar F. Holcombe to the meeting, Judge Wharton obviously expected a strong voice of support from the city's chief executive. He did not get it. Instead, Mayor Holcombe, like Judge Wharton himself, assumed a neutral stance. "As mayor, I am neither advocating nor opposing the bond issue. My position is this: I want it if the people want it." When the meeting finally adjourned, Judge Wharton must have realized that his belated effort had achieved little.[10]

On the eve of the voter canvass that would, in essence, determine whether Houston would submit a viable bid for the exposition, the *Houston Post* issued one of the more positive statements made during the course of the discussions. It called the centennial "the greatest civic opportunity that has been made available to this city since congress . . . authorized a deep water port. . . . The city will obtain publicity of incalculable value and in its wake will come new money for investment, new industry, and new population for at least a decade after the observance closes. . . . When the Centennial workers call

[9]Clarence R. Wharton to George A. Hill, Jr., August 8, 1934, George Hill Collection, Houston Metropolitan Research Center, cited hereafter as Hill Collection.
[10]*Houston Post*, August 11, 1934.

on you, give them a courteous hearing. . . . Your signature will be a renewed pledge of your faith in Houston."[11]

On August 13, a thousand volunteers began a house-to-house canvass of some nineteen thousand property owners. They received a courteous hearing. Partial returns tabulated a week later showed a two-to-one margin favoring the issue. The people had spoken. Houston's future role in the celebration rested with Judge Clarence R. Wharton and his committee of fifteen Houstonians. Now was the time for decisive action: the deadline for submitting exposition proposals was less than two weeks away.

Judge Wharton, however, continued to vacillate. On August 21, he wrote Lowry Martin, acting chairman of the Texas Centennial Commission, stating that unless arrangements could be made for the Houston Centennial Committee to meet with the planning and finance committees prior to September 1, they would not be able to submit Houston's bid for the centennial by the deadline. Two days later Judge Wharton directed a similar message to all members of the commission. The fundamental issue was money. The Judge objected to the commission's ultimate control of local funds raised for the central exposition. In addition, he feared that unless the state and federal governments made substantial appropriations, the celebration would become essentially "a local affair . . . [which] we do not want." Judge Wharton argued that the only solution to the matter was to await a legislative appropriation before any city had to commit a sum of money. He concluded that since "it will be absolutely impossible to get a credible celebration ready by the early part of 1936 . . . we are . . . going to ask our friends in Dallas and elsewhere to join us in postponing these matters until these questions can be more thoroughly threshed out."[12]

Judge Wharton's attempt to postpone the selection process drew immediate fire. R. L. Thornton, president of the Dallas Chamber of Commerce and veteran civic leader, took marked exception to the judge's suggestion. The judge, Thornton thought, was expecting far too much from friendship. To await legislative action, either state or

[11] Ibid., August 13, 1934.
[12] Clarence R. Wharton to Amon G. Carter, August 23, 1934, Centennial Collection, Texas State Archives.

federal, would be detrimental to the entire program. Thornton argued that any further delay would make it impossible for the host city to clear the necessary political, legal, and financial hurdles in order to open the exposition in 1936. And furthermore, this delay would "permit all the publicity to die out . . . and the entire enthusiasm throughout the state would slacken to the extent that it would be almost fatal." Thornton apparently anticipated this action of Judge Wharton. He scribbled across the bottom of his letter to Martin, "It happened quicker than I thought, RLT."[13]

Thornton reinforced his argument the following day with a two-page telegram to Martin, stating that he felt it was important that the legislature know the identity of the host city and its commitment to the celebration before considering any supplementary state appropriation. Unlike either San Antonio or Houston, Dallas had organized a solid base of community support for hosting the central exposition, and they were prepared to act; any further delay would be unacceptable. Later that same day Martin telegraphed Thornton that rumors of postponing the September 1 deadline were absolutely without foundation.

Time had about run out on Judge Wharton and his Houston committee. If they submitted a bid to host the central exposition, it would have to be in accordance with the provisions already established by the commission. There would be no exceptions. The ineptitude exhibited by the Houston committee did not go unnoticed. Amid the hesitancy and indecision over the changes and delays, the *Houston Post* editorially admonished those responsible for Houston's civic embarrassment. It pointed out that Texas should take note of San Diego's preparations for the California-Pacific International Exposition scheduled to open there on June 1, 1935. Five million dollars was being spent preparing the exposition site. The editor suggested: "The people of Texas would do well to acquaint themselves with this ambitious venture on the Pacific coast. . . . If the people of San Diego have sufficient faith in the pulling power of an exposition of this kind . . . there can be little ground for fear that a great Centennial celebration in this State will not be a financial success. The enterprise and courage of the City of San Diego, a community much smaller

[13]R. L. Thornton to Lowry Martin, August 24, 1934, ibid.

than Houston, provide an illustration of what can be accomplished through united action."[14]

The selection process proceeded as mandated by the commission. On Saturday, September 1, a centennial commission subcommittee met in Austin and received bids from Houston, Dallas, and San Antonio. Total secrecy surrounded the meeting. Only one representative from each city was permitted to appear before the subcommittee to present that city's bid. Each representative submitted maps, drawings, and photographs of the proposed sites, with architectural renderings of exposition structures plus listings of civic attractions that city offered. Commission chairman Cullen F. Thomas admonished each delegate not to reveal the amounts offered by their cities. Houston brought the largest delegation to Austin and installed a special exhibition of its exposition plans in a hotel suite for the subcommittee to inspect. In addition, groups from Galveston, Bryan, Liberty, Huntsville, Beaumont, and Nacogdoches accompanied the Houston delegation, to urge that city's selection as the exposition site.

With the bids submitted, an on-site inspection followed. The tour began in Dallas on September 6, 1934. Twenty-one members of the commission assembled in a Baker Hotel ballroom to hear R. L. Thornton present Dallas's claim to the exposition. They quickly realized that his would be a hard act for anyone to follow. Selling Dallas to the nation had become Thornton's driving passion.[15] He recognized that within that crowded ballroom lay his opportunity to achieve his ultimate goal — sponsoring a world-class fair that would gain global recognition for Dallas and the untapped economic resources of the great Southwest. His position, however, was not totally defensible. Compared with Houston and San Antonio, Dallas had little to recommend it historically. At the time of the siege of the Alamo and the Battle of San Jacinto, Dallas was an unoccupied spot on a treeless plain. But for Thornton that was not the issue, and he quickly moved to resolve once and for all the ongoing philosophical conflict between patriotism and progress. "We can only picture history and romance where history and romance exist," he argued. "We must pic-

[14]*Houston Post*, August 27, 1934.
[15]As chairman of the Industrial Dallas, Inc., Committee, Thornton had led the drive to raise $474,412 to advertise Dallas nationally as a favorable industrial center. In this capacity he became known as "the general sales manager of Dallas." *Dallas Times Herald*, March 24, 1928.

ture its great economical development from an economical point of view." He reasoned that the centennial should be about progress, progress made possible through the patriotic sacrifice of the state's founders. And there was no better place to celebrate this century of progress than in Dallas.[16]

Thornton gave a compelling presentation. Surrounded by six of architect George L. Dahl's highly romanticized color renderings (Dahl called it "eyewash"), Thornton made his pitch. The former candy salesman was in his element; the customers were ready to make a purchase and he had something to sell. Referring to a bank of maps, graphs, and charts, he itemized Dallas's assets as the exposition site: a central location, abundant peripheral population, excellent transportation facilities, more than adequate visitor accommodations, financial resources and responsibility, and a city unified behind its offer to host the exposition. Architect Dahl, Mayor Charles E. Turner, banker Nathan A. Adams, and Otto Herold, president of the State Fair of Texas, also addressed the commission. In addition, the Dallas Hotel Association offered a pledge to maintain the present rates during the centennial year. These would not exceed five dollars per day for a single room and six dollars for a double room; the minimum rate would be two dollars.

One of Dallas's greatest assets remained the facilities of the State Fair of Texas. Thornton explained that "for over forty-six years . . . we have constantly, without a single exception, portrayed to the commonwealth of Texas, the greatest economical and agricultural exposition in the name of the State Fair of Texas. . . . Ladies and Gentlemen, that forty-six years of experience . . . with our physical abilities . . . makes us competent to undertake this great undertaking."[17] The members of the commission were then taken on a two-hour tour of the fairgrounds and shown the 95-acre proposed addition to the existing plant which was included in the Dallas offer. (The addition was subsequently reduced to 26.5 acres.) Before departing, commission member Walter Cline posed a question which he stated would be asked all competing cities: "Assuming that Dallas is chosen as the Centennial city, would Dallas carry on without any State or Federal

---

[16]R. L. Thornton's address to the Centennial Commission subcommittee, copy in R. L. Thornton Scrapbook, Dallas Historical Society.
[17]Ibid.

aid?" To this Thornton replied: "Dallas has already said 'Yes.' . . . The Dallas bid stands firm as it is for the Centennial."[18]

Thornton emerged as the star of the Dallas presentation. Probably no one was more impressed with his performance than Dallas banker George Waverley Briggs, who telegraphed the following account to the vacationing Mrs. Thornton: "It was a masterpiece of vivid color and cogent argument and enraptured everyone who heard it. He talked for an hour and his audience called for more. . . . Dallas was proud of him . . . if we win it will be attributed to him."[19]

Later that night the members of the commission boarded a train at Dallas's Union Station for an overnight trip to Houston to inspect that city's facilities. Thornton, however, was not one to leave anything to chance; he wanted to know what the competition had to offer. The Houston committee, unknowingly, was about to host two uninvited guests for breakfast. Thornton and architect George H. Dahl drove most of the night, arriving in Houston just in time to meet the official entourage for an early morning reception at the Rice Hotel. Following that session, the commission toured the 200-acre centennial site near Sam Houston Hall, after which they boarded two yachts for a cruise down the ship channel for lunch at the San Jacinto Inn. Thornton and Dahl followed, arriving in time to hear Judge Wharton deliver a patriotic address and urge the selection of Houston as the central centennial city. For the judge, that fleeting moment of glory was, unfortunately, all too short-lived. The greatest embarrassment of the campaign was about to befall him. A half-century later George Dahl recalled the event vividly with wry amusement. It was a hot, humid autumn day, and following lunch the judge led the Commission on a tour of the San Jacinto Battlefield, pausing at one point to describe the event that won Texas' independence. The judge ascended an improvised dais (Dahl called it a soapbox) and began to speak:

> "Over there—you see that stone wall? There's where Santa Anna was. Over here [Wharton pointing] General Houston stood with his soldiers. . . . Here's where Houston won the Battle of San Jacinto." After about a half hour . . . the wind shifted. It came in off

18Secretary's Report, January 8, 1935, p. 6.
19Thornton Scrapbook.

the swamps and [brought in] a bunch of long gallinippers [mosquitoes]. And they came in and almost made the sky like a cloud. And these women with low neck dresses, these gallinippers were landing on them. They had newspapers, [and] they [began] hitting themselves all over to keep these gallinippers off. And Wharton says, "How can I deliver a romantic speech to you people as long as you are waving those damn newspapers at me?" He said, "It's those fellows here that came down from Dallas; there're the ones that brought these gallinippers in." And that broke up the meeting.[20]

Following the gallinipper invasion, the commission returned to Houston and boarded a night train for San Antonio, the last stop on the inspection tour. Before departing, however, Cline posed the question about Houston's hosting the exposition without state and federal appropriations. Mayor Holcombe responded that Houston would not be interested as "in that case it would be a Houston fair and not a Texas Centennial, in reality." When Cline asked the minimum amount Houston would accept as state participation, Holcombe replied approximately $3 million.[21]

The day in San Antonio began with a breakfast at the Plaza Hotel, followed with a tour of Brackenridge Park, the Alamo, the Spanish Governor's Palace, Olmos Basin, the Spanish missions, and Riverside Park. During a luncheon held in the St. Anthony Hotel, several people spoke in favor of San Antonio's bid for the exposition: Henry B. Dielman, chairman of the local centennial committee; Perry S. Robertson, president of the Chamber of Commerce; and Mayor C. K. Quinn. And then something unexpected, and unfortunate, occurred. By noon, news reached the entourage that a story in the Saturday, September 8, edition of the *Dallas Morning News* proclaimed: "Dallas Bid Wins Centennial, Claim Campaign Leaders . . . San Antonio Deal; In Return for Support Dallas Will Assist Alamo Exposition." The San Antonio committee understandably was furious. Had the local tour been conducted as merely a perfunctory exercise? And who had made a deal? Embarrassed, commission chairman Thomas quickly denied the *News* report as absolutely false. "I desire to say in this presence and to the world," Thomas explained, "that the commission

[20] Interview with George H. Dahl, Dallas, Texas, April 6, 1978.
[21] Secretary's Report, January 8, 1935, p. 7.

as a body has not considered for one moment the question of location of the Texas Centennial."[22]

With Thomas forced on the defensive, Mayor Quinn saw an opportunity to gain some points for his committee. Returning to the "highest bidder" argument, he registered his displeasure that the Texas legislature had enacted into law "a provision which placed the commission in the attitude of obtaining applications based on the highest monetary bids." Thomas took immediate issue with his host, stating it was the duty of the commission to see that the celebration was held in the proper way and to "forget sentiment."[23] San Antonio, when queried, placed the minimum state and federal subsidy at $1 million.

Under a cloud of suspicion and embarrassment, the commission embarked for Austin on the final leg of the tour. The following day the full commission would meet to consider all of the data, make a decision, and, they hoped, let the matter be closed and forgotten. On Sunday morning, September 9, twenty-four members of the commission convened, as usual, in the Driskill Hotel. Large delegations from Dallas and Houston were waiting in the hotel lobby when the commission arrived. They immediately went into executive session and deliberated from ten o'clock until noon, then adjourned until two o'clock when the session resumed. At 4:30 P.M. Chairman Thomas summoned newspaper reporters and members of the visiting delegations to the meeting room and explained he had been instructed by the commission to announce the results of the deliberation. Dallas had submitted the successful bid with a total offer of $7,791,000. Houston had submitted a bid of $6,507,000, and San Antonio, $4,835,000. Thomas explained further that the decision was made on the second ballot, whereupon every member of the commission, including the commissioners from Houston and San Antonio, stood in unanimous approval of the Dallas choice.[24] R. L. Thornton delivered the acceptance speech for Dallas: "We accept this honor in a spirit of humility and thankfulness. . . . It is a heavy obligation. It will require all we have

[22] *Houston Post*, September 9, 1934.

[23] *Fort Worth Star-Telegram*, September 9, 1934.

[24] Commission Secretary Will H. Mayes recorded the balloting as follows: "On the first ballot, Dallas received thirteen votes, Houston eight, San Antonio six. Neither place having received a majority, a second ballot was taken with Dallas receiving sixteen votes, Houston eight, San Antonio three. [J. E.] Josey moved that the selection of Dallas be made unanimous; [H. H.] Ochs [of San Antonio] seconded the motion, and it was adopted by a unanimous rising vote." Secretary's Report, January 8, 1935, p. 8.

of strength, of cash and of credit to portray faithfully and adequately the century of achievement in this great empire state of Texas."[25]

The Dallas victory brought mixed reactions from the other competing cities. Houston commission member Jesse H. Jones telegraphed his regrets for being unable to attend the meeting, but pledged his assistance in future work of the commission. Gus Wortham, president of the Houston Chamber of Commerce, stated that no resentment existed in Houston. The *San Antonio Express*, likewise, editorially accepted the commission's decision and challenged every community in the state to support the celebration. Although that newspaper had advocated a historical celebration, "the Legislature saw fit to adopt a compromise between such a view and that advocating another 'Century of Progress' for Texas. Under the lawmakers' mandate, the Centennial Commission had no choice but to award the main event to the highest bidder."[26] The San Antonio Centennial Committee, however, refused to accept defeat with dignity. In an undated broadside entitled "The Centennial Contest," committee chairman Morris Stern, Mayor Quinn, and chamber general manager Whaley expressed deep bitterness over the commission's decision, which they believed was based on regional considerations and San Antonio's opposition to a commercial exposition. The writers argued that two-thirds of the commission members were located in cities and towns in the northern half of the state, and "no one in San Antonio or Houston were [sic] asked who should be on the Commission." And when the commission met in Austin for the final vote "there were only two members of the Commission living south of San Antonio who actually had a vote." Although San Antonio remained perfectly willing "to have a commercialized exposition in Dallas," they challenged the Texas Legislature to amend Senate Bill 22, specifying adequate appropriations for historical celebrations which "we insist . . . must be held in some city in the historical region of Texas."[27]

Despite these smoldering animosities, another milestone in centennial history had been reached. Texas would have a centenary celebration, and Dallas would host a central exposition "Texanic in proportion, continental in ideals, and international in scope." The

[25] *Houston Post*, September 10, 1934.
[26] *San Antonio Express*, September 11, 1934.
[27] "The Centennial Contest," Farnsworth Collection.

commission's decision, however, was important not only for what it achieved, but for what it revealed about Texas in the mid-1930s. During the campaign the four major Texas cities displayed vastly different urban personalities, determined largely by the men and women who were at the forefront of the decision-making process. Fort Worth, for reasons that only Amon Carter knew, withdrew from competition early on, while San Antonio, possessing the greatest historical assets, submitted an almost inconsequential offer, obviously in defiance of the statute authorizing the celebration. That left the state's two largest metropolises, Dallas and Houston. Here the contrasts become even more striking. That Dallas enjoyed the advantage of Fair Park, its monetary value, plus forty-six years of exposition experience, did not preordain its selection, given Houston's superior size, strategic location, and greater economic resources. At that particular point in time, the stature and vision of Houston's decision-makers were simply not commensurate with the city's potential for urban leadership, especially in the matter of sponsoring a world exposition. Some local citizens recognized this. Following Dallas's selection, J. E. Josey, a commission member and chairman of the board of the *Houston Post*, wrote R. L. Thornton, "I want to congratulate you on your successful effort in bringing to Dallas the Texas Centennial. . . . When I returned from Dallas Friday morning with the Commission, I told the Committee of Houston citizens that Houston stood no chance in their half-hearted, unorganized effort against the united support of Dallas, led by such men as you."[28]

Houston's loss to Dallas also caused great concern to the Houston Chamber of Commerce. As Judge Wharton had warned belatedly, Houston's statewide leadership did indeed hang in the balance. On September 15, chamber secretary Bill Blanton dispatched a three-page communication to chamber members. In "Can We Capitalize Defeat to Launch Greater Houston Campaign," he also cited the lack of unity for Houston's failure to win the central exposition. "Dallas does not possess a single historical asset," Blanton asserted, "while other contestants were rich in that respect. . . . But the real factor that swayed the Centennial Commission was the absolutely solid front presented by Dallas."[29]

[28]J. E. Josey to R. L. Thornton, September 12, 1934, Thornton Scrapbook.
[29]Hill Collection.

While the solid front presented by the Dallas community was an obvious factor in winning the exposition, fulfilling that obligation to the State of Texas demanded that such concerted effort be maintained during the critical months that lay ahead. The big question that now confronted Thornton and the commission was how much supplementary funding the state and federal governments would appropriate to help pay for the celebration. Suddenly June 6, 1936, seemed frighteningly close, and awaiting government appropriations could be terribly time-consuming.

5

WAR OF WORDS
IN THE TEXAS LEGISLATURE

On September 9, 1934, the centennial spotlight switched suddenly from Corsicana to Dallas, where it would remain throughout the celebration. With the new location came a new cast of performers creating new character roles seldom seen in the Lone Star State. Little more would be heard from Lowry Martin and the *Corsicana Sun-Times*. For eleven years he had carried the centennial mantle with fervor and dedication, and now it was passed to new hands. Immediately following the Austin meeting, Martin advised State Comptroller George H. Sheppard that he was closing the Corsicana office and transferring the records to Dallas. He had served the cause well; his account was in order. Of the $15,000 allocated the publicity campaign, he had spent approximately $14,500.[1]

In that brief moment in an Austin hotel room, Dallas became the host city for the world-class exposition. And while the city had campaigned vigorously for it, the honor carried staggering responsibilities. Dallas, however, possessed a citizenry equal to the assignment. The primary leadership roles fell ultimately to a triumvirate of bankers: R. L. Thornton, Fred F. Florence, and Nathan Adams. Their past contributions as civic leaders account largely for their selection; they represented a good balance of skills and attitudes. With Dallas the designated centerpiece of the celebration, they were intent on bringing worldwide recognition to their city.

The leaders lost little time preparing for the great event. Florence called a meeting for Friday, September 14, to complete the local organization and map out a campaign for a $3 million bond issue. To further expedite the matter, Walter D. Cline scheduled a September 21 meeting of the State Centennial Commission's executive committee in Dallas, where both Thornton and Florence were added to that body.

---

[1] *San Antonio Express*, September 10, 1934.

At the same meeting the committee accepted an invitation to appear before the Senate Committee of the Whole on September 24, to request a state appropriation for the celebration. Seven commission members, including Thornton and Dallas Mayor Charles E. Turner, addressed the Senate committee at 10:00 A.M. and the House committee at 8:00 P.M. Each made patriotic appeals for an appropriation and urged immediate action by the legislature. Their pleas went unheeded; unemployment relief remained the lawmakers' primary concern. The Third Called Session of the Forty-Third Legislature adjourned the following day, having taken no action on the centennial matter.

The members of the legislature apparently did not share the commission's sense of urgency. With the centennial year only fifteen months away, awaiting action until the next regular session would reduce the lead time to only twelve months. It was a time for drastic action. Walter D. Cline assumed the initiative, dispatching the following telegram to 1,430 individuals, urging another special legislative session to act on the centennial issue:

> It is vital that you, the mayor, chamber of commerce, or other bodies in your city, immediately wire the governor expressing the necessity for a special session of the legislature in order that centennial plans may be perfected immediately, and that you have personal contact with your representatives and senator, urging them to support energetically centennial measures presented to the legislature. . . . Please wire us collect by Western Union tomorrow night, results of your efforts. Your personal cooperation will be greatly appreciated.[2]

This effort yielded immediate results. At an executive committee meeting held in Dallas on October 3, Cline exhibited a sheaf of telegrams and letters from both legislators and centennial supporters indicating their support for a special session. Public opinion expressed in this magnitude was too much to ignore. On October 12, 1934, lame duck Governor Ferguson convened the Fourth Called Session of the Forty-Third Legislature in Austin. In her proclamation she cited five priority items for the lawmakers' consideration. Four items involved huge appropriations; two — the centennial and emergency relief —

[2](Author's punctuation.) Undated, Carter Archives.

dominated her message. As the session progressed, these two contrasting subjects became intertwined emotionally and philosophically as well as financially. By the time her message was read, the outcome of each was virtually predictable. The governor, however, spoke positively to the centennial issue, acknowledging the cost, "perhaps Five Million Dollars," while emphasizing the economic benefits that would accrue to the state: "The Texas Centennial will bring in my opinion ten million new people to Texas, which will spend an average of Ten Dollars each for the manufactured products of our natural resources. . . . No matter how you figure the Centennial it means a Hundred Million Dollars [of] new money turned loose in Texas. I am for it."[3]

The governor obviously saved the most critical item for last: her emotional appeal for aid for the indigent. Against a centennial appropriation, this appeal gave lawmakers virtually no choice in their decision. She estimated that 267,000 Texas families were then receiving relief. That number was increasing daily, she explained, and would probably reach three hundred thousand families or 1.5 million people. "I want no honor for economy at the expense of hungry mothers and fathers and crying babies," she demanded. "The last Legislature . . . set aside One Million Dollars a month for the next five months for relief. I submit this is grossly inadequate."[4]

On October 13, the day following the opening of the called session, the full commission met in Dallas to develop legislative strategy. Cline made two requests; both were granted. The commission allocated $10,000 to wage a publicity campaign during the next thirty days and accorded the executive committee, under Cline's direction, plenary powers to represent the commission before the legislature. Two days later Sen. George C. Purl of Dallas introduced Senate Bill No. 4, an appropriation measure to fund the centennial.

As the bill made its way through the legislative process, a new issue emerged igniting an entirely new complex of sensitivities. Some three weeks prior to the bill's introduction, members of the Dallas Negro Chamber of Commerce had begun developing a strategy to gain black representation at the central exposition. At a September 22 meeting, A. Maceo Smith, a Dallas high school teacher who held degrees from Fisk, Columbia, and New York University, reported he had

---

[3]*Journal of the Senate of Texas, Fourth Called Session, Forty-Third Legislature*, pp. 21–23.
[4]Ibid.

discussed the matter with members of the legislature. Smith's plan included "gaining state aid for a Negro display at the main exposition in Dallas and for the creation of a special advisory committee on Negro affairs to represent the state's Negroes during the centennial preparation."[5] Senator Purl, who appeared responsive to Smith's plan, suggested that a delegation from the Dallas Negro Chamber of Commerce appear at the forthcoming hearing on the centennial appropriation bill. Joining the other Dallas representives, Smith and Houston architect J. L. Blount appeared in Austin on October 23 to present the black proposal. Armed with schematic drawings and statistical data on blacks in Texas, Smith outlined plans for a $500,000 "Africa Museum" at the Dallas exposition and a statewide survey to gather materials on the black experience in Texas. The committee appeared interested, allowing "Smith to talk for an hour rather than the allotted twenty minutes."[6]

Although both Cline's committee and the black spokesmen made determined presentations to the legislature, their efforts yielded little. They nevertheless learned a valuable lesson. Far more than patriotic rhetoric was needed to penetrate the legislative barrier; regional jealousy and fiscal conservatism would emerge as major stumbling blocks. During early debates, however, prospects for favorable action appeared bright. On Saturday, November 3, three weeks into the session, the Senate, sitting as a Committee of the Whole, approved Senator Purl's centennial appropriation bill and ordered it printed for consideration on the following Monday. The tone of the bill was definitely pro-Dallas. Of the proposed $5 million, Dallas would receive $2.7 million for the central exposition, with $300,000 tentatively earmarked for the Fort Worth livestock coliseum. The remaining $2 million would be available for other statewide centennial events.[7]

If Cline's committee interpreted this action as a good omen, they were unaware of the obstructive forces that lurked across the hall.

[5] John D. Boswell, "Negro Participation in the 1936 Texas Centennial Exposition," p. 2. This is an unpublished term paper that was submitted in History 389 in 1969 at the University of Texas at Austin. Photocopy in author's files.

[6] Ibid., p. 3. Historian Michael L. Gillette described Smith as "a gifted practitioner of the political arts of compromise and consensus; he combined the administrative talents of the bureaucrat with the promotional skills of an insurance executive. Confident and charismatic, he was above all an organizer." "The Rise of the NAACP in Texas," *Southwestern Historical Quarterly* 81 (April, 1978): 393.

[7] The bill in its original form called for a $8,972,174 appropriation.

While the Senate prepared to act on an appropriation bill, Rep. Vernon Lemens of Somervell County offered a resolution to prohibit any legislative appropriation for the centennial, recommending instead that it be financed from private funds. This produced an immediate confrontation with the Dallas delegation, which proposed obtaining the necessary funds through special corporation taxes rather than a state appropriation. Journalist Harry Benge Crozier reported that this touched off "a war of words that occupied the House for three-fourths of Friday, [in which] Dallas as a Centennial site was liberally lambasted and a few harsh words were thrown in the general direction of San Antonio."[8]

The ongoing Dallas-San Antonio conflict appeared to polarize the members of the House. A middle ground no longer existed. If Dallas wanted to host an exposition, it apparently had come to the wrong place for money. Rep. Joseph F. Greathouse of Fort Worth claimed that holding a "Centennial celebration at Dallas, is like celebrating Washington's Birthday at Buckingham Palace. . . . You don't have to put your filthy hands in the Treasury for $5,000,000 to be patriotic." Rep. Pat Dwyer of San Antonio, still smarting from his city's loss to Dallas, claimed: "If we want to perpetuate Texas history, for God's sake let's don't go to Oklahoma to do it. If Dallas wants a fair, let it pay for it. If you want a historical fair, come to San Antonio." Rep. Walter E. Jones of Jourdanton agreed that "San Antonio is the logical place for a Centennial, but in doing things and in money power, it compares with Dallas as a Model T does with a twelve-cylinder car." Taking a dim view of the Alamo City's role in the entire matter, Rep. Oscar F. Chastain of Eastland claimed "there isn't enough patriotism in San Antonio to bury a dead soldier. Mrs. Clara Driscoll Sevier had to save the Alamo and the Forty-First Legislature was called on to appropriate $200,000 to make it fit for visitors to look at." The House finally voted to postpone consideration of the Lemens resolution until Wednesday, November 7, thus ending the carnival of words. Crozier observed: "There was a difference of opinion as to whether the vote was a victory for the sponsors of the Centennial. At least it constituted a stay of execution."[9]

The latter proved correct. House consideration of the Lemens reso-

[8] *Dallas Morning News*, November 3, 1934.
[9] Ibid.

lution the following Wednesday developed into another day of ora-
torical bludgeoning that brought the centennial appropriation issue
to a crisis. The resolution weathered a point of order, but the seventy-
two-hour rule went into effect the following day. When the measure
failed to muster the necessary two-thirds vote, Lemens' bill died a
procedural death. A similar fate awaited across the hall, where Sen.
George C. Purl of Dallas scrambled for support for his appropriation
bill in the upper house. Sen. Joe Moore of Greenville, who opposed
all centennial bills, called up, as privileged, the House resolution calling for sine die adjournment at noon on Saturday, November 10, thus
cutting twelve hours off of the session. "That caused another wrangle,"
Crozier reported, "during which Moore said he wanted to see Saturday's Texas-Baylor football game, as did Clint Small of Amarillo, who
has a son playing in the Longhorn line." (Senator Small had every
reason to be proud. Texas won the game 25 to 6.) Thus the session
ended without passage of a centennial appropriation measure. Its supporters, however, salvaged some consolation. Before adjournment the
Senate passed Senator Small's resolution thanking the centennial commission for its efforts, endorsing the selection of Dallas as the central
exposition site, and expressing hope the state would ultimately make
ample financial provisions for the celebration. Even the optimism im-
plied in the resolution did not go unchallenged. Tom DeBerry of Bo-
gata, another perennial opponent of centennial appropriations, and
E. J. Blackert of Victoria, his ardent supporter in such measures, cast
the two dissenting votes. Although the 20 to 2 tally constituted an
oblique vote of confidence (one senator called it "crocodile tears"),
it nevertheless indicated that when the measure was taken up again,
a formidable opposition would still have to be dealt with.[10]

The name-calling and accusations did not cease with adjournment.
The Dallas committee felt, apparently with some justification, that
San Antonio had obstructed passage of the appropriation measure.
When Morris Stern, chairman of the San Antonio committee, learned
this, he wrote Fred Florence, his Dallas counterpart, a four-page epistle denying San Antonio's role in the legislative miscarriage. Stern
claimed that while his group wanted to see the centennial bill passed,
they nevertheless wanted a bill that would grant reasonable recognition to their city. The reasonable recognition his city sought, Stern

[10]Ibid., November 8, 1934.

explained, turned out to be "somewhat more than the $250,000" provided in the original bill. While denying that he was "one of those 'I told you so' individuals," Stern turned once again to the old patriotism versus commercialism debate as the real reason for the bill's defeat. "That ill-conceived scheme which created the [original] Centennial Bill under which the Commission was working," he wrote, "cheapened the real spirit of this wonderful event, commercializing it and putting patriotism and recognition of our heroic pioneers second. . . . Our Legislators, in their hearts, felt that Texas wanted a dignified historical celebration centered around the Alamo and San Jacinto."[11]

Recent legislative oratory provided some basis for Stern's sometimes questionable rationale. However, the state's other financial obligations and the prevailing aura of fiscal conservatism in the mid-1930s were also factors that should not be dicounted. During a Senate hearing, McDonald Meacham of Houston, an independent oil operator and former state senator, spoke of the poor timing of the forthcoming celebration and recommended an indefinite postponement. "Hungry men don't believe in shows," he said. "I'm for a Centennial and I'm not against it being in Dallas, but the hour for such a celebration is not at hand." Many of the state's lawmakers apparently agreed, at least temporarily.[12]

While the legislature wrangled over the centennial bill, Dallas moved ahead with its plans for the exposition. The city council scheduled the $3 million bond election for October 30, 1934. The matter received enthusiastic editorial support from both the *Morning News* and the *Times Herald*. The *News* considered the bond issue "a sound expenditure, a necessary piece in the Centennial mosaic. A vote for the bond issue Tuesday is a vote for Dallas."[13] The black business community, encouraged by the apparent support of Dallas's business and political leaders, also joined the campaign for passage of the bond issue. The *Dallas Express*, the city's major black newspaper, added its support to the measure while issuing a prophetic warning to its readers: "Dallas Negroes will support the organized efforts of Dallas in observing the Centennial, but we ought to be sure we are not over-

[11]Morris Stern to Fred F. Florence, November 15, 1934, Farnsworth Collection.
[12]*Dallas Morning News*, November 1, 1934.
[13]Ibid., October 29, 1934.

oked."[14] The electorate, both black and white, responded with a
record turnout, approving the issue overwhelmingly. The $3 million
bond was earmarked for land and permanent improvements, including buildings, parks, parkways, boulevards, and other beautification
work at the exposition site. Attempting to gain legislative support,
the *Morning News* cited passage of the bond issue as an example for
the lawmakers to follow. The message, however, went unheeded.

The same day Dallas passed the bond issue, the Chicago world's
fair, the Century of Progress, ended its second year's run. This exposition's statistical record gave the Dallas business community reason
for optimism. The more than thirty-eight million people attending
the fair produced $160 million in additional income and gave direct
and indirect employment to five hundred thousand persons. Hoping
to sustain this business bonanza, the Chicago Real Estate Board petitioned Mayor Edward J. Kelly to continue the fair on an annual basis. Members of the Dallas Real Estate Board foresaw a similar up-
swing in local property values and supported the local bond issue in
the belief that real estate would benefit more than it would be taxed.
The business community lost little time in translating these words
into positive action. By mid-September Ralph Hitz, president of the
National Hotel Management Company, was in Dallas to plan extensive renovations of the Adolphus Hotel in anticipation of the exposition boom.

Despite R. L. Thornton's "go it alone" pronouncement, the ultimate success of the celebration remained contingent on both state
and federal subsidies. The latest news from Austin was not encouraging. However, by the time the Forty-Fourth Legislature convened on
January 8, 1935, several changes had occurred that would influence
the session's outcome. First, the people of Texas had elected a popular young governor, James V. Allred, who evolved as the celebration's
greatest supporter and most visible asset. Second, the Texas Centennial Commission, in cooperation with the Dallas Centennial Executive Committee, had helped redraft an appropriation bill reducing
the state's proposed expenditures to $3 million. And third, the Texas
Press Association again came to the centennial's rescue. At Walter
Cline's request, the bureau launched a three-week intensive statewide
publicity campaign to stimulate renewed interest in the celebration

[14]Boswell, "Negro Participation," p. 3.

concurrent with the legislature's consideration of the appropriation measure. The campaign cost only $4,700 and turned out to be the commission's greatest bargain.[15]

It was obvious from the beginning of the session that getting the reduced appropriation through the new legislature would not be easy. The economic news remained dismal. By March, 1935, some six weeks into the session, 163,926 persons were receiving direct relief in Texas, while 146,337 were engaged in work relief programs. This data alone gave centennial opponents a formidable weapon to use against the Dallas area's six House members. Rep. Jeff Stinson, a third-term veteran, headed the Dallas delegation that included four freshman representatives (Rawlins Colquitt, Jimmy Collins, Sam Hanna, and Fred Red Harris) and one sophomore (W. O. Reed). Stinson moved with dispatch. On January 11, 1935, four days into the session, he introduced House Bill No. 11, which was read the same day and referred to committee. The last lap of the centennial legislative race was on. The Texas Press Association again flooded the state with pro-centennial news releases while the Dallas Chamber of Commerce literally "camped on the doorsteps" of the legislature during the session. Robert Pool, Adolphus Hotel executive and former manager of Dallas radio station WFAA, was a member of the Dallas entourage that R. L. Thornton brought to Austin to help entertain the legislators. Pool later remembered that he sang for the lawmakers on several occasions.[16]

Noticeably absent from this session of the legislature were members of the Dallas Negro Chamber of Commerce. Something unexpected had happened in the interim. Early in 1935, Governor Allred had appointed Dallas County Rep. Sarah T. Hughes as judge of the Fourteenth District Court. A general election was called for March 16, 1935, to fill the vacancy in the legislature. When an unprecedented seventy-four candidates entered the race (sixty were actually listed

---

[15]One phase of this publicity campaign consisted of a series of daily news releases entitled "Dusting the Covers of Texas History." These historical vignettes covered a wide range of Texas history topics: January 1, 1935, "Stephen F. Austin's and Joseph Hawkins' Trek to Texas in 1821"; January 4, "Good and Bad Indians"; and January 9, "Wedding in Austin's Colony."

[16]Robert Pool was also a pioneer in radio broadcasting. He created the "Early Birds Program," a popular early morning program during the 1930s and 1940s on WFAA, supervised the first remote control broadcast of a Texas football game (Abilene versus Cleburne), and the first "live" broadcast of a governor's inaugural (Ross S. Sterling).

on the ballot), the black community decided to support black Dallas attorney A. S. Wells. The Dallas *Express* editorialized: "Mr. Wells' friends feel that he stands a good chance of being elected, and especially so if one thousand qualified Negro voters in the county can be aroused to go to the polls and vote."[17] The Dallas business and political community also recognized that possibility and acted accordingly. Maceo Smith remembered they began applying pressure, verbally at first, "to get the nigger out of the race . . . their condition was that if we pulled him out, they could assure us that we'd get our money to put on this Negro exhibit." Smith, however, refused to compromise, and Dallas blacks suffered a double defeat. Wells lost the race, placing fifth, "and when we refused to pull our man out . . . then we lost the interest of the people who were sponsoring us." No mention of the black exhibit appeared in the bill then under consideration in the Texas legislature.[18]

Defeat, however, was only temporary. "We weren't going to be outdone," Smith explained, "because we'd set up a state committee" to generate interest in the black exhibit. Although Dallas and Austin had rejected the proposal, black participation in the Texas centennial was merely dormant, not dead. It was destined to surface again in the near future as a vital factor in the forthcoming celebration.[19]

The sponsors of the centennial measure were forced to grapple with many negative issues other than race before finally getting the bill through the legislature. Dallas Rep. Fred Red Harris explained:

It was a hard, hard fought bill. . . . Those who didn't want the bill referred to it as another Dallas fair. And the lines were drawn pretty quickly. Those who were not gettin' any money, you knew exactly where they were goin'— to oppose it! We couldn't even depend on Fort Worth. They had the Fat Stock Show over there, and they thought they oughta get some money. And we did finally get some help out of Houston. But there was an awful lot of tradin' around in those days. . . . Trade your life out, practically. . . . I voted for every squirrel bill brought up in the State of Texas. I could no more

[17]*Dallas Express*, March 2, 1935. As this was a general election, blacks who had paid their poll tax could vote.

[18]Interview with A. Maceo Smith, Dallas, Texas, November 3, 1977; Boswell, "Negro Participation," p. 4.

[19]Smith interview, November 3, 1977.

go huntin' anywhere because I didn't remember whether or not I voted to close the squirrel law or open it.[20]

Rep. Vernon Lemens, who had introduced the controversial resolution in the preceding session, ultimately joined the fight for the centennial appropriation. He explained the reduction from $5 million to $3 million "was the main thing. It was pretty obvious that there was some sentiment in having a bill. And most of us were tightwads at that time. And we wanted to get off as light as we could." Representative Lemens further credits Rep. Jeff Stinson for personally overcoming the "what history is there in Dallas?" stigma and ultimately gaining most of the opposition's support. "He had an uphill fight all the way," Lemens explained. "He was a good, wholesome, fine representative . . . and I helped him on the thing because of him."[21] Stinson also gained the support of Governor Allred. On March 12, Edward Clark, secretary to the governor and later ambassador to Australia, appeared at the bar of the House and read the following message from the governor:

> Due to the pressure of official duties I have not had time to prepare a message of such nature as to adequately do justice to this great project. After all, however, no stronger recommendation could be made than that contained in the constitutional amendment and in the platform of the [Democratic] party. I trust this Legislature will make adequate provision, including a reasonable appropriation, for a real Centennial celebration.[22]

The San Antonio legislative delegation also gave its support to Stinson's bill. On March 15, the day following House passage of the measure, Rep. R. L. Reeder reassured Mrs. O. M. Farnsworth that he "voted for the bill and helped every way possible to put it over. As the bill passed the House, San Antonio will receive three hundred and fifty thousand dollars." (That amount was subsequently reduced to $250,000.)[23]

[20]Oral Memoirs of Fred Red Harris, September 7, 1977–December 5, 1977, Texas Judicial Systems Project, Baylor Program for Oral History, Baylor University.

[21]Interview with Vernon Lemens, Austin, Texas, October 11, 1984.

[22]*Journal of the House of Representatives, Regular Session, Forty-Fourth Legislature*, p. 619.

[23]Rep. R. L. Reeder to Mrs. O. M. Farnsworth, March 15, 1935, Farnsworth Collection.

Yet the long-standing opposition to a centennial appropriation remained active throughout the session. The measure initially passed the House by a vote of 102 yeas to 32 nays. After the House refused to concur with Senate amendments, the bill went to a conference committee. Both houses voted final passage of the bill on April 25 by comparatively slim margins, 78 to 63 and 17 to 12. Governor Allred signed the $3 million appropriation bill into law on May 7, 1935.[24] His signature assured, at last, that Texas would stage a creditable centennial celebration.

The essential provisions of House Bill No. 11 are as follows:

(1) Appropriated $3 million for conducting celebrations commemorating the historic period of Texas, during the period to December 31, 1936.

(2) Created the Commission of Control for Texas Centennial Celebrations, a nine-member commission chaired by the lieutenant governor, with broad authority to supervise disbursement of the $3 million appropriation. This allocation was to include the selection and administration of local celebrations and the erection of historical markers, monuments, and memorials.

(3) Allocated $1 million to erect exposition buildings on the site of the centennial central exposition in Dallas, plus $200,000 to equip and furnish the structure. This evolved as one structure, the present Hall of State.

(4) Allocated $225,000 to gather and prepare exhibits at the yet-to-be-built Texas Memorial Museum in Austin. (This museum, now located on the campus of the University of Texas, was to be constructed at a cost of $750,000 from funds raised by the Texas Centennial Committee of the Texas American Legion.)

(5) Allocated $250,000 to restore the Alamo and stage a celebration commemorating that historic shrine.

(6) Allocated $250,000 to erect and equip a permanent memorial at the San Jacinto Battlefield.

(7) Authorized the Commission of Control to expend "an appro-

[24]*House Journal*, pp. 435–36. It seemed ironic that Theodore H. Price, who advanced the idea of a Texas centennial celebration in Corsicana in 1923, died in New York City on May 4, 1935, only three days before the governor signed the centennial measure into law.

priate amount" for a memorial to Texas' pioneer women at some suitable place in Texas.

(8) Provided that $1,075,000 and such other sums as might be reallocated under the terms of this act, be allocated for celebrations and expositions outside Dallas County.

(9) Created a three-member Advisory Board of Texas Historians to make recommendations to the Commission of Control on proposed commemorative celebrations, expositions, markers, and memorials.

(10) Created the three-member Advisory Board for Advertising, with a $500,000 budget, to formulate a program of state and national publicity and advertising.

(11) Limited salaries to $4,000 per year. Commission and board members would serve without pay, receiving only a per diem allowance.

(12) Provided that the Texas Centennial Central Exposition would repay the $100,000 that the Second Called Session of the Forty-Third Legislature had advanced to the Centennial Commission.

(13) Authorized the Commission of Control, immediately after the passage of this act, "to make formal application for the participation of the Federal Government in the Texas Centennial celebration . . . and for adequate appropriation . . . of Federal funds for that purpose."[25]

Two days after Governor Allred signed the appropriation bill into law, the legislature approved a concurrent resolution making the $3 million immediately available. Without that action no money could have been used until August 9. Little of the bitterness that attended other centennial debates surfaced when this resolution was offered in the House on May 9. Several former opponents of the measure requested unanimous acquiescence in the final vote. This, however, did not occur. The House voted 110 to 22, while the tally in the Senate was 21 to 6. Sen. T. A. DeBerry of Bogata in Red River County led the Senate opposition, composed largely of an East Texas farming bloc. Over in the House, Rep. Leonard Westfall also accepted defeat with

[25] General and Special Laws of the State of Texas, Forty-Fourth Legislature, Regular Session, January 8, 1935 to May 11, 1935, 1:427-37.

bitterness, claiming "this Centennial bunch and the Governor, in signing this bill, are taking money away from the ragged school children
of the State. It is planned to give the Centennial the first dive into
the State Treasury and if anyone has to take a 5 or 10 per cent dis-
count on their warrants it will be the $30 a month girls working for
the eleemosynary institutions."[26]

The passage of House Bill No. 11 remains a landmark in Texas political history. This enactment cleared the way for the state to embark on an unprecedented $3 million adventure, sponsoring the first
world's fair ever staged in the Southwest.[27] Once again the legislature maintained its consistency by its inconsistency, enacting a nonessential appropriation measure at a time when state funds were steadily being drained away by emergency aid for the unemployed and
the destitute. Probably the greatest anomaly of this action was allocating $500,000 to advertise the celebration, especially the central ex-
position, both statewide and nationally. In taking this action, however, the legislature attempted to draw a compromise between the
patriotic and commerical purposes of the celebration. The $500,000
advertising budget, one-sixth of the total appropriation, was sufficient
to please the commercial advocates. They were assured that the national spotlight would be turned primarily on Dallas and the Texas
Centennial Central Exposition, dramatizing Texas' progress toward
the future. That would be the primary statement issued to the nation
and the world in 1936. Commission member John H. Shary undoubtedly relished the decision. He was now assured that they would "get
people from outside our state to come and look us over."

The governor's signing the centennial bill on Tuesday morning,
May 7, touched off a chain reaction in Dallas. Programs that had been
held in abeyance for several weeks were now cleared for action, free-
ing Dallas civic leaders for a three-pronged attack: to push for immediate federal participation, to establish a working procedure with
the city council, and to stimulate the sale of the remaining Centen-

[26]*Dallas Morning News*, May 10, 1935.

[27]Other state legislatures had previously appropriated funds for world's fairs. The Penn-
sylvania state legislature appropriated $1 million for the 1876 United States Centennial
Celebration in Philadelphia, and the State of Missouri voted a like amount for the 1904
Louisiana Purchase Exposition held in Saint Louis. See also Frederick M. Crunden, "The
Scope and Features of the Louisiana Purchase Exposition," *Review of Reviews* 86 (May,
1903): 547–56.

nial Corporation bonds, of which $579,950 were unsubscribed. Walter D. Cline, who recently had been appointed executive director of the exposition, spent most of the afternoon in the corporation's temporary offices in the Baker Hotel, talking long-distance with Sen. Tom Connally and Fort Worth Congressman Fritz Lanham in Washington. They agreed to introduce in both houses of Congress a bill authorizing federal participation in the Texas centennial with a $5 million appropriation. Late that afternoon Mayor George Sergeant invited the corporation's executive committee to meet with the new city council to discuss condemnation of twenty-six acres of land adjoining Fair Park and the sale of $3.5 million in bonds. The mayor, however, declined to give a specific date when the first exposition contracts would be let or when construction would get under way. Nonetheless, it had been a very busy Tuesday afternoon in Dallas.

As spring gave way to summer, the entire city seemed to catch the spirit of the great transformation that was about to engulf that North Texas metropolis. In the pulpits, at business luncheons, at country clubs, on the radio, and in the newspapers, the Texas Centennial Central Exposition became the primary topic of interest. None were more interested than the three members of the corporation's executive committee: Thornton, Florence, and Adams. The exposition was now a reality. It was their challenging task to convert the some 185 acres of residences and obsolete exhibit halls into a world-class exposition. This required the right combination of management, manpower, and money. Management was in place, unemployed labor was in abundance, yet the financial mosaic was still incomplete. The State of Texas had at last made its financial commitment. Now it was the federal government's turn to help honor the once-independent republic that had voluntarily accepted statehood. The congressional wheels had already begun to turn, but time, obviously, was critical. The June 6 opening day of the exposition was only one year away.

6

THE DALLAS TRIUMVIRATE:
ADAMS, FLORENCE, AND THORNTON

Federal participation in the Texas centennial celebrations had been a long-standing assumption. The movement's leaders based their belief on established precedent; the 1903 Louisiana Purchase Exposition held in Saint Louis received a $5 million federal appropriation, plus a $1,575,000 loan.[1] Even before the selection of Dallas as the exposition city, commission members had begun speculating on the amount of a federal request. Roy Miller wrote finance committee chairman John A. Hulen on July 20, 1934, that "considering the magnitude of our state and the epochal character of the proposed celebration, it seems to me that our request for an appropriation of not less than $5,000,000 is sound and reasonable."[2] That amount remained in the commission's financial projections through most of 1934; however, when Congressman Fritz G. Lanham drafted House Joint Resolution 293, he reduced the request to $3 million.

In addition to the $3 million federal appropriation, the resolution authorized the president of the United States to invite foreign countries to participate in the Texas Centennial Exposition, created the United States Texas Centennial Commission (composed of the secretaries of state, agriculture, and commerce and, by subsequent amendment, Vice-President John Nance Garner), created a United States Commissioner General for the Texas Centennial Exposition, and authorized the heads of various executive departments and independent governmental offices to cooperate in the procurement, installation, and display of governmental exhibits at the exposition.[3]

---

[1] House Joint Resolution 293, *Hearings Before the Committee on Foreign Affairs, House of Representatives, Seventy-Fourth Congress,* p. 19, cited hereafter as House Joint Resolution 293.

[2] Roy Miller to John A. Hulen, July 20, 1934, State Archives.

[3] Foreign participation at the Central Exposition was minimal; there were no foreign pavilions. Peru, Spain, Chile, Honduras, and Nicaragua sent either representatives or small delegations, and France sent a portrait and a medallion of Cavelier de La Salle. Great

Hearings on House Joint Resolution 293 began before the Committee on Foreign Affairs on May 23, 1935. Speakers on behalf of the resolution included Texas Senators Tom Connally and Morris Sheppard; Congressmen Fritz G. Lanham, Maury Maverick, and Richard Kleberg; Texas State Senator H. L. Darwin; and Cullen F. Thomas, president of the Texas Centennial Commission. Each addressed the proposition positively, tracing the historical background for the commemoration. Only Rep. George H. Tinkham of Massachusetts challenged the resolution, objecting to the appropriation and the precedent its passage might establish. Addressing Senator Connally, he argued, "If we passed this resolution [and other states] should feel that they should receive a contribution for an exposition, it would be pretty hard to deny them. What have you to say about that?" Senator Connally responded emphatically: "Well, I will say to that this: What other State is there that can have a centennial of its own independence as a republic? That is the distinction. . . . There is no parallel. There is nothing for which this could be pointed as a precedent."[4]

Senator Connally obviously won his point. Although the Massachusetts opposition remained active, the measure's supporters did not regard it as a serious obstacle, and for good reason. With a native son serving as Vice-President, Texas' political influence in Washington was at an all-time high. Vice-President Garner's congressional experience, high position, and personal interest in the centennial celebrations became key factors in the measure's ultimate passage. How-

---

Britain, being a signatory of the 1928 Paris "Convention Regarding International Exhibitions," had to decline. United States diplomats in Mexico reported that the Mexican government preferred not to receive an invitation. Militant student groups, however, expressed that country's attitude through a "Manifesto to the Nation by Reason of the Centenary Loss of Texas" and requested that April 21, 1936, be considered a national day of mourning. Anti-Texas sentiment also surfaced among Mexican American groups living in the state. The Club Femenino Chapultepec issued a ten-part complaint that stated: "Texas cannot, due to Chamber of Commerce and patriotic society activities, forget that Texas lost a tragic battle at the [A]lamo in San Antonio and won a battle at San Jacinto. This causes teachers to teach a patriotism not kind to Mexican children." When a Laredo, Texas, centennial committee announced it would not participate in the celebration, Edward Clark, secretary to Governor Allred, attempted to project Texas' relationship with Mexico in a broad historical perspective. "The Texas War of Independence was not waged against either the Mexican Government or Mexican people," he explained. "Rather it was against tyranny in the form of one despot" whom the Mexican people later overthrew. Thomas H. Kreneck, "The Letter from Chapultepec," The Houston Review 3 (Summer, 1981): 268–71; Edward Clark to Mrs. Wm. Prescott Allen, January 7, 1936, State Archives.

[4] House Joint Resolution 293, p. 13.

ever, a close parallel to the political drama that had been played out in the Texas legislature less than two months before soon developed in Washington, as well. The Sheppard-Connally resolution encountered little opposition in the Senate but met both regional and fiscal resistance in the House. The Massachusetts and New York delegations emerged as the main stumbling blocks to the centennial appropriation. Bay State Representatives Joseph M. Martin, Jr., and Edith N. Rogers led the Republican assault, largely on arguments for economy. The Texas centennial measure, however, eventually cleared the congressional hurdles. Vice-President Garner signed Public Resolution No. 37 on June 26, and two days later, with President Franklin D. Roosevelt's signature on the document, the United States Texas Centennial Commission became a reality. Only one legislative hurdle remained: congressional appropriation of the $3 million. This would not be an easy task; unexpected obstacles still lurked along the path that led to the exposition's opening on June 6, 1936.

Meanwhile in Dallas, plans were getting under way to build the "Magic City." At noon on Thursday, June 13, the board of directors of the State Fair of Texas Association met with city and Centennial Corporation officials in the Baker Hotel to transfer Fair Park to the new tenants. The unexpected harmony that pervaded this legal transaction stands as another milestone in centennial history. This critical meeting, clearing the way for construction to begin on the exposition site, brought face to face a group of civic leaders who, until recently, had been locked in a bitter political struggle. Dallas had just experienced the trauma of a complete change in city government.

The key issue in the recent campaign was the ouster of City Manager John N. Edy. Edy himself had come to power as the result of an earlier political struggle. A campaign for political reform, promoted by the local newspapers and spearheaded by the Dallas Citizens Charter Association, had led to establishment of the council-manager form of government in 1931. The Charter Association council had appointed Edy, an experienced and highly qualified municipal executive, as Dallas's first city manager. In terms of expertise, Edy was probably the best qualified man in the nation to revamp a city government. Directing the changeover to the new system while grappling with steadily declining tax revenues (collection had fallen below 88 percent), Edy made some difficult and unpopular decisions. He proposed new taxes, staff reductions, and competency examinations to upgrade the police force. He also possessed a fatal personality quirk: he treated everyone alike. He once kept First National Bank executive Rosser Coke waiting in his office while he interviewed several job applicants. According to former Dallas Health Officer Dr. J. W. Bass, "Harry Lawther [another banker and prominent civic leader] was treated just like the others. The important Dallas people had always gotten and expected special treatment at City Hall."[5] Barry L. Bishop, former *Dallas Morning News* city hall reporter, added, "Nobody liked him [Edy] because he had a job to do and he did it . . . he brought Dallas [city government] into the twentieth century."[6]

Edy, however, was not the fundamental issue in the campaign. A proposal by the city planning department to widen Field Street had touched some sensitive nerves among the city's financial elite. Several prominent businessmen and bankers regarded the Field Street expansion as favoring growth northward. Since many of them owned property to the east, they, of course, opposed it. The downtown property owners, on the other hand, believed the northbound corridor would further enhance their downtown property values. According to one contemporary observer, this created a break in the established power structure, forcing former friends and allies into opposing political camps. Therefore, the widening of Field Street and the general dissatisfaction with Edy together spawned an unlikely political coalition of the "haves" and "have-nots." Together they launched a campaign to "throw the rascals out of city hall."

Slogans and sobriquets are part and parcel of the American political process; their use and application frequently influence the public's perception of political issues. Such was the case in Dallas in 1935. The local establishment — the Citizens Charter Association primarily — regarded these political renegades with amused derision, referring to them as "catfish politicians." The term backfired; the "Catfish Club" became the catchword in a heated campaign that gave the underdog candidates an unintended popular advantage.

The "Catfish" launched their campaign with a parade from the union hall. A union band made up of unemployed musicians led the entourage of supporters carrying signs demanding "Oust Edy" and "Carpetbag Edy." The electorate heeded their message of "reform";

---

[5]Dr. J. W. Bass, Canton, Texas, to Kenneth B. Ragsdale, undated.
[6]Interview with Barry L. Bishop, Austin, Texas, April 27, 1978.

the political newcomers, actually commission-type leftovers, swept the election and installed a completely new city council. But once in control, the "Catfish Council" failed to fulfill its campaign promises; the city hall purge never materialized. City Manager John Edy became the only casualty of the administrative change. (The police chief was also dismissed; however, Edy had scheduled that dismissal prior to his own departure.) Edy's replacement, A&M College chemical engineering graduate Hal Moseley, proved equally efficient as his predecessor. L. B. Houston, a recent employee in the public works department, witnessed the administrative change with apprehension. "Everybody thought they were returning to the spoils system," he recalled later, "but . . . when they tried to force [the] appointment of inferior people [on Moseley], he said, 'Hell no . . . civil service jobs are going to be filled with civil service people.'"[7] Moseley's policy prevailed. One of his successes included the appointment of Jim Dan Sullivan as chairman of the park board. Remembered by one journalist as "honest as the Bank of England," Sullivan occupied a critical position as the Centennial Corporation began the arduous task of renovating Fair Park.[8]

The day the "Catfish Council" took office, — May 1, 1935 — marked one of the most dramatic political changes in Dallas history and a crucial point in centennial history. The Citizens Charter Association, which had supported the local centennial effort and helped engineer the recent $3 million centennial bond election, was out, and a brash young band of political newcomers was in power. The task of building a world's fair from the ground up in just one year depended largely on this virtually unknown and politically inexperienced group. The unproved leadership of the "Catfish Council" added to the complex problems centennial leaders faced throughout the summer of 1935.

American cities develop unique personalities according to individ-

---

[7]Interview with L. B. Houston, Dallas, Texas, April 3, 1978. L. B. Houston had participated in another Edy innovation, an in-service training program for talented young men entering municipal government. James W. Aston, president of the Republic National Bank of Dallas, was another Edy apprentice who later became the Dallas city manager; at twenty-nine years of age, Aston was the nation's youngest. For a comprehensive study of the "Catfish era" in Dallas politics, see Harold A. Stone, Don K. Price, and Kathryn H. Stone, *City Government in Dallas* (Chicago: Public Administration Service, 1939).

[8]Jim Dan Sullivan was well schooled in Dallas politics. His father, Dan F. Sullivan, a prosperous plumbing contractor, had served as that city's first water commissioner in the early 1900s.

ual urban environments. Kansas City's stockyards, Pittsburgh's steel mills, San Francisco's Golden Gate, New York's skyscrapers, and New Orleans's French Quarter give these cities their individual and un-mistakable identity. In addition, geographic locations and natural resources — climate, agriculture, mining, forestry, seaports, and water-ways — have enabled these cities to prosper economically. Dallas, the Southwest's major trade center, possessed none of these — no special identity and no natural resource base. Other than being where John Neely Bryan parked his covered wagon on the east bank of the Trinity River in 1841, there was no logical reason for a city to develop there. Reflecting on Dallas's geographic deficiency, Stanley Marcus com-mented: "The Lord must have created Dallas on Sunday when he was resting because there's no mountains, no lakes, no water, just a flat piece of land with no reason for being."[9] Yet Dallas grew and pros-pered. By 1935, with a population of 260,475, Dallas ranked second to Houston's 292,352 individuals (according to the 1930 United States census). In addition, the city could boast of two major universities (one a medical school), a federal reserve bank, ten national and state banks, and the largest inland cotton market in the nation. Dallas also ranked third nationally in the distribution of farm machinery and had become the fourth largest insurance center and dry goods distri-bution center in the nation. In addition to five hundred wholesale firms and seven hundred manufacturing outlets, three thousand for-eign corporations maintained branch offices in Dallas. Annual whole-sale transactions of $700 million and $179 million in retail trade at-test to the city's economic vigor duing the early Depression years. Pe-ripheral oil deposits constituted Dallas's only mineral resource; in the mid-1930s 65 percent of the nation's petroleum was produced within a two-hundred-mile radius of the exposition city. Culturally, Dallas could boast of forty theaters, a municipal auditorium, a symphony orchestra, an art association, two community theaters, a historical society, the Dallas Museum of Fine Arts, and a public art gallery. But most importantly, a varied transportation network brought the state and nation within a few hours' travel time to Dallas. Eleven steam railroads, four electric interurbans, fifteen bus lines, forty-one freight lines, ten airlines, and eleven state and five federal highways served the city on the eve of the centennial celebration.

[9]Interview with Stanley Marcus, Dallas, Texas, July 26, 1978.

After the railroads reached Dallas in the early 1870s, the village became a "terminal town," a trade center for the redistribution of merchandise arriving by rail from Galveston and later from the Northeast. Consequently, during the late nineteenth century, Dallas evolved as a sales-oriented, self-promoting distribution center for the northern half of the state. That was its only reason to exist and its only method of survival. This tradition of necessity persisted, and boosterism became a way of economic life in Dallas. A national advertising campaign launched in the mid-1920s to attract new industries brought in 484 new businesses in 1926, 364 in 1927, and 704 in 1928. This led to the formation in 1928 of Industrial Dallas, Inc., a half-million-dollar promotional undertaking to further expand the Dallas manufacturing community. "Payrolls bring populations and prosperity," trumpeted the *Dallas Times Herald*. "It all adds to the future value of Dallas real estate. We have opened the gates and hung up our welcome sign where all will see it."[10]

From boosterism evolved another local tradition: the spirit of collective leadership. Dallas business and civic leaders learned early that the community's economic health was everyone's responsibility. It therefore became an unwritten law in Dallas that, while local firms competed individually for profits, civic welfare and urban progress were matters to be shared jointly. George B. Dealey, publisher of the *Dallas Morning News*, and Edward J. Kiest, publisher of the *Dallas Times Herald*, are cases in point. As publishers of the city's two leading newspapers, they engaged in an intense, ongoing battle for advertising linage and circulation supremacy. Yet on issues of civic welfare they formed an inseparable bond to promote the city's social, cultural, and economic betterment. (The council-manager form of city government resulted from their joint efforts.) The same held true for other segments of the Dallas business community, including the three bankers—Adams, Florence, and Thornton—who headed the Texas Centennial Central Exposition Corporation. Felix McKnight, managing editor of the *Dallas Morning News* and later editor of the *Dallas Times Herald*, recalled that during the planning stages of the exposition, "every morning [they] would call [each other] . . . like you call about the weather. . . . And once they got off the phone and Mission 'A' was accomplished, they'd fight like hell all day long for that bank-

[10]*Dallas Times Herald*, March 24, 1928.

ing business."[11] And when the "Catfish" threw out the Citizens Charter Association council, the same triumvirate helped minimize the political breach by providing a stabilizing element.

Although closely associated personally and professionally, and jointly committed to producing a world's fair in record time, the three bankers displayed widely contrasting styles and personalities. Nathan Adams, president of the First National Bank of Dallas, was the senior member of the triumvirate and chairman of the board of the Texas Centennial Central Exposition, Inc. Born in Pulaski, Tennessee, in 1869, he was sixty-six years old when construction began on the exposition. He moved to Dallas in 1887 and served in a number of clerical positions before joining the First National Bank of Dallas. After he became president of that institution in 1929, Adams gained recognition as a dedicated leader in both civic affairs and the banking profession. He pioneered the organized solicitation of national accounts for his bank, advocated placing community credit reserves at the disposal of the oil industry in the early 1930s, and helped organize President Herbert C. Hoover's Home Loan Bank system to aid distressed homeowners in the early Depression years. He also became known as a knowledgeable and sympathetic consultant to the state's banking community. During the March, 1933, bank holiday crisis, he helped raise $900,000 to shore up faltering Dallas banks. In 1913, the Texas Bankers' Association honored Adams with its presidency. Although Adams occupied a key role in the centennial triumvirate, his contemporaries recall he was less visible and more conservative than his more ebullient colleagues.

Fred F. Florence, president of the exposition corporation, was the youngest member of the trio. He was born Fred F. Fromowitz to emigrant Lithuanian parents in New York City on November 5, 1891. The next year the family moved to New Birmingham, Texas, near Rusk, and had their name changed legally to Florence. After graduating from high school at the age of fifteen (he reportedly skipped one or two grades), Florence entered the banking profession in Rusk. In 1920, he was appointed vice-president of the Guaranty Bank and Trust Company, forerunner of the Republic National Bank of Dallas. In 1929, at the age of thirty-eight, he became president of the Republic Bank. James W. Aston, later a president and chairman of the board of that

<hr />

[11]Interview with Felix McKnight, Dallas, Texas, October 20, 1977.

institution, described Florence as a "very aggressive, enthusiastic personality, and anything that he became a party to, he assumed a position of leadership. He was just a dynamic leader. . . . And of course, we're talking about a dynamic group of really dynamic leaders."[12]

Of the centennial triumvirate, Robert Lee Thornton, who served as the corporation's chairman of the executive committee, was the only native Texan. He was born on August 18, 1880, in a half-dugout in Hamilton County on the banks of the Bosque River. He later moved to Dallas, where he sold candy and operated a bookstore, but in 1916, with the aid of his two brothers-in-law, he raised $20,000 ($6,000 of it in cash), to establish the Stiles, Thornton, and Lund Bank at 704 Main Street. With Thornton as president, the bank lent money on mules, automobiles, and other collateral, grew rapidly, and in 1925 became the Mercantile National Bank, the third largest in Dallas. Thornton quickly ascended the ladder of professional and civic responsibility. By 1930, he ranked among Dallas's civic captains. Two years later he helped raise $100,000 to feed the city's hungry and in 1933 was elected president of the Dallas Chamber of Commerce. In his presidential address to the Texas Bankers' Association in 1925, Thornton stated his guiding principle of civic responsibility. "It is certainly possible to be a good citizen and not be a banker, but it is impossible to be a good banker and not be a good citizen."[13] "Uncle Bob" became the ideal public servant, crisply efficient but also warmly human. His verbal syntax reflected his rural upbringing, but for the most part it was a self-conscious effort to reveal his down-home genuineness. His homilies became his trademark: "You've got to pick the peaches when they're ripe," "You've got to catch the fish when they're bitin'," and "Boys, if you ain't movin', make way for someone who is." When a friend once admonished Thornton for saying "ain't" in a public address, he retorted, "Them that ain't sayin' ain't, ain't eatin'!" Thornton often referred to the city he loved as "Dy-damic Dallas."

Throughout his almost four decades of serving Dallas, Thornton became the symbol of civic dedication. "American cities have always had their cheerleaders, their civic dynamos," wrote journalist William Murchison. "None could have more profoundly loved his city,

[12]Interview with James W. Aston, Dallas, Texas, May 12, 1978.
[13]Reprint, President's Annual Address, Texas Bankers' Association, Houston, May 19, 1925, in Thornton Scrapbook.

or perhaps have toiled more effectively than Bob Thornton . . . who embodied — flesh, blood, and jutting cigar — the spirit of an explosive city."[14] By 1935, Thornton had proved himself as a leader and a doer. He had orchestrated the plan that won the central exposition for Dallas and had assembled a talented and dedicated team committed to creating a world's fair in just twelve months. Although many believed he had at last taken on an impossible task, Thornton did not think so. Neither did John Stemmons, who explained some four decades later that Thornton was the "quarterback of the team and . . . the matador [as well] and anybody that got in his way, goddam, he'd kill 'em with the bull."[15] Centennial architect George Dahl interpreted Thornton's leadership somewhat differently: "He hitched his wagon to a star and kept on driving."[16]

Thornton obviously was the quarterback or matador of the triumvirate, but they did not work alone. The Dallas pattern of collective enterprise provided a second echelon of business leaders who shared their interest and concern for the civic welfare. "They were not independent operators," explained James W. Aston. "Thornton wouldn't take a position until he'd conferred with people like Florence" and Adams; Karl Hoblitzelle, president of Interstate Circuit, Inc.; Jean Baptiste Adoue, Jr., president of the National Bank of Commerce; or John W. Carpenter, president of the Dallas Power and Light Company. And once they agreed on an issue, it received their uniform support. In assessing the success of this relationship, Robert Cullum, a later civic leader, explained, "They worked very unselfishly together."[17]

All great cities have great leadership; that is a metaphor for urban progress in America. But in the 1930s Dallas was endowed with a cadre of unusually talented and dedicated business executives who labored in concert for the civic, cultural, and economic betterment of their city. When examined within the context of the 1930s, Dallas as a civic entity appeared unique in Texas. The contest for the central exposition had revealed a widely varying quality of urban leadership. Houston's urban bureaucracy appeared lacking in both leadership

[14]Wayne Murchison, "Remembering Uncle Bob," Scene (Dallas Morning News Sunday Magazine), December 5, 1976.

[15]Interview with John Stemmons, Dallas, Texas, May 29, 1978.

[16]Dahl interview, April 6, 1978.

[17]Interview with Robert Cullum, Dallas, Texas, May 16, 1978.

and direction; San Antonio, suffering from the same malady while languishing in its historic past, was unable to reach unanimity on any issue; and Fort Worth, overshadowed by Amon Carter, wanted no part, at least temporarily, in the major celebration. Boosterism prevailed in Dallas and won the central exposition.

In meeting this challenge Dallas would, indeed, produce an exposition of consummate quality. It would bring national publicity to the city and the state, along with new population, new wealth, and ultimately new growth. These would be the by-products of the Dallas tradition of collective enterprise. The same team with the same commitment already cared for the indigent, fed the unemployed, and built the hospitals, parks, and libraries. The same leadership—some would refer to it as the Thornton Era—would ultimately provide the city with an unsurpassed quality of government. Some four decades later John Stemmons paid his highest tribute: "Cousin, the genius of this town has been good government, good clean, honest government. You don't have to pay any son of a bitch a nickel to do anything in this town."[18]

But in May of 1935, the triumvirate and their supporters faced the immediate task at hand: a mandate to produce an exposition commensurate with the century of freedom and progress that prompted the commemoration. Dallas had spoken, the Texas legislature had spoken, the federal government had made a commitment, but as yet no money was forthcoming. And there was the matter of the "Catfish Council." As the triumvirate looked toward June, they realized full well a number of knotty problems awaited their immediate attention.

[18]Stemmons interview, May 29, 1978.

7

MIRACLE AT SECOND AND PARRY

When Governor Allred and President Roosevelt affixed their signatures to the two key centennial appropriation measures, basic funding for the Texas centennial celebrations was assured. But legislative enactment marked only the latest step in a statewide process to commemorate Texas' hundred years of progress and independence. The coming months would witness a great transformation throughout the state: erection of scores of permanent historical markers, restoration of the state's major historical shrines, construction and expansion of several historical museums, presentation of hundreds of local pageants and celebrations, and construction of the first world's fair to be held in the Southwest.[1] And there would be an invisible benefit to accrue from the centennial celebrations: the heightened awareness of and appreciation for the state's history. While such claims defy scholarly documentation, it appears in retrospect that during this period the average individual's perception of Texas' heritage reached an all-time high.

The central exposition in Dallas constituted the celebration's major undertaking. It required the greatest financial outlay (a reported $25 million), the largest physical plant (185 acres), the largest construction program (some seventy buildings either remodeled or constructed especially for the exposition), and the assemblage of a design, contracting, and labor force to create virtually a new city in less than one year. (The press ultimately labeled the exposition the "Magic City.") With the arrival of the first warm days of summer, the Dallas City Council (the "Catfish Council") and Exposition Cor-

---

[1] The Texas Centennial Central Exposition did not have the endorsement of the Bureau of International Expositions; none had been requested. The bureau was established in Paris in 1928 by thirty-five countries to regulate the staging of global expositions. The United States was not a signatory; it did not consider foreign participation essential to an exposition's success. The scope and magnitude of the Texas Centennial Central Exposition, however, justified the sponsor's "world's fair" designation.

poration officials came face to face with the realities of constructing a world exposition: (1) condemning the 26.5-acre addition to Fair Park, (2) planning and designing the exposition complex, (3) calling for bids and issuing contracts for the construction program, (4) launching the largest short-term peacetime construction program in Southwest history, and (5) awaiting the funding of the $3 million federal appropriation. It proved to be a long hot summer.

Centennial officials lost little time in getting the program underway. On Saturday, June 8, 1935, two days less than one year from the opening date, members of the state Centennial Commission of Control met with the Centennial Corporation in Dallas to release $1 million to construct the state building at the central exposition. John Singleton, building director for the State Board of Control, announced that both groups had approved the general plans for that structure and the board would let the contract in the near future. Singleton, unfortunately, was overly optimistic. The directors of the Exposition Corporation also presented the Board of Control with written assurances that they were financially able to fulfill their commitment to produce the exposition and were prepared to begin immediately. Lieut. Gov. Walter F. Woodul, chairman of the Centennial Commission of Control, stated that "with the approval of the $1,000,000 for Dallas, the rest of the State appropriation becomes available, under the interpretation of the law." Looking forward to beginning the other statewide commemorative projects, Woodul challenged the Advisory Board of Texas Historians, on the eve of its first meeting, "to do its work so thoroughly and fairly that no community could complain and none find it necessary to appeal to the Commission."[2] The lieutenant governor had no way of knowing that this body would become the spawning ground for some of the celebration's more heated controversies.

Those attending the Dallas meeting participated in another important moment in centennial history. Cullen F. Thomas, chairman of the Texas Centennial Commission, announced that its powers and administrative duties had been assumed by the Centennial Commission of Control, but the commission would continue to serve in a supportive and advisory capacity. That appointive body had served both efficiently and economically. Commission Secretary Will H. Mayes's final

[2]*Dallas Morning News*, June 9, 1935.

report revealed that in approximately one year's service, the commission had spent only $28,116.63 of the original $100,000 appropriation.[3]

The obligations assumed jointly by the Centennial Corporation and the City of Dallas under the terms of the June 8 contract were formidable. Cost estimates for the permanent structures to be erected and services to be provided, excluding the state building, were: Travel and Transportation Building, $365,000; Varied Industries, Electrical, and Communications Building, $440,000; Aquarium, $180,000; Natural History Museum, $250,000; Horticultural Hall, $75,000; Home Planning Building, $75,000; Band Pavilion (Amphitheater), $50,000; Fine Arts Museum, $550,000; Food and Agriculture Building, $200,000; Livestock Building, $410,000; landscaping, $250,000; paving and sidewalks, $350,000; utilities, $500,000; electrical equipment, $350,000; and entrance gates and fences, $100,000.[4] In addition, the Exposition Corporation, according to the enabling act, was to (1) repay the original $100,000 promotion appropriation from the first 10 percent of the exposition's gross receipts, (2) carry all insurance and maintenance expense, and (3) repay the full $3 million appropriation from 75 percent of the exposition's net receipts. If there were no net receipts there would be no repayment.

Following the signing of the contract, Dallas began making immediate preparations to build its exposition. One of Thornton's famous homilies keynotes the occasion: "Keep the dirt flyin'." On Monday morning, June 10, Dallas Public Works Director A. P. Rollins began organizing survey crews to plan street widening in the Fair Park area. The following day Ray Foley, the Exposition Corporation's director of the Department of Works, submitted to Otto H. Herold, assistant managing director of the exposition, a $266,300 budget for utility changes in the same area. These included extending existing gas service lines in the park, constructing a new electrical transformer and distribution station in the same area, and relocating streetcar and railroad tracks along the streets bordering the proposed exposition grounds. The latter item was budgeted at $209,000.[5]

[3]Secretary's Final Report, January 7, 1935, State Archives.

[4]Centennial Corporation News Release, October 1935, Texas Centennial Central Exposition Collection, Dallas Historical Society, cited hereafter as Centennial Collection, DHS. This listing did not include the police-fire-hospital building, estimated originally at $20,000.

[5]Centennial Collection, DHS.

One of the more critical issues was acquisition of the designated 26.5-acre addition to the park complex. This responsibility fell largely to Jim Dan Sullivan, the newly appointed chairman of the Dallas Park Board. Sullivan gradually emerged as a positive symbol of the "Catfish" administration. He is remembered as blatantly honest and fair, one of the driving forces behind the exposition construction. As chairman of the Park Board, he oversaw all city funding for constructing the Fair Park civic center. While Rollins and Foley grappled with the practical problems of public works, Sullivan turned his attention to a more sensitive and volatile matter, eminent domain. It became apparent early on that acquisition of the park expansion property would not be a simple matter. People do not easily relinquish family businesses and homesteads, no matter how humble, especially when the purchaser is a city government recently funded by a multimillion-dollar bond issue. This matter would plague the "Catfish Council" throughout the summer and fall of 1935 and would further delay construction at the exposition site.

The exposition era brought to the forefront several individuals whose names remain synonymous with this great undertaking. If Adams, Florence, and Thornton deserve major credit for bringing the central exposition to Dallas, then architect George L. Dahl must be remembered as the person most responsible for designing and building the 1936 Texas Centennial Central Exposition. Fair Park stands today as a monument to his vision, creative imagination, and total dedication. When the Centennial Corporation launched the construction program in the spring of 1935, Dahl's office, located in the downtown Southland Life Building Annex, became the nerve center of that operation. It was there, at the insistence of R. L. Thornton, that Dahl developed the original concept for the fair, and when Dallas was selected to host the central exposition, he continued working on the project. By February 1, 1935, he had completed his original layout of the exposition grounds, including tentative floor plans and profile renderings of the major buildings. To this point he had no formal agreement with either the city or the Exposition Corporation. "They hadn't hired me," Dahl explained. "[They said], 'You're going to have to gamble with us.' [I said], 'All right, I'll gamble with you. I think it'll go.'" History proved him correct.[6]

[6]Dahl interview, April 6, 1978.

Dahl first arrived in Dallas in 1926. He had earned two degrees in architecture (the bachelor's from the University of Minnesota and the master's from Harvard University) and completed a two-year appointment to the American Academy in Rome, then joined a distinguished Los Angeles architectural firm whose projects included two West Coast landmarks, the Huntington Library and the Ambassador Hotel. Dallas architect Herbert M. Greene learned of Dahl's work and invited him to join his firm, which evolved as Herbert M. Greene, La Roche, and Dahl. Dahl had never been to Texas but liked the environment immediately. "I walked up and down the streets . . . and talked to some of the businessmen," he remembered. "And I said, 'I'll take it. . . . I'll take Texas.'" His initial meeting with Dallas businessmen influenced his decision: "They were all successful. Working like hell." So he joined them and also began working like hell.[7]

Dahl was eminently qualified for his new assignment with the corporation. In addition to his architectural and design experience, he had visited and studied several major expositions: the 1924–25 British Empire Exhibition at Wembley, England, the 1933 Chicago Century of Progress, and the 1935 San Diego California-Pacific Exposition. Accorded a title — Chief of the Technical Division and Centennial Architect — and a salary commensurate with the assignment — $1,500 a month — Dahl set about planning the greatest project of his career. At the outset he faced three major problems: assembling a technical staff, providing them with working quarters on the exposition grounds, and developing an initial program of work for the demolition, excavation, and utility crews already converging on Fair Park.

Dahl needed staff assistants to free him for the overall planning. For his chief designer he chose Chicago-born Donald S. Nelson, who also possessed outstanding credentials. After graduating from the Massachusetts Institute of Technology, he had received the *diplome* of the Fontainebleau School of Fine Arts as one of its scholarship students. In 1926 he was among five finalists in the Paris Prize in Architecture, and the following year he won that distinguished award. Returning to Chicago in 1929, Nelson joined the architecture and planning firm of Bennett, Parsons, and Frost. When work began on

---

[7] Ibid. Other than the Texas Centennial Exposition complex, Dahl designed more than three thousand projects, including the Dallas Public Library, the *Dallas Morning News* building, the Neiman-Marcus building in Dallas, RFK Stadium in Washington, and Memorial Stadium at the University of Texas at Austin.

the Century of Progress, Nelson represented that firm in designing four major exposition buildings.

In April of 1935, Dahl invited Major Lennox Lohr, former manager of the Chicago exposition, and Louis Skidmore, that exposition's chief of design, to consult with him on the Texas exposition. At that time Lohr recommended Nelson for the chief designer's position. When Dahl invited him to Dallas for an interview, Nelson came reluctantly, purchasing a round-trip ticket in the likelihood he would return shortly to Chicago. When, during the ensuing conference, the two architects failed to agree on a salary, Nelson triumphantly displayed his ticket and walked out of Dahl's office. Dahl interrupted Nelson's dramatic departure; after a few moments of embarrassed hesitation, the technical director acknowledged defeat in his attempt to conserve some of the Dallas bond money. In yielding to Nelson's $500-per-month salary demand Dahl had, nevertheless, served his employers well; he had just added to his staff one of the top young architectural designers in the nation.

With Nelson busy developing the designs for Dahl's original layouts, Dahl was free to begin hiring his technical staff. Nelson was pleased with his Dallas colleagues. "He [Dahl] assembled men of real stature," Nelson recalled. "He got Harry Overbeck, the architect of the criminal courts and jail buildings [in Dallas] . . . and Doug Coburn, whose firm . . . did the city hall. All men of that caliber."[8] Dahl engaged a Dallas consulting engineering firm, Myers, Noyes, and Forrest, to plan and supervise street grading, paving, and laying out the underground utilities network. With that firm's expertise limited to civil engineering assignments, Dahl also hired Robert Ross, a structural engineer, and Gregory Taylor, a mechanical engineer. Since Dallas had no landscape architects capable of designing and executing the exposition grounds, that assignment went to a Kansas City firm, Hare and Hare.

One of the first major on-site problems Dahl encountered was to identify the dimensions and locations of twelve existing structures he planned to renovate for the exposition. On June 15, 1935, he wrote the Myers firm an urgent memorandum stating that "we must have the corners of all structures definitely located to coordinate points. . . . We need this information now, and if you do not have all of it

[8]Interview with Donald S. Nelson, Dallas, Texas, April 5, 1978.

available we suggest you take the necessary steps to secure it."[9] With that information in hand, Dahl ordered demolition of the park structures he declared unusable. Urgency was the name of the exposition game; this phase of the operation began less than twenty-four hours after the contracts were signed. The date was June 19 (the anniversary of emancipation for Texas' slaves); the first structure to fall was a frame building formerly used to house black exhibits. As the demolition crews moved ahead with their work, engineer T. C. Forrest began planning for the next phase of park conversion, excavating lakes and lagoons and generally altering the park grounds. This would require moving 150,000 yards of earth, largely by men and mules.

Throughout the initial phase of work, Dahl housed his skeleton staff in his downtown offices. However, he wanted his staff nearer the construction site and chose an unlikely setting, the 1909 Fair Park Coliseum, for his staff. Thus, the future Centennial Administration Building came to be known affectionately as the "horse barn." Remodeling plans for the administration building were accepted on July 10, Walter Cline approved the $100,000 appropriation the same day, and the carpenters began the interior construction the following day. Dahl's design included flooring a second-story balcony area and dividing the space into private offices with temporary partitions. Nelson remembered this as another rush job: "We were already in our new offices before the renovation was complete. The noise! I don't see how we worked. And the heat! No air conditioning. That came later. But it was a good working space. We were all together with George's office in the far back corner."[10]

As the multiple units of the exposition team gained momentum, their forces began to mesh. Negotiations had been completed in late June with the American Telephone and Telegraph Company for the exposition's first major exhibit. And at the same time George Dahl was moving his technical staff into the "horse barn," Dallas Mayor George Sergeant announced that all contracts had been signed, releasing millions of dollars for construction work on the exposition. Under these agreements the city would spend up to $3,198,900, while the Central Exposition Corporation was committed to at least $2,860,500. Each organization had reserved approximately $250,000

[9]George Dahl to Myers, Noyes, and Forrest, June 15, 1935, Centennial Collection, DHS.
[10]Nelson interview, May 24, 1985.

for contingencies. At the same time the city council ordered the acquisition of the 26.5-acre proposed park addition, purchasing properties whose value had been approved and condemning acreage when the council considered the price exorbitant.

The mayor's announcement translated into a timely economic boon for Dallas. Applying for a $1,412,100 grant from the Public Works Administration, the city outlined a work program employing 8,331 persons to construct roads, buildings, and communication facilities at the exposition site. The application designated the eight months from October 1, 1935, to May 31, 1936, as the construction period, during which employment would be provided for 5,760 unskilled laborers, 2,000 intermediate types, 524 skilled laborers, 7 persons in technical and clerical positions, and 40 in professional and supervisory capacities. The estimated 10,664,840 man-hours would generate $1,273,260 in new money for the Dallas economy.[11]

The lead time necessary to design and plan such a construction program placed enormous pressure on Dahl's technical staff. Dahl, however, set the pace. "I worked from eight in the morning until about midnight every night," he recalled. I had to show them [his staff] by example. . . . I have to give it the best I can because they're giving it the best they can."[12] Donald Nelson remembered that during the summer of 1935, "I would work thirty hours straight and never bat an eye. *We had to.* And we loved what we were doing. And when you got through with something, you'd get a little praise, especially from George Dahl. . . . He was a good man to work for."[13] The pressure of the assignment was reflected in various ways among his staff; the long hours ultimately took their toll. On one occasion when Dahl was consulting with architect Harry Overbeck, he discovered a milk bottle under the latter's desk. When asked what it was for, Overbeck explained: "That's the best thing you have given me yet. . . . When I got to urinate, I urinate in that milk bottle and go to the window and throw it out!"[14]

Since Ray A. Foley's Department of Works was responsible for initiating and supervising all phases of exposition construction, his office became the "heartbeat" of the Central Exposition. By August, 1935,

[11]*Dallas Morning News*, August 13, 1935.
[12]Dahl interview, April 6, 1978.
[13]Nelson interview, April 5, 1978.
[14]Dahl interview, April 6, 1978.

fifty-eight employees comprised the departmental staff with a monthly budget of $14,435. Salaries ranged from Dahl's $1,500 a month to the porters (listed specifically as "colored") who earned $50 a month. Foley, the department's director, was paid second highest with $625. Secretaries received $125, clerk-typists $100, and file clerks $65. The twenty-five employees in the Technical Division made up the largest staff in the Works Department; their salaries ranged from Donald Nelson's $500 a month to model-maker Jack Hubbell's $90. Architectural designers' salaries ranged from $250 to $400, while draftsmen earned from $130 to Chief Draftsman Walter Gray's $325. When Managing Director Cline inquired if Foley could reduce his staff in order to cut costs, he responded that "instead of reducing the force we will be obliged to make some additions thereto." Foley paid high tribute to the effort and productivity of Dahl's personnel. "The employees of the Technical Division . . . are averaging a minimum of seventy (70) hours per week," he explained, "and in many cases this figure is being exceeded." Foley pointed out further that, instead of exceeding his budget, he had achieved an underrun "due to our receiving more production per dollar of expenditure than was originally anticipated."[15]

Toward the end of August, however, it appeared that the fierce pace being set by Dahl had become counterproductive. Foley advised his technical director on Saturday, August 17, that when the Poultry Building specifications had been typed and delivered to the Finance Department for processing, "I wish all employees in the Technical Division released until Monday morning. . . . I see no reason why any of our staff should be employed tonight [Saturday], tomorrow or tomorrow night [Sunday], and this means *you* personally."[16]

Foley was obviously attempting to conserve human resources, not save dollars. Technical Division employees understood they would receive no additional compensation in excess of their forty-four-hour base weekly salary. Foley established this policy during the early spring hirings. He explained to Cline that "if the necessity for extended overtime occurs, an adjustment can be made in the base rate per week rather than through the payment of actual overtime."[17] Employers in the mid-1930s enjoyed the luxury of an eager, sometimes hungry,

[15] Ray Foley to Walter Cline, August 15, 1935, Centennial Collection, DHS.
[16] Ray Foley to George L. Dahl, August 17, 1935, Centennial Collection, DHS.
[17] Ray Foley to Walter Cline, May 20, 1935, Centennial Collection, DHS.

and always abundant labor force. This was an era when hard work was considered a virtue, a necessity as well as a stepping-stone to personal success. People wanted to work, needed to work, and took pride in their achievements. The result was maximum human productivity. Nelson speculated that "today [1978] you'd have to have 175 [people] to do one-half the amount of work" produced by the twenty-five member Technical Division. Unknowingly, the Texas legislature had, through procrastination, created a near-impossible task for the exposition builders. Without that personal commitment and dedication, the Texas Centennial Central Exposition could never have been completed within the allotted time. "At Chicago [the 1933 Century of Progress] we had four years to design and build that exposition," Nelson explained. "At Dallas, ten months. But by golly, *we did it!*"[18]

[18]Nelson interview, April 5, 1978.

8

NOT MANY PEOPLE CARE FOR ANSON JONES

s George Dahl and Ray Foley forged ahead toward 1936, other critical centennial dramas were being played out, one in Austin, Texas, and the other in Washington, D.C. The day before the Fair Park demolition crews began their chore on June 19, 1935, the Advisory Board of Texas Historians held its first meeting in Austin. House Bill No. 11, creating the Commission of Control for Texas Centennial Celebrations, established this three-member panel to receive and evaluate applications to the commission for local centennial projects (exclusive of those specified in the bill) and to recommend which items should be funded. The recommendations of the board were advisory only; the final decision in all cases rested with the commission.[1]

The creation of this board, its membership, and its activity in the celebrations remain among the more significant aspects of the centennial experience. Writing this recognition of local history into the law was obviously a compromise between the state's business and professional interests, who advocated a major exposition primarily to promote the state's economic interests, and those who believed the centennial should emphasize and preserve the state's regional heritage. The latter was the sole objective of the advisory board, which would ultimately recommend expenditures of more than $750,000 for this purpose (in addition to the $575,000 state appropriation and $200,000 in forthcoming federal funds). Most of these funds would be invested in permanent structures and memorials commemorating the heroic period of Texas history.

[1] The legislative act provided that the commission be composed of nine members; the lieutenant governor served as chairman, and the speaker of the house, vice-chairman. Governor Allred appointed Karl Hoblitzelle, former governor Pat M. Neff, and John Boyle (and upon Boyle's resignation, Wallace Perry); Lieut. Gov. Walter F. Woodul appointed Joseph V. Vandenberge and James A. Elkins; and Speaker Coke R. Stevenson appointed Gen. John A. Hulen and John K. Beretta. All were confirmed by the senate.

The enabling legislation provided that the three board members be selected by the Commission of Control. It is of some historical significance that none of the members selected were professionally trained historians. The chairman, Louis Wiltz Kemp, was a lay historian who spent his entire professional life with Texaco, Inc. His research on the citizens of the Republic of Texas resulted in two books, *Signers of the Texas Declaration of Independence* and *The Heroes of San Jacinto*, which he coauthored with Sam Houston Dixon. Kemp served as president of the Texas State Historical Association, the Sons of the Republic of Texas, the San Jacinto Museum of History, and as historian-general of the National Society of the Sons of the American Revolution. He was also responsible for the reburial of more than one hundred prominent early-day Texans in the state cemetery in Austin.

Another advisory board member was Rev. Paul J. Foik, a Canadian-born Roman Catholic priest who had received his doctorate from Catholic University in 1912 and served as professor, librarian, and historian at Notre Dame before coming to St. Edward's University in Austin to chair the foreign language department in 1924. A charter member of the American Catholic Historical Society, he founded the Texas Catholic Historical Association and edited four of the seven volumes of *Our Catholic Heritage in Texas*. Father Foik was elected a Fellow of the Texas State Historical Association and served two terms as vice-president of that organization.

The ultraliberal and frequently controversial J. Frank Dobie was the third member of the advisory board. His prominence in the field of southwestern folklore probably accounted for his appointment. Born and raised in the ranching country of Live Oak County, Texas, Dobie studied English and prelaw at Southwestern University, taught school, did some summer newspaper work, and entered Columbia University, where he received his master's degree in 1914 (his doctorate was honorary). He later served as chairman of the English Department at Oklahoma A&M College and as adjunct professor of English at the University of Texas, where he became editor and secretary of the Texas Folklore Society. Dobie's real passion was writing; he wanted to "open the eyes of the people to the richness of their own tradition." By the time he was asked to serve on the advisory board, he had achieved this goal; publication of *A Vaquero of the Brush Country* (1929) and *Coronado's Children* (1931) had made Dobie a national literary figure.

A liberal Democrat, Dobie was often at odds with the University of Texas administration and state officials. He vociferously opposed the firing of University President Homer Price Rainey and served two days in jail (doing office work) to protest a parking ticket. Had the members of the commission known the three appointees personally, they could have foreseen how their philosophical differences would affect their work as members of the board. In expressing their divergent views, however, Dobie and Kemp provided some of the more colorful and entertaining rhetoric of the centennial era.

When Chairman Kemp convened the first meeting of the Advisory Board in Austin on the morning of June 18, he probably did not anticipate the enormous number of applicants waiting to present their claims. At that point the board had at its disposal the $550,000 state appropriation; that figure would be surpassed before noon. Senator W. K. Hopkins of Gonzales spoke first. He contended that Gonzales's role in Texas history entitled it to as much ($250,000) as had been allotted San Antonio (the Alamo) and Houston (San Jacinto Battlefield) but agreed to accept the maximum amount given any other city, be it $50,000 or $75,000. Senator Hopkins stated he wanted to erect a heroic monument on the site where the first shot was fired in Texas' war for independence, asserting his committee wanted "no pageant to blow away with the wind, but something enduring so the world would know our wonderful history."[2] Contrary to Senator Hopkins's proposal, Mrs. C. D. Kelly of Groesbeck, chairman of the pageantry committee of the Texas Women's Clubs, recommended that historical pageants be encouraged and that a five-dollar prize be given for the best pageant in each of the seven federation districts, as well as a fifteen-dollar state prize. She proposed optimistically that these pageants be held on rotating dates so tourists could see most of them. Limestone County representative E. L. Connolly also favored the pageant format. He requested $50,000 to fund an outdoor production portraying the capture of Cynthia Ann Parker. This would be staged in a permanent Indian village setting to be erected on a 1,500-acre state park.

While most local representatives appearing before the advisory board presented some comprehensive plan, the knowledge that government funds were available usually escalated the project's cost. For

[2] *Texarkana Gazette*, June 19, 1935. While the Advisory Board of Texas Historians undoubtedly kept minutes, no record of that document has been found.

example, Judge J. A. White of Goliad, the person credited with discovering Col. James W. Fannin's burial site, requested $50,000 —
$30,000 to erect a monument to Fannin and his martyred men; $5,000
for a memorial to Señora Francisca Alvarez, the "Angel of Goliad";
and $15,000 for "other purposes." Dr. L. H. Hubbard, president of
Texas Woman's College at Denton, argued that a $30,000 monument
to pioneer women should be placed on the college campus, while
former state legislator Phil Sanders recommended restoration of the
Old Stone Fort on the campus of Stephen F. Austin State College at
Nacogdoches.

The largest requests were for memorial buildings and historical
museums. Two officers of the Panhandle-Plains Historical Society asked
for $50,000 to enlarge the museum at West Texas State Teachers Col-
lege at Canyon, while a Polk County representative sought $65,000
for a museum, memorial tower, and various historical markers. Judge
Joseph McGill of El Paso asked for $150,000 to erect an exposition
building in that city's Washington Park. The judge, however, broke
the pattern established by other applicants: he offered $100,000 in
matching funds, added that El Paso would spend $50,000 on a his-
torical pageant, and proposed a meeting of the presidents of the United
States and Mexico as part of that city's celebration. Alpine and Lubbock were other West Texas towns requesting museum grants. Dr.
W. C. Holden of Texas Technological College headed a three-man
committee presenting the Lubbock proposal. They requested $150,000
to erect a museum on that campus.

At the conclusion of the two-day hearing, chairman Kemp recessed
the board subject to his recall. They had accumulated an enormous
amount of data that merited careful study and evaluation. Kemp,
however, was appalled by the number and amount of the applications. He announced that the two-day hearing had yielded approximately $3 million in requests, and "the surface has just been scratched."
He estimated that the final total would exceed $5 million, or approxi-
mately ten times the amount allocated. In order to achieve a more
equitable distribution of these funds, Kemp discouraged all further
museum applicants, explaining that the legislature had already provided $225,000 for a museum to be erected on the University of Texas
campus.[3]

---

[3] *Dallas Morning News*, June 19, 1935.

The period of harmony and tranquility that characterized the early meetings of the board soon drew to a close. There were too many local interests to be served for the initial concept of regional equality to prevail. The advisory board meeting in San Antonio on July 5 forecast troubles to come. When a local committee requested a portion of the original $250,000 Alamo allocation to produce a historical pageant, the chairman balked. He declared that the entire amount should be applied to a permanent commemoration at that historical shrine. That, however, did not resolve the issue. San Antonio would evolve later as an urban battleground for control of that city's centennial appropriation.

The first public rejection of the advisory board's function occurred following the July 20 meeting of the Commission of Control in Austin. At that meeting the commission, without consulting the advisory board, allocated $250,000 to Fort Worth for a memorial to the livestock industry and $50,000 each to Gonzales and Goliad. In terms of historic preservation, the commission's decision placed Fort Worth above Gonzales and Goliad and on a parity with Houston (San Jacinto) and San Antonio (the Alamo), to which the legislature had previously allocated $250,000 each. The commission vote, held in executive session, was five to one. James E. Elkins, Karl Hoblitzelle, and Gov. Pat M. Neff were absent. Elkins sent a written protest.

Lieut. Gov. Walter Woodul, the commission chairman, announced, however, that should Fort Worth receive a portion of the pending federal appropriation, the state fund would be reimbursed for the $250,000. To most capital observers, the commission's action smacked of a political payoff; the firm but subtle hand of Amon Carter appeared to be in control of the matter. This was later confirmed by J. M. North, Jr., editor of the *Fort Worth Star-Telegram*. In a letter to Ted Dealey, vice-president of the A. H. Belo Corporation, publisher of the *Dallas Morning News*, North took exception to a *News* story condemning the commission's action in the Fort Worth matter. In defending the Fort Worth position, North described the behind-the-scenes maneuvers that led to passage of the centennial bill. He explained that

if Fort Worth's Senator [Frank H. Rawlings] had not yielded and withdrawn its demand for an earmarked sum in the latter stages of the fight, *there would have been no appropriation whatsoever* [author's italics]. Walter Cline and Bob Thornton both insisted that unless Fort Worth withdraw, every other community with a historical background would insist on an earmarked fund. . . . I sat in a session with these gentlemen from morning to midnight. . . . both agreed that if Fort Worth would withdraw, the then Centennial Committee would support Fort Worth's application for an appropriation out of the lump sum. I believe both will verify these statements.[4]

Their confirmations were unnecessary; by Sunday morning, July 21, the story was front-page news. Advisory board members responded predictably; they regarded the commission's action as an attempt to destroy the board's integrity. Kemp announced his immediate resignation in Houston and said Father Foik had done likewise. Dobie, who heard the news in Dallas, said he would also resign "if the funds on which he and his associates on the advisory board are to recommend allocation are to be used in settling political trades and furthering the ambitions of politicians."[5]

Whatever changes Kemp and Foik hoped to achieve by their actions were never forthcoming. When the commission refused to accept their resignations, they agreed to serve until the United States Centennial Commission made a decision on replacing the Fort Worth allotment.[6] Kemp proceeded with his assignment, convening the next meeting of the advisory board in Austin on July 30. It evolved as another study in futility. With only $200,000 remaining for distribution and a $5 million backlog of grant requests, board members had no choice but to listen patiently as additional applications continued to pour in: Temple wanted a $50,000 museum; Jacksonville, a ninety-two-foot monument depicting local historical events; New Braunfels, a $50,000 monument to German pioneers; San Antonio, a $70,000 monument to the Canary Islanders; Anderson County, $3,000 annually to maintain the John H. Reagan house; ad infinitum. The Lubbock Chamber of Commerce, ignoring Kemp's earlier admonition to withhold museum requests, filed an amended application for $118,750 (down from $150,000) for the Texas Technological College museum.

---

[4]J. M. North, Jr., to Ted Dealey, July 26, 1935, Carter Archives.

[5]*Dallas Morning News*, July 21, 1935.

[6]The Commission, however, would again overrule the advisory board in executive session. On September 4, the commission changed the advisory board's recommendation on the Gonzales application.

Kemp finally announced in frustration that the remaining funds were "totally and pathetically inadequate to meet the demands of the bona fide historical spots."[7]

The conflict and dissension that began to envelop the advisory board characterized much of the precentennial preparations. Recognition of local and regional interests formed the crux of this discord. As one contemporary observer explained, "Everyone seemed to be grabbing for a government tit, and the problem was, there just wasn't enough to go around." While this philosophy applied to most towns and counties in the state as they competed for a centennial appropriation, Lubbock's amended application added a different dimension to the contest — regional paranoia. The West Texas Chamber of Commerce had previously articulated the High Plains isolationist credo during the 1932 campaign to pass the constitutional amendment. And while spokesmen varied, the theme remained unchanged; West Texas was a frontier island separated from the remainder of the state by a psychological moat. In declaring his opposition to a 1934 centennial appropriation measure, Sen. Walter C. Woodward of Coleman County claimed the bill provided "not one penny . . . for any purpose West of a line extending from Fort Worth to Laredo," while the people living in those 150 counties would have to pay approximately 40 percent of the proposed appropriation. As an alternative to this injustice, the senator offered a resolution requesting that "the citizens living west of said line *be at least invited to attend* said Centennial in the northeast, East, and southeast portions of Texas."[8] While Senator Woodward probably offered this resolution in jest (it passed 22 to 2), it is historically significant that none of his colleagues living in the "northeast, East, and southeast portions of Texas" made similar proposals.

The proposed museum on the Texas Tech campus became the focal point of a verbal battle that developed between Tech's Dr. W. C. Holden, chairman of the West Texas Museum Association, and advisory board chairman Kemp. Kemp believed that the appropriated funds should be distributed on the basis of historical significance; Holden stood firm in his belief that the monies should be apportioned on a pro rata basis. On September 25, 1935, the Texas Tech history

[7] *Dallas Morning News*, July 26, 1935.

[8] (Author's italics.) *Senate Journal, Fourth Called Session, Forty-Third Legislature*, pp. 22–23.

professor sent Kemp his formula for distributing the local funds. He argued that the sixty-seven county area supporting the museum project had a population of 742,493, which was roughly 15 percent of the total state population. On that basis, he reasoned, West Texas was entitled to $116,255 of the available funds. When projected on a square mile basis, that region, containing approximately 29 percent of the states's area, was entitled to $230,000. According to Holden's formula, the total request for $162,750 "is only nine percent more than we are entitled to on a per capita–per acre basis."[9]

Even if Kemp understood the professor's rationale, he was both unmoved and unimpressed. On October 3, he responded emphatically, but not briefly: "We are not concerned in the least about how any county in the state may have been discriminated against in the past; how great its population is; how much taxes it pays or how much cotton, corn or wheat it raises. We are concerned only in marking or improving historic places and in honoring the memory of pioneer men and women who have rendered outstanding services to Texas. . . . We shall not make the slightest attempt to have the funds distributed equally." Kemp concluded his three-page epistle, "You informed me that you lacked but one vote of being elected a member of the board of which I am chairman. Knowing your reputation as an historian I do not believe that had you been elected you would have recommended that more than three times the amount of money be spent at Texas Tech than at Goliad."[10]

Holden, also unmoved and unimpressed, continued his campaign to gain an appropriation for the Texas Tech museum. He suggested relinquishing future funds for other West Texas memorials and applying those amounts toward the museum. To achieve a consensus, he canvassed the members in the sixty-seven county area. The responses were uniformly in agreement. One member writing from Abernathy, Texas (signature illegible) seemed to speak for the majority: "We want a museum or nothing." A Brownfield, Texas citizen (signature illegible) also favored Holden's proposal for museum funding while articulating the West Texas party line: "West Texas has been discriminated against and we are willing to do our part in giving the Centennial Commission Hell, even to refunding what has been offered to us."

[9]W. C. Holden to Louis W. Kemp, September 25, 1935, State Archives.
[10]Kemp to Holden, October 3, 1935, State Archives.

W. R. McDuffie, another Brownfield resident, stated, "I agree entirely with your local committee and endorse return of the appropriation to State Board." Tom W. (last name illegible) of Floydada, Texas, was even more emphatic in his response: "If West Texas does not receive more consideration, I am in favor of a New State."[11]

Funding for the local commemorative projects remained contingent, in part, on a supplementary allocation from the $3 million in federal centennial funds previously authorized but not yet appropriated by Congress. On July 23, 1935, the Senate adopted without amendments a deficiency appropriation bill containing the $3 million Texas centennial allocation. House concurrence remained the final step to presidential approval, but adjournment came before the bill could be called up for a vote. With funding virtually assured, however, the United States Texas Centennial Commission began planning the government's role in the celebration.[12] To structure and administer federal policy within the state, President Roosevelt, with the advice and consent of the Senate, named Cullen F. Thomas the United States Commissioner General. The Dallas attorney and veteran centennial leader appointed three assistant commissioners who were approved by the United States Commission: Ernest J. Altgelt, attorney, realtor, and member of an old San Antonio family; J. Percival Rice, another Dallas attorney; and Paul Wakefield, an Austin newspaperman and publicist. Three of the four had important political affiliations.[13] W. B. Yeager served as executive secretary to the United States Commission. This five-man body became the federal government's link to the Texas Centennial.[14]

With Thomas and the United States Commission responsible for allocating the federal funds, the nation's capital, during the summer

[11]Sixty-one returned postcards are in the Centennial Collection, Texas State Archives.

[12]Public Act No. 260, Seventy-Fourth Congress, approved on August 12, 1935, appropriated the $3 million for the Texas celebrations.

[13]Thomas was the brother-in-law of Texas Senator Morris Sheppard; Rice had managed Senator Tom Connally's political campaigns; and Wakefield had served on Vice-President Garner's staff and as an assistant to Jesse H. Jones. The enabling legislation set Thomas's salary at $10,000 a year; each of his assistants received $7,500 a year.

[14]Commissioner Thomas appointed a committee of nine Texas civic leaders to serve in an advisory capacity to the United States Commission. They were George Waverley Briggs, Dallas, chairman; John E. Owens, Hugh E. Prather, Edward T. Moore, Hilton R. Greer, Nelson Phillips, and W. E. Wrather, all of Dallas; Galloway Calhoun, Tyler; and John D. Middleton, Greenville.

of 1935, became Mecca for everyone "seeking a piece of the action." Lieutenant Governor Woodul, apparently under pressure, appeared first before the commission to request that $250,000 of the federal appropriation replace the controversial state allotment to Fort Worth. Commission chairman Garner was noncommittal. Amon Carter also spoke to the issue but from a different perspective. He wanted to retain the state's allocation and to obtain a like amount from the federal commission for the Fort Worth celebration. The West Texas Museum Association also refused to be denied a share of federal money. Lubbock Congressman George Mahon pleaded its case, requesting $120,000, while central exposition director Walter D. Cline asked that $2 million of the $3 million federal appropriation be designated for the Dallas Exposition. That amount, he explained, was necessary to bring the desired capital structure to $15 million.

Cline also reintroduced a centennial theme that had been purposely omitted from the recent proceedings — official black participation at the central exposition. His interest in the project stemmed from the urging of A. E. Holland, a black professor and close friend of Cline. The Wichita Falls oilman had previously met with thirty-one Dallas black leaders, who agreed to sell $50,000 in Central Exposition Corporation bonds in return for his pledge to support their project. Cline used this commitment to convince Fred Florence and R. L. Thornton that the Wells matter should be closed.[15] They, in turn, contacted Congressman Sam Rayburn about supporting the black project, while Cline interceded with Congressman Wright Patman and Vice-President Garner. The initiative in the matter, however, would remain primarily with the black community, namely with A. Maceo Smith and John L. Blount.

On Saturday, August 17, the United States Texas Centennial Commission announced the allocation of the federal appropriation as follows: Texas Memorial Museum in Austin, $300,000; central exposition in Dallas, $1.2 million; San Jacinto Battlefield, $400,000; the Alamo, $400,000; Goliad, $50,000; the Texas Centennial Commission (Commission of Control), $200,000; Southwestern Fat Stock Show and Exposition at Fort Worth, $250,000 (returned to the Commission of Control for a similar amount previously allocated to that project);

[15] Boswell, "Negro Participation," p. 7. This information was based on an interview with A. Maceo Smith on December 23, 1969.

and $200,000 reserved for contingencies. Not everyone was happy with the announcement. Amon Carter objected to having to return the $250,000 to the Commission of Control, while Jesse H. Jones expressed his disappointment that the federal commission denied his request for $2 million to commemorate "the bloody history made at San Jacinto, the Alamo, and Goliad." Jones characterized as sacrilegious the $2 million allocation for the Dallas exposition (actually $1.2 million), which he termed a waste of money, just "another fair for strictly commercial purposes."[16]

Smith and Blount were also distressed to learn that the United States Commission had made no specific provision for black participation at the exposition. Refusing to depend any longer on peripheral support, they assumed personal initiative in the matter. On August 30, Blount wrote the United States Texas Centennial Commission in Washington, citing the Negro Centennial Commission's displeasure with the recent allocation of federal funds.[17] He considered the bond selling requirement discriminatory, explaining that "we do not recall that San Antonio, San Jacinto, Fort Worth, or groups sponsoring any other project, were required by anyone to buy or sell bonds."[18] The following day Blount sent a copy of the letter to Secretary of State Cordell Hull, explaining briefly that he felt the federal allocation was not being fairly adjusted. Secretary Hull apparently had already inquired into the matter. On September 7, Richard Southgate, Chief of the State Department Division of Protocol and Conferences, wrote the secretary of state: "The sum of roughly $50,000 has been tentatively considered as adequate for the construction of a building to house Negro exhibits at the Exposition, and approximately $25,000 more has been tentatively ear-marked for administrative expenses. However, until the allocation has definitely been made by the Commissioner General and approved by the Commission, I am sure that you will agree that we should not give out any information on the subject."[19]

[16]*Dallas Morning News*, August 18, 1935.

[17]The Negro Centennial Commission was composed of W. R. Banks, Prairie View, general chairman; A. Maceo Smith, general secretary; and Jno. L. Blount, Houston, promotion and exhibits.

[18]John L. Blount to U.S. Texas Centennial Commission, August 30, 1935. State Department Decimal File 811.607, Texas Centennial/29.

[19]Richard Southgate to Cordell Hull, September 7, 1935, 811.607, Texas Centennial/33.

Meanwhile more trouble had been brewing back in Dallas, where there was growing concern over mounting exposition costs and a seeming overgrowth of top management. The corporation's executive committee decided it was time for change. Cline's Washington appearance to plead the case of the central exposition marked his final service in behalf of the centennial movement; the executive committee had already agreed that he was expendable. After Cline announced that he would resign if his salary was reduced by as much as one dollar, they cut his salary from $25,000 to $15,000 on September 20 and limited his authority to promotional work with state and federal officials. The committee further removed from his control all development work at the exposition site. This made his departure inevitable; on September 24, he submitted his resignation effective October 1. With Cline out, the interim management group — R. L. Thornton, Arthur L. Kramer, and Harry A. Olmsted — assumed temporary control of the operation.

The corporation's management, however, remained in flux; efforts at economy appeared to be the underlying factor. With Cline's departure, assistant director Otto Herold became acting director, but his tenure was also brief. When the management committee reduced his $10,000 salary and curbed his authority, the veteran president of the State Fair of Texas also resigned. Thereupon the executive committee appointed William A. Webb "executive representative of the executive committee" at a salary of $6,000 a year. On assuming his position, Webb announced that a third executive, concessions director Nat D. Rodgers, had also resigned, and Paul M. Massmann, previously exhibits director, had assumed Rodgers's responsibilities with the title of chief of exhibits and concessions. This move to consolidate the corporation's management team resulted in a net eight-month saving of $100,000. At that time the corporation had 141 employees.[20]

Webb filled a crucial administrative void. The quiet-spoken former Dallas city councilman and railroad executive brought a wealth of experience and administrative skill to his new assignment. He had served as operating vice-president of the Missouri, Kansas, and Texas Railroad System from 1911 to 1919 and was appointed to the United States Railroad War Board during World War I. On the recommendation of the United States Department of State, he served a ten-year

[20] *Dallas Morning News,* October 25, 1935.

assignment as commissioner of the Southern Australian railway system. In appointing Webb as executive director, the executive committee made a wise decision; he fulfilled their expectations in abundance.

Controversy, however, was not limited to the Dallas-Washington scene. Back in Austin a mutiny had been developing in the Advisory Board of Texas Historians. This apparently came as no surprise to the board chairman. Although Kemp and Dobie respected each other personally, they remained poles apart in their individual views of the board's responsibility. In a letter to Kemp on September 11, 1935, Dobie explained: "I am writing you in all friendliness, but I realize that there is a fundamental gulf between the ways our minds work. I live more by imagination; you more by literal facts." As the date approached for the Advisory Board to make its final recommendations, Dobie realized that his views would be diluted by Kemp's and Foik's votes. "Father Foik will vote straight through with you any way you vote," Dobie continued. "That makes two votes for one mind. I have but one vote, but I (also) have a mind. In the beginning you said that a minority report would be permissible. Unless this schedule is revised and revised radically, I am going to make a minority report."[21]

Dobie also disagreed with Kemp over the policy of assigning markers and monuments. Probably unknowingly, he agreed with Holden in his preference for a geographic consideration rather than the senatorial district orientation. He explained to Kemp on September 11: "I think that our principle of putting up various monuments merely because they are handy to certain senatorial districts is wrong. Let us place something, yes, in every district, but let us concentrate on geographical districts. . . . Personally I am not concerned with helping get certain senators re-elected. . . . I doubt if you will agree to much of this. But merely because the figures balance up evenly is no indication that we have a just and civilized report."[22]

The fundamental source of this disagreement was neither mathematical nor geographic, but philosophical. While Kemp thought primarily in terms of memorializing the Republic period of Texas history, Dobie viewed the Texas experience within an expansive concept; while Kemp focused primarily on the factual, the practical, and the spe-

    [21] Dobie Papers, Box 2B149, Barker Texas History Center, University of Texas at Austin; Jeffrey Mason Hancock, "Preservation of Texas Heritage in the 1936 Texas Centennial," Master's thesis, University of Texas at Austin, 1962, pp. 22–23.
    [22] Hancock, "Preservation of Texas Heritage," p. 24.

cific, Dobie wanted to honor men who had contributed to the various currents of culture and civilization of the state — cowboys, Texas Rangers, poets, and writers — not just political and military figures. Student author Jeffrey M. Hancock explained that Dobie "was primarily concerned that the heroic, the legendary, the epic phase of Texas history was not ignored. He was eager to let the sculptors reflect the personality of the subject concerned, and to present history to the public in as broad a perspective as possible."[23]

The convergence of strong wills seldom leads to compromise; on October 7 the Commission of Control received two reports from the advisory board. They differ mainly in areas of emphasis and total recommendations. Dobie pointed out, however, that fiscal economy was not the objective, as "$771,000 had been more money than we really needed for strictly centennial purposes. The fact that $8,000,000 or so has been asked for means no more than [if] a child asks for a barrel of chocolate candy." He noted further that while many requests have been "uniformly reasonable" in efforts toward "preserving history and forwarding culture," the bulk of the applications came from communities "merely joining in the national Democratic movement to grab from the public barrel while it is open."[24]

To Dobie, this local scramble for funds to honor those whom he regarded with historical skepticism violated the purpose of the centennial. Anson Jones was a case in point. "I know positively that the people away out on the Clear Fork of the Brazos care nothing for a $14,000 statue of Anson Jones, as recommended in the Majority Report," Dobie stated in his report. "Not many people anywhere, as matter of fact, care for Anson Jones." Basing his evaluation on Carlyle's definition of history as the projected shadows of a few individuals, Dobie concluded, "We should be where we are today had Anson Jones never been born. His shadow was never very long, and has grown less and less until it is now invisible." Dobie argued, however, that people all over West Texas as well as the people in Jones County would take pride in a memorial to Larry Chittenden, the cowboy poet of Jones County. Dobie and Chittenden both lost. Anson Jones stands today memorialized on the courthouse square in the town and county

[23] Ibid., p. 23.
[24] Minority Report, p. 7, in *Reports of the Advisory Board of Texas Historians to the Commission of Control for Texas Centennial Celebrations, Majority and Minority Reports,* October 7, 1935, State Archives.

that jointly share his name—the beneficiary of federal, not state, money.[25]

The Commission of Control began a three-day meeting in Austin on October 17 to act on the advisory board's recommendations. After considering both reports, the commission recommended $759,000 of the $775,000 in state and federal funds allocated for permanent memorials to Texas history. These expenditures fell within the scope of House Bill No. 11, which provided that $1,075,000 be used to fund celebrations outside of Dallas County. No appropriated funds were allowed for pageantry.[26] Aside from the allocations specifically provided for in the legislation, the Commission of Control designated ten different categories of memorials to Texas' past. These were exposition buildings, memorial museums, community centers, restorations, park improvements, statues, monuments, historical markers, grave markers, and highway markers. Comparatively little was spent for historical restorations. Major projects consisted of $50,000 for a memorial museum at the College of Mines at El Paso; $25,000 each for museums at West Texas State Teachers College in Canyon, Texas Technological College in Lubbock, and Sul Ross State Teachers College in Alpine; and $41,200 to construct and equip the Sam Houston Memorial Museum and Shrine in Huntsville. These were part of a list of thirty-seven major monuments for which the state legislature had appropriated $375,000.[27]

A smaller series of memorials identified as "X" and "Y" monuments (for example, "X," a memorial to Mahan's Chapel in Sabine County, cost $327, and "Y," a memorial to the City of Jefferson in Marion County, was $777) cost a total of $13,068. The largest category of historical monuments and markers consisted of more than seven hundred smaller memorials placed throughout the state; 758 had been completed by February, 1939. These were produced in three sizes and marked battle sites, old forts, missions, homes of Texas patriots, old

[25]Ibid., p. 10.
[26]The allocations specified in the legislation included: repairs to the Alamo, $250,000; San Jacinto monument, $250,000; Goliad monument, $50,000; Gonzales projects, $50,000; major monuments, $375,000; and historical markers, $100,000. Some of this work remained incomplete at the time of Tom C. King's official accounting. Tom C. King, *Report of an Examination of the Texas Centennial* (Austin: Office of the State Auditor and Efficiency Expert, 1939), p. 56.
[27]Ibid., pp. 68–75.

towns, schools, churches, and other sites important in Texas history. A slightly smaller marker was used to mark graves of Texas patriots; the remains of twenty-four were removed from former locations to the state cemetery in Austin. The cost of this series of memorials was $130,715.[28]

The actual federal allocation for historical sites, monuments, museums, and restorations totaled $1.9 million and was divided among thirty-one separate projects. Many of these fell within the province of the advisory board. Major expenditures within this category include: federal portion for erecting the memorial at the San Jacinto Battlefield, $385,000 (plus an additional $202,927 P.W.A. grant); Texas Memorial Museum, $300,000; Alamo restoration, $75,000; Fort Worth Livestock Centennial Exposition, $300,000 (not expended through the Commission of Control); cenotaph to the heroes of the Alamo, $100,000; Trail Drivers Memorial at San Antonio, $98,000; and San José Mission repairs and restoration, $20,000. Statues and monuments ranged in cost from $776 for a monument giving the history of Burnet County to the controversial $25,000 memorial to the pioneer woman erected on the campus of Texas State College for Women at Denton. There were two categories of statues to Texas heroes: seven cost $14,000 each, and eight were allotted $7,500 apiece. Anson Jones was accorded one of the latter.[29]

For the many dedicated people responsible for planning the forthcoming celebrations, the summer of 1935 had been a period of controversy, compromise, and progress. Much of the failure and frustration stemmed from inexperienced people dealing with the unfamiliar; no one in Austin or Dallas had ever before organized a celebration of this magnitude. Planning for 1936 opened up a new and unexplored frontier; those in the vaguard were modern pioneers coming face-to-face with both the unknown and the unexplored. Failures there were indeed, but in the final assessment the major performers should be accorded high marks. If Walter Cline, obviously hired in haste, was an unwise choice for the exposition's first executive director, then W. A. Webb far more than compensated for any of his predecessor's shortcomings. And while the black community's $50,000 federal allo-

[28] Ibid., pp. 85–121.
[29] For a complete accounting of all state and federal centennial expenditures, see King, *Report of Texas Centennial*.

cation for an exhibit hall fell far short of their expectations, they nevertheless would erect an edifice to their progress and culture that remains a milestone in race recognition.[30] Likewise, neither Jesse H. Jones, Amon Carter, Walter Cline, nor W. C. Holden were granted all the funds they requested, yet each community they represented received something enabling them to fulfill some projected goal benefitting their respective constituencies.

The summer of 1935 must also be remembered as the time of victory for those who believed the celebration should emphasize patriotism as well as commercialism. In addition to Texas' $1,075,000 designated for use "outside of the County of Dallas," the federal government allocated $1,335,000 to the Commission of Control for thirty-seven projects memorializing local history. And whatever the controversies and disagreements that developed within and beyond the Advisory Board of Texas Historians, the program developed by that three-man panel produced some of the celebration's more enduring benefits. Kemp and Dobie may have differed on the philosophy of memorializing the past (the board, unfortunately, developed no uniform philosophical objectives), but they gave the Commission of Control an outline for memorializing Texas history, most of which will remain throughout the ages. Thanks to the work done by many people in Texas and in Washington during the summer of 1935, future generations were assured that the past would always remain a part of the present.

It had been a long hot summer. But with the approach of autumn came the stark realization that another summer — the centennial summer — lay less than ten months away. It was a time for great preparations.

---

[30]On January 28, 1936, Dr. J. W. Studebaker, commissioner of education, Department of the Interior, received notice that the U.S. Texas Centennial Commission was transferring $50,000 to his credit for preparing the Negro exhibit (Thomas to Studebaker, State Dept. Decimal File 811.607/92, Texas Centennial).

9

A BEAUTIFUL FACE AND A WELL-KNOWN GIRL

Architects, builders, politicians, and historians alone could not ensure the success of the Texas centennial celebration. This observance needed people, out-of-state visitors especially, to witness the wonders of the state's century of progress and independence. It was the idea of attracting nonresidents to Texas that first sparked the centennial movement. Theodore Price's 1923 challenge to the media executives to use their "gloriously romantic history . . . [to] attract the attention and presence of the world" set forth the two-fold nature of the movement—patriotism and commercialism—which persisted throughout the celebration. The commercial theme emerged as a major factor in planning the celebration; the organizational structure deemed it so. With newspaper and advertising executives promoting the centennial idea and politicians, businessmen, and professional leaders carrying the movement to fruition, it was inevitable that boosterism would emerge as an all-pervasive force. Commercialism led three Texas cities to compete for the central exposition, and the same impulse created the three-member Advisory Board for Advertising, which House Bill No. 11 authorized to formulate a half-million-dollar program of state and national publicity. Thus the spirit of Theodore Price was destined to prevail.

At the same time George Dahl was moving his architectural staff into the "horse barn" and the fund-seekers were converging on Washington, the three-man Advisory Board for Advertising was presenting its initial report to the Commission of Control. These three forces—the builders, the fundraisers, and the advertisers, all subtly interrelated—would ultimately converge with the opening of the central exposition on June 6, 1936.

Exactly one month prior to the August 8, 1935, meeting at Palacios, Texas, the commission had appointed to the board three prominent Texas business executives with outstanding credentials. They were Roy Miller, chairman, a Corpus Christi businessman with strong political affiliations, who had spearheaded the development of the Gulf Intercoastal Waterway; Gen. John A. Hulen, Fort Worth, president of the Burlington, Rock Island Railroad;[1] and Arthur L. Kramer, Dallas, president of A. Harris and Company, a major department store in that city. During the month interim the three board members met on several occasions to formulate an advertising and publicity campaign for the forthcoming celebration. They made the following recommendations which the Commission of Control accepted unanimously:

(1) creation of a Department of Publicity as a subdivision of the Commission of Control;

(2) division of the $500,000 appropriation for advertising and publicity as follows:

Radio advertising	$40,000
Paid space advertising in Texas newspapers and other Texas media	$50,000
Paid space advertising in publications outside of Texas	$160,000
Printed literature, posters, folders, travel posters, booklets, outdoor bulletins, etc.	$65,000
General publicity and staff personnel	$50,000
Reserved for future allocation	$135,000

(3) separation of the publicity and advertising campaigns into two distinct divisions: (a) general publicity and (b) paid newspaper, magazine, billboard, and radio advertising; and

(4) appointment of advertising counsel as official agents and representatives to carry out these recommendations.[2]

The advertising board lost little time in implementing the program. On August 15, 1935, they announced the appointment of Charles Roster, a Corpus Christi advertising executive, as director of the Department of Publicity. He closed his Corpus Christi office immediately

[1] Hulen was a general in the Texas National Guard; Camp Hulen, the National Guard training field at Palacios, Texas, was named for him.

[2] King, *Report of Texas Centennial*, pp. 44–46.

and by Monday, August 26, was conducting business from a room in the Adolphus Hotel in Dallas. His first order of business was to assemble a publicity staff. On Monday night he telegraphed *Corpus Christi Caller-Times* reporter William P. Elliott: "Ready to get going. Report at once. Salary $250." He also wrote Elliott the following day explaining that since they were embarking on a crash program, he was to begin work while en route to Dallas. Roster instructed Elliott to stop in Gonzales and Goliad to gather information about the celebrations planned for those two points. He urged Elliott to "get enough information to enable you to plug the celebration for sixty days. . . . Our job is going to be a hard one. For the next six months we will have to build up a background for the whole Centennial idea, and this we will have to do by colorful, romantic, and historical stories. I am counting on you, old fellow."[3]

Roster's one positive asset in organizing the department was staff availability. With hundreds of journalists and public relations people out of work, he was inundated with quality job applications. There were old friends seeking work, young people just out of college, and displaced Texans hoping to return home. By late October, Roster had assembled a skeleton staff that was turning out centennial information from a new suite of offices on the second floor of the Administration Building. By then he had established six divisions in the Department of Publicity and engaged directors for each. They were Dale Miller, Dallas, press;[4] Roger M. Busfield, Fort Worth, periodicals; Robert G. Coulter, San Antonio, travel and advertising tie-in; Merle H. Tucker, Fort Worth, radio; Elithe Hamilton Beal, Coleman, school and club; and Melissa Castle, Dallas, research. The department staff totaled seventeen employees and was eventually increased to twenty-eight, including five half-time employees. Roster earned the top monthly salary, $333.33, while Miller and Coulter each received $250 and Melissa Castle, $175. Elithe Hamilton Beal, field representative Mrs. Hulen R. Carroll, and Florentine Fernandez, chief clerk and secretary, earned $150 a month; secretaries received $125 and stenographers $105.

Dallas became the center for all centennial publicity and advertis-

---

[3] Charles Roster to William P. Elliott, August 26 and 27, 1935, State Archives.

[4] Dale Miller, who led the *Texas Weekly's* patriotic crusade for the constitutional amendment, took a leave of absence to join the centennial publicity staff. He also took with him his secretary, Bess Harris [Mrs. Judge Herman] Jones.

ing. On October 15, 1935, the Commission of Control entered into a contract with Tracy-Locke-Dawson, Inc., of Dallas, designating that firm as the official agent and representative to conduct a state and national advertising campaign. The $315,000 contract covered paid space advertising, both in-state and national; printed materials; and radio advertising. The advertising board later allocated an additional $23,544 for national advertising and transferred funds from the radio budget to provide increased coverage in national publications. Thus the spirit of Theodore Price indeed prevailed; more than three-fifths of the advertising budget was planned to lure out-of-staters to visit Texas.[5] In addition to the state Department of Publicity and the Tracy-Locke-Dawson contract, the Texas Centennial Exposition Corporation also established a separate promotion department to publicize Dallas and the central exposition. Frank N. Watson headed this department, which also had offices in the exposition Administration Building.

Roster developed his publicity campaign around the same theme from which the centennial movement originally emerged—Texas history and the Texas experience. He first articulated this theme to William Elliott, and it became the publicity staff's guiding principle. Robert Coulter, in turn, conveyed the same message to staff writer Ayres Compton prior to his joining the department. "The entire state —with its wealth of history and romance— is the field from which our writers will draw their material," he explained. But whatever Ayres wrote, he should "bear in mind that it must have a Centennial slant."[6]

By the time Roster assumed his new responsibilities, the state was alive with centennial preparations. Local beautification programs topped the popularity list. On April 1, 1935, the *Dallas Morning News* reported that, "with the Texas Centennial celebrations in 1936 in mind, every progressive community in the State, it would seem, is busy with some landscaping enterprise or other."[7] The citizens of Leonard, Texas, had already set out 208 rosebushes on the courthouse lawn, while the Mount Pleasant Boy Scouts were planting shrubs and flowers around their cabin in that town's fair park. The mayor of Galveston proclaimed

[5]King, *Report of Texas Centennial*, pp. 48–49. The final breakdown in coverage was: ads in Texas, 16.6 percent; ads outside Texas, 61.7 percent; printed materials (posters, lists, etc.), 19.5 percent; and radio advertising, 2.2 percent.
[6]Robert Coulter to Ayres Compton, September 23, 1935, State Archives.
[7]*Dallas Morning News*, April 1, 1935.

the week of November 18, 1935, as Oleander Planting Week. Through the efforts of the Galveston Women's Civic League, five thousand free oleander plants were distributed daily through the cooperation of local merchants. The mayor explained this was part of "the city's beautification program for the Texas Centennial next year."[8]

During July and August of 1935, the *Dallas Morning News* ran a series of photographs of dilapidated farm structures with the suggestion that these should be either repaired or razed as part of the centennial effort. The caption line below a photograph of an abandoned tenant farm house stated: "No Asset for a Main Highway. . . . It is unlikely that it will be of any service in attracting visitors to Texas."[9]

Shamrock, in Wheeler County, regarded the future as well as the past as an appropriate precentennial theme. The community leaders believed that establishing a system of good parks would "create a mental attitude, especially among the boys and girls of the communities, that will be conducive to good citizenship." They believed this, in turn, would contribute toward "a proper mental attitude [that] can serve as a stimulus to broadmindedness, loyalty, and all other attributes composing a true patriotic character."[10] Roster entered the centennial publicity campaign riding the crest of a great ground swell of public interest. He could, therefore, enjoy the luxury of an eager, receptive, and patriotic audience.

Dallas became the wellspring of centennial information. The methods employed by both the state and exposition divisions (including the Tracy-Locke-Dawson firm) fell roughly into seven categories: printed material, print media releases (newspapers and periodicals), radio production, paid advertising, tie-in advertising, field work (including school and club promotion), and "stunts" (contrived or planned news events designed to gain free media exposure). Each method helped disseminate the message that Texas was celebrating its centennial and everyone, from everywhere, was invited.

The primary media blitz began in September. The exposition's promotion department launched its campaign on September 7 with the *Centennial News* (1935–36 version), a weekly four-page news flyer that focused primarily on the central exposition. It traced the prog-

[8]*Galveston Tribune*, November 19, 1935.
[9]*Dallas Morning News*, August 18, 1935.
[10]Texas Centennial Commission News Release, State Archives.

ress of exposition construction, reported the signing of each major exhibitor, and described in spectacular terms the modern wonders that awaited exposition visitors. The *Centennial News* immediately became popular with the transportation companies and travel agencies, and regular deliveries were made to their branch offices throughout the United States.

Roster initially focused his publicity campaign within the state, highlighting both local observances and the central exposition. To promote the many burgeoning state and local activities, Roster's staff established a weekly newsletter, the *Texas Centennial Review* (mailed to 750 Texas newspapers), which evolved as a clearinghouse for centennial information, ideas, and suggestions. One priority of the department was to include every local activity within the state with a centennial theme. Each issue of the *Review* carried a regular feature, "Texas Centennial Calendar," listing all the statewide activities. A February, 1936 issue (undated) mentioned 111 local activities, while an early April issue listed a total of 212 scheduled events. One month later that had grown to 238 events. The *Review* soon became one of the department's more popular undertakings. Roster ordered 7,500 copies of the first issue. Weekly orders averaged 12,000 copies until June 17, when, during the second week of the exposition, the press run totaled 14,700 copies. One issue suggested: "Enclose this week's copy of the *Review* in a letter to an out-of-state friend." Dale Miller, director of the press division, later explained the publication's economic purpose: "Our job was to keep out-of-state visitors traveling throughout Texas by incorporating into our Centennial observance such widely dispersed activities as the Tyler Rose Festival, the Stamford Rodeo, the Mission Citrus Fiesta, and many, many others."[11]

Other printed materials also contributed to much of the department's publicity saturation of the state and nation. All were keyed to promoting travel to and through Texas in 1936. The most ambitious project was *This is Texas*, a 187-page illustrated history of Texas and preview of the 1936 Texas centennial celebrations. This was, in essence, Texas' official "press book" extolling the state's heroic past, its scenic beauty, the exciting present, and its virtually unlimited economic potential. The Department of Publicity ordered one thousand copies from the Steck Company in Austin at a cost of $4,629. Nine

[11] Dale Miller to Kenneth B. Ragsdale, March 9, 1980, in author's possession.

hundred copies were bound in fabricoid; a special edition of one hundred copies was bound in leather. These were distributed by Governor Allred as formal invitations to distinguished individuals.

The publicity department also produced a steady stream of less pretentious brochures and pamphlets. Much of this literature was distributed by railroads, bus lines, airlines, and travel agencies, which were all actively promoting travel to Texas in 1936. Roster regarded this type of promotional literature as one of his more potent promotional techniques. According to his records, the department distributed 8.75 million pieces of literature promoting the state and the centennial celebrations. "Inquiries from every State and from fifty-six foreign countries sometimes reached more than 2,500 a day," he explained, "and each was expeditiously answered within twenty-four hours."[12]

The paid advertising campaign being developed by the Tracy-Locke-Dawson agency and the concurrent general publicity releases distributed by Roster's publicity department complemented each other. Centennial ads began appearing in national publications in December, 1935. Tracy-Locke-Dawson's billings for that month totaled $13,202.76 and $24,115.49 for January, 1936. Charges thereafter increased each month, peaking at $66,349.38 in April, one month prior to the exposition's opening.[13] Roster explained later that "the paid advertising helped pave the way for publicity releases, which, normally, were distributed to Texas dailies twice a week, Texas weeklies once a week, and national dailies once a week."[14]

The cover of one of the most widely distributed centennial brochures resulted from a publicity "stunt." The beautiful blonde girl wearing western attire and waving a white cowboy hat became the symbol of Texas' welcome to the nation, while inviting the reader to peruse the thirty-two colorful pages of "A Pictorial Parade of Texas." The lovely lady was San Antonio native Janice Jarratt; the image was the creation of press director Dale Miller. In assessing the effectiveness of the publicity campaign, Miller had decided they needed a sym-

---

[12]*Dallas Morning News,* December 4, 1936.

[13]King, *Report of Texas Centennial,* p. 54. Part of this expenditure included the production of printed promotional materials such as posters, flyers, and the popular windshield stickers for automobiles: "Texas Centennial Bound" and "We Enjoyed the Texas Centennial."

[14]*Dallas Morning News,* December 4, 1936.

bol, a person with a high identity factor whose appearance at centennial functions would assure immediate news coverage. "I thought what we needed was a beautiful face and a well-known girl," Miller recalled. "I got in touch with Janice." Thus, the "Sweetheart of the Texas Centennial" was born.[15]

In 1935, Janice Jarratt was America's most photographed model. After she achieved national recognition as "the Chesterfield girl," her career skyrocketed. By the mid-1930s she had become a national symbol, seen regularly in newspaper and magazine ads, on billboards, and on magazine covers. At the pinnacle of her career Miller called her in New York and asked if she would like to come back to Texas "to be the Sweetheart of the Texas Centennial. The title? Just thought it up." Surprisingly, she liked the idea, even without a salary, and agreed to investigate the matter. The following week she called Miller and announced that the model agency agreed to a leave of absence. They thought that further exposure through the Texas centennial would heighten her value to them. Miller, of course, was delighted. He did not know it at that time, but he had just pulled off one of the great publicity stunts of the centennial year.[16]

Miller managed Jarratt's new career adroitly; her arrival in Texas rivaled Hollywood at its gaudy best. Even the governor of Texas joined in on the stunt. As Miss Jarratt stepped from the Missouri Pacific train in San Antonio, a welcoming committee presented her with a huge bouquet of roses while a band played "The Eyes of Texas." She was whisked away in a waiting limousine to the St. Anthony Hotel, where Miller had arranged a dinner dance that evening, following her presentation as the official centennial sweetheart. San Antonio Mayor C. K. Quinn introduced her to Governor Allred, who delivered the presentation speech. The thirty-minute ceremony was broadcast over the Texas Quality Network.[17]

In addition to posing for the now-famous photograph in the patio of the Governor's Palace in San Antonio (Miller snapped the photograph while Miss Jarratt waved his official centennial hat), Miss Jarratt fulfilled Miller's expectations in abundance. From that moment on the state became her beat (though she made an official appear-

[15]Miller interview, Austin, Texas, July 21, 1978.
[16]Ibid.
[17]WOAI, San Antonio; WBAP, Fort Worth; WFAA, Dallas; and KPRC, Houston, all NBC affiliates, comprised the Texas Quality Network.

ance at the Democratic National Convention in Philadelphia), and wherever she appeared she made news—centennial news. But the publicity saga of the "Sweetheart of the Texas Centennial" had just begun. During Miss Jarratt's reign, Universal Pictures Corporation offered her a movie contract which Miller arranged to have signed in the governor's office. He telegraphed Universal corporate headquarters in New York: "Governor agrees to have contract signing in his office Friday morning, eleven o'clock and he personally will sign contract as witness. . . . I suggest you order Universal Newsreel coverage of Austin ceremonies which I think are unprecedented. Now working on Dallas stunts for Friday night and am confident everything will work out well. . . . You of course, are at liberty to use governor's telegram in publicity."[18] And the publicity ball kept rolling. Hundreds of clippings bearing Miss Jarratt's image attest to the success of Miller's "sweetheart stunt."

The publicity department relied heavily on radio to convey the centennial message to the masses in Texas and across the country. This coverage included remote broadcasts of local celebrations, tie-in plugs on commercial broadcasts, and radio programs produced especially to stimulate centennial interest. Merle H. Tucker, director of the radio division, coordinated these activities. He was well qualified for the assignment; he had begun his radio work in 1930 at WBAP, Fort Worth, and had served as announcer, production manager, and studio director at various other major outlets, including a special assignment with the National Broadcasting Company in New York.

Tucker's first assignment after joining the publicity department was launching a weekly series of thirty-minute radio programs over the Texas Quality Network. These broadcasts originated from various locations around the state and were planned specifically to generate local interest in the centennial. The initial broadcast, which Tucker wrote, rehearsed, and produced himself, originated from Houston on November 11, 1935. All programs followed a similar format: an orchestral overture, vocal selections (many on Texas themes), local dignitaries speaking on the centennial, and periodic announcements promoting the forthcoming celebrations. Considering that these broadcasts reached a statewide audience, the publicity department was

[18] Telegram from Dale Miller to Paul Gulick, Universal Pictures, New York, July 1, 1936, State Archives.

richly rewarded for the investment. The November 11 Houston broadcast cost only $226, including the cast, a fifteen-piece orchestra, an engineer, and production costs. The most expensive broadcast originated from San Antonio on March 30 and cost $331. The series continued through April 6, 1936.[19]

Commercial tie-ins, guest appearances, and special programs dedicated to the Texas Centennial reached a far greater listening audience on national radio. Much of this coverage resulted from Tucker's extensive field work. In January, 1936, he conferred with civic leaders and business and radio executives in the major eastern markets concerning centennial publicity. At Cincinnati he arranged a radio salute to Texas with executives of the Crosley Radio Corporation. In Washington and New York he met with representatives of the major advertising agencies and executives of both the National Broadcasting Company and the Columbia Broadcasting System regarding network tie-in publicity.

Results were immediately forthcoming. On February 21, station WLW in Cincinnati dedicated a special broadcast to Texas and the centennial. Weekly radio programs on the national networks also began airing salutes to the Lone Star State. When baritone John Charles Thomas, star of a popular network radio show, announced he would plug the centennial, Texas Gov. James V. Allred quickly responded: "All Texas is appreciative of the deep national interest being shown in our centennial celebrations. . . . I am pleased to know you contemplate a salute to the Lone Star State. Texas will be grateful to you."[20] The Maxwell House Coffee Company, sponsors of the NBC program "Show Boat," agreed to salute the Texas centennial with a dramatization of the fall of the Alamo. Miller, the master of the stunt, quickly recognized another opportunity. Knowing that "stars" make news, he aimed for the pinnacle of the galaxy, the vice-president of the United States, only to be denied. Miller received the vice-president's refusal in a telegram: "Garner expresses keen regret he is unable to establish precedent permitting his name on commerical programs despite merit of this one." Jesse H. Jones, chairman of the Reconstruction Finance Corporation, came to Miller's rescue. He (or was it Miller?) drafted a telegram to be read on the air during the presentation:

[19]Centennial Collection, State Archives.
[20]Gov. James V. Allred to John Charles Thomas, April 10, 1936, State Archives.

"The Texas Centennial marks one of the great events in the history of our country, the winning of the independence of approximately one-third of the territory of the United States at the Battle of San Jacinto. . . . The centennial is worthy of the recognition you accord it. Best wishes to Captain Henry [actor Charles Winninger] and his splendid troupe."[21]

While the publicity department used the airwaves to carry the centennial message to the nation's millions, Roster also realized that stimulating group and community involvement required person-to-person contact. In October, 1935, he engaged Mrs. Hulen R. Carroll as a field representative and later added Mrs. R. F. Martin to a similar position on his staff. For the next ten months they literally canvassed the state, community by community, helping local citizen groups plan their centennial celebrations. While Mrs. Carroll concentrated on Northwest Texas, Mrs. Martin began a county-by-county solicitation in South Texas communities. (The Trans-Pecos and Northeast Texas areas appear to have been omitted.) They found an eager clientele. In late November Mrs. Martin was helping Crystal City plan a spinach festival, Carrizo Springs stage a strawberry festival, and Del Rio citizens develop plans for the Val Verde County anniversary celebration. She later returned to Crystal City to discuss plans for presenting the operetta "Rose Window of San José." By mid-December Mrs. Martin had worked her way to Central Texas, where she had appointments with centennial advisory boards, school superintendents, and chamber of commerce presidents at Luling, Lockhart, Georgetown, and Austin. She explained in her report: "Due to Xmas activities was unable to get committee together after Dec. 20th." Mrs. Carroll began the new year with an equally hectic schedule. Between January 7 and February 3, she worked the communities between Fort Worth, Wichita Falls, Lubbock, and Abilene. During that period she traveled 1,861 miles by private automobile and was reimbursed $177.35 for her mileage, room, and board.[22]

Elithe Hamilton Beal, director of the school and club division, also spent much time in the field. She was in Fort Worth on October 14 to consult with officials of the Southwest Broadcasting Company on centennial publicity; she left the following day for Austin to discuss

[21] Telegram, February 18, 1936, State Archives.
[22] Travel Authorization Forms, Publicity Department, State Archives.

the same matter with officials of the University Interscholastic League and the State Department of Education. On November 3 she had an appointment with President W. J. McConnell at North Texas State College in Denton to discuss centennial educational materials, and she appeared in Jacksonville the following day to address a Federated Women's Club luncheon. Mrs. Beal targeted public school administrators as key individuals in implementing the centennial education program. In early February she returned to Austin to distribute centennial materials at the state convention of city school superintendents, while later that month she attended the National Education Association annual convention in Saint Louis to discuss the department's educational programs.

While most publicity staff members traveled by private automobile, bus, or train, Melissa Castle, director of research, chose Braniff Airways for a trip to Austin on December 2, 1935. This appears to be the first use of air travel by the publicity department staff. The afternoon flight required one hour and thirty minutes and cost $11. She returned to Dallas via Pullman service; this trip required six hours and thirty minutes and cost $8.89.[23]

Tom L. James and J. P. Murrin, the publicity department's sign-posting crews, became the most traveled of all staff personnel. Traveling in separate automobiles, they visited twenty-four states to post large colored waterproof banners displaying the invitation "Visit Texas in 1936 and Enjoy the State-Wide Centennial Celebrations." In addition, they called on newspaper editors along their routes to distribute centennial news releases. Both departed Dallas on January 16, 1936. James worked the Deep South and the Middle Atlantic states, while Murrin traveled up the Mississippi Valley to the Great Lakes area, later canvassing the Great Plains and the Rocky Mountain states. James returned to Dallas on May 18, while Murrin did not complete his itinerary until June 1, 1936. Combined they traveled 38,467 miles promoting the Texas centennial celebrations.[24]

Although publicity staff members who were confined to the Administration Building in Dallas missed the excitement of an entire state gearing up for its big birthday bash, they were nevertheless eye-

[23] Ibid.
[24] Ibid.

witnesses to an equally electrifying human drama — a world's fair in the making. Whatever direction they looked — west toward Parry Avenue, south and east across the recent excavations and sprouting superstructures, up the stairs, or down the hall — something exciting was always happening. Engineers with rolls of building plans and survey plats under their arms came in asking for George Dahl's office, while important-looking business types carrying briefcases were always waiting to see either General Manager W. A. Webb or Paul Massmann, head of the exhibits and concessions department. Massmann headed a staff of merchandising specialists — for food, petroleum, transportation, electronics, automobiles — who traveled the nation soliciting exhibitors for the exposition. Maps, charts, and photographs of exposition buildings covered the walls of Massmann's office, each area bearing a different color indicating its current availability. A profusion of red spelled success; by October 1, unexpected demands for exhibits space in the Foods and Agricultural buildings necessitated expansion of those structures. Throughout October and November, 1935, contracts with new exhibitors — Westinghouse, Standard Brands, Kraft-Phoenix, Beech-Nut, and Dr. Pepper — were announced almost daily, while both Texaco and Gulf Oil Corporation had leased space to construct their individual exhibit facilities. Automobile companies, however, proved to be the exposition's major exhibitors. In late November, while sales representatives were finalizing contracts with both General Motors and the Chrysler Corporation, Webb and Massmann were in Detroit conferring with Ford Motor Company executives about the company's projected $1,250,000 exhibit.

Massmann's other role as concessions head insured a daily replay of the human comedy. One journalist reported that a visitor to his office "might just run into a young ape attired in cowboy regalia, whose owner wants a concession to exhibit him on the midway. Or possibly, a visitor would unavoidably stare at a pretty and well-endowed girl who was there with her manager, investigating the 'fan-dance' possibilities."[25] On October 12 Governor Allred added a different brand of excitement. He appeared at the exposition site to help launch the largest five-month building program in the state's history. As hundreds of construction workers, centennial employees, and invited guests

[25] *Dallas Journal*, March 23, 1936.

looked on, the governor pushed the switch to touch off a dynamite blast that broke ground for the $1.2 million Texas Hall of State. In an age of construction dependent upon men, mules, and some mechanization (a mechanical trenching machine was used to dig piers for the Foods Building), George Dahl was able to report to Ray Foley on October 23 that the building program was proceeding on schedule. The exposition building completion dates were as follows: Administration Building, December 15; Agriculture Building, Foods Building, Livestock Building, Unit 2, and the Varied Industries Building, March 15; Transportation and Petroleum Building, March 20; and the Livestock Building, Unit 1, April 1, 1936.[26]

With the exposition grounds closed to visitors since mid-October (and the State Fair of Texas canceled for the first time in forty-nine years), Webb announced weekly Sunday afternoon "open houses" to begin on December 1. This public relations ploy enabled visitors to view construction progress firsthand. The thousands who turned out were baffled but impressed by what they saw. Most familiar landmarks were gone, streets had been removed, and in their place were gaping excavations upon which new structures would soon appear. Signs were placed on all buildings under construction and on sites where others would be raised. Many Texans first became aware of the exposition's true magnitude from these visits. Most liked what they saw and vowed to return. The following day brought another centennial milestone. United States Texas Centennial Commissioner Cullen F. Thomas, who had established offices in Dallas on October 2, met with the central exposition executives to sign a contract authorizing that corporation to prepare plans and award contracts for the $350,000 federal exhibits building and the $50,000 Hall of Negro Life. Thomas explained that this action cleared the way to begin construction of these facilities, possibly by early January, 1936.

To R. L. Thornton and all exposition executives, the year-end news appeared as a good omen: President Roosevelt announced he would attend the exposition, the title transfer of the disputed 26.5-acre park addition was completed, construction was proceeding on schedule, and 2,500 men were working in three shifts to ensure that the exposition would open as scheduled. Economically, both the exposition and

---

[26]George L. Dahl to Ray Foley, October 23, 1935, Centennial Collection, DHS.

the city were doing well. On Monday, December 23, Dallas's street-car company reported one of the busiest days in its history, and local merchants were predicting that the 1935 Christmas season would be the best in at least five years. Out at Fair Park the exposition was operating on a cash basis. The November financial statement showed a cash balance of $231,349, with $86,671 in receivables from concession and exhibit contracts. The concessions and exhibits yielded $148,769 for the month. Bond income also remained strong, with collections of 98 percent of maturities to November 30.[27] Speaking at the annual Chamber of Commerce banquet on December 3, Thornton appeared equally upbeat about "Dy-damic Dallas" and its recent industrial growth, some obviously tied to exposition construction. "We have acquired more than 1,000 new business and manufacturing plants in the last ten months and should run well over 1,100 for the full year," he explained. "This will be the greatest acquisition of new businesses in our history."[28] Then two days later, writing as guest columnist for the *Dallas Morning News,* Thornton foresaw the centennial exposition as the catalyst for even greater growth in the future. He predicted optimistically: "There will be 8,000,000 visitors in Dallas next year. They will see a Centennial Exposition that has not been surpassed on the American continent. . . . These will be people of means. They will represent millions of dollars in wealth. . . . The Southwest is the promised land of the Nation. . . . They must find here a citizenry united in a common purpose. They must find pride in city ownership that will make them want to become one of us, to cast their economic lots with us, to live among us as neighbors and friends."[29] Urban boosterism was running at high tide.

As Thornton stood at the threshold of the new year, he could at last envision the growth benefits he had prophesied when he led the fight to host the central exposition. He saw history, romance, and a big show as the media through which a city and a state could be merchandised to the nation. And the combined publicity forces were disseminating the Texas message far and wide. The nation, which still harbored a great curiosity about Texas, was intrigued by the glowing invitations to visit this land of vastness, myth, and mystery; at the

[27]*Dallas Morning News,* December 10, 1935.
[28]Ibid., December 3, 1935.
[29]Ibid., December 6, 1935.

same time, the native Texans were becoming increasingly aware of their history and devising individual methods of celebrating their centennial locally. Thus, the masters of the media — Roster, Miller, Tucker, and Watson — were well along on their mission of setting the stage for the greatest historical drama in modern Texas history.

10

TEN GALLON HATS,
SIX SHOOTERS, BLUEBONNETS, AND SEX

The nation greeted the new year, traditionally, with football. And as if by some preordained miracle, three Texas teams appeared in bowl games on the first day of the centennial year. Hardin-Simmons University played New Mexico A&M College in the Sun Bowl Classic (Fiesta del Sol) at Phoenix, the Texas Christian University Horned Frogs met the Louisiana State University Tigers in the Sugar Bowl, and the Southern Methodist University Mustangs, Southwest Conference champions and winners of the Knute Rockne Memorial trophy, faced the Stanford University Indians in the Rose Bowl, "the granddaddy of 'em all."[1] Roster and Miller were quick to perceive that, with millions of the nation's sports fans tuned in to the latter two contests, another publicity blitz awaited the referees' whistle. Thus, they joined the pigskin parade in their campaign to sell Texas and its centennial.

The project became a publicity man's dream-come-true. In addition to the current collection of Saturday's heroes, the cast of newsworthy celebrities included a host of motion picture and radio stars and Texas' two top-ranking executives, the governor and lieutenant governor. Probably never again would the State of Texas receive such well-planned, well-coordinated, and widespread publicity as it did on January 1, 1936. Originally, Governor Allred had planned to be in Livingston, Texas, on New Year's Day to preside at an Alabama-Coushatta Indian tribal ceremony, but Roster convinced him otherwise. On December 14, 1935, the governor wrote Roster that "I feel . . . that I owe it to the State as a whole and the Centennial to make the California trip." He explained that since Lieutenant Governor Woodul would attend the Sugar Bowl Game, he had arranged for Sen. Wilbourne Collie of Eastland, president pro tem of the Senate

---

[1] The Knute Rockne Memorial was tantamount to a national championship in 1935.

and acting governor in their absence, to represent him at Livingston.[2]

Roster was prophetic in his vision; the West was still the land of opportunity. Movie stars in the mid-1930s were certain newsmakers. Thus the primary stunt on the West Coast trip, in addition to the Rose Bowl appearance, was Governor Allred's presentation of Ginger Rogers's commission as admiral in the Texas Navy. Roster laid his plans carefully. On December 10, he telegraphed the Pendleton Dudley agency in Washington to arrange to "have Ginger wire acceptance [of her commission] and thanks to Governor Allred expressing continued interest in Texas Centennial and hopes for its success. This is the angle we want now. Commission awarded because of this interest, although Ginger may not know it."[3] Miss Rogers, one of the ten top box-office stars of the mid-1930s, responded as programmed, and Governor Allred headed west, stopping en route at El Paso to crown a queen at the annual Sun Carnival. Before leaving the state, however, the governor issued a centennial year proclamation, drafted by Charles Roster, appealing "to the people of Texas and to all Texans in the world to dedicate themselves to the task of making the Centennial observance of our State's stirring history 'bold enough to please the still hearts of Austin, Travis and Houston, and big enough to mirror the accomplishments of Texas to the sons and daughters of the earth.' . . . So today, as we stand upon the threshold of our State's Centennial, we must not forget that its purest concept lies in a reverence for the past, and a devotion to the perpetuation of that past through an endless future."[4]

Miller arrived in Los Angeles in advance of the governor's party to complete the arrangements. He orchestrated Allred's every moment with infinite care and perception. Probably no foreign head of state ever received such a star-studded reception. Ginger Rogers received the governor and her commission on New Year's Eve on the RKO Studio set as Miller, studio executives, and publicity writers looked on approvingly.[5] Later that day California Gov. Frank Merriman held a reception for the visiting Texans. Although the Stanford Indians "scalped" the favored Mustangs 7 to 0 the following day (one sports-

[2]Gov. James V. Allred to Charles Roster, December 14, 1935, State Archives.

[3]Charles Roster to Pendleton, Dudley Agency, December 14, 1935, State Archives.

[4]Proclamation No. 16409, December 27, 1935, State Archives.

[5]Roster had planned for the governor to invite Miss Rogers to join his party at the Rose Bowl Game but discovered that "tickets here [were] positively unavailable."

writer described them as "the most jittery eleven that ever represented SMU"), the national spotlight belonged to Texas. For the first time in Rose Bowl history, the visitors were allowed program time between halves of the game. The *Centennial News* reported the Southern Methodist University Band presented five minutes of entertainment that thrilled the "lucky game goers and . . . [provided] radio millions a words-to-music picture of some of the glories of history of Texas as it comes of centennial age."[6] In addition, Governor Allred was allocated ninety seconds at halftime to extend New Year's greetings to the nation over the NBC network and invite everyone to attend the Texas centennial.

And there was still more to come. The governor's subsequent tour of the motion picture studios added another dimension to the publicity orgy. Miller telegraphed Ayres Compton in Dallas, instructing him to release a wire story covering the governor's filmland activities: "Yesterday we were guests of Admiral Ginger at RKO Studios and of John Boles and Wallace Beery at Fox. Today guests of Ernest Lubitsch, Joan Bennett, Fred MacMurray, Gladys Swarthout at Paramount luncheon and later of Mary Pickford at [her palatial home] Pickfair. Guest tonight of Mrs. Will Rogers at Rogers Ranch."[7]

Miller also did a little West Coast promoting on his own. He visited a rehearsal of the Jack Benny radio show, presented Benny with an official Texas centennial hat, and suggested a Texas theme for that radio series. Benny agreed. The "Buck Benny Rides Again" comedy routine between Benny and actor Andy Devine became an on-going sequence on radio's most popular prime time program. Nothing was too good for Texas in 1936.

Texans were accorded an equally cordial reception in New Orleans on New Year's Day. New Orleans Mayor Semmes Walmsley held a pregame reception for Lieut. Gov. Walter F. Woodul and his party, later accompanying them to the Sugar Bowl where they witnessed the Texas Christian University Band saluting the Texas centennial during the halftime show. The theme was six flags over Texas; the pub-

---

[6]*Centennial News*, December 14, 1935. The Southern Methodist University Band, led by Tom Johnson, gained national recognition as the first major university band to abandon the military format in favor of the current swing idiom. The band preceded the football team on the West Coast trip in order to fill a week's professional engagement in a Los Angeles theater.

[7]Dale Miller to Ayres Compton, January 2, 1936, State Archives.

Dale Miller, Texas Centennial press representative, visits the Jack Benny radio
show rehearsal during the 1936 Rose Bowl publicity tour. Cast members are, left
to right, vocalist Kenny Baker, Mary Livingston, Miller, announcer Don Wilson,
Benny wearing Miller's Texas centennial hat, and orchestra leader Johnny Green.
(Courtesy Dale Miller)

Dale Miller, left, introduces unidentified officer to actress Ginger Rogers and Gov. James V. Allred at a gala dinner during the 1936 Rose Bowl weekend in Hollywood. RKO studio publicity staff is in the background. (Courtesy Dale Miller)

Janice Jarratt, "Sweetheart of the Texas Centennial," wears a Texas centennial hat as she poses for a publicity photograph in the patio of the Spanish Governor's Palace in San Antonio. (Courtesy Dale Miller)

Janice Jarratt signs a long-term movie contract in Gov. Allred's office, with, left to right, J. Cheever Cowdin, chairman of the board, Universal Pictures; Harry Evans, Universal publicity director; Governor Allred; and Louis Novy, Austin theater executive. (Courtesy Dale Miller)

Dale Miller (left), wearing centennial hat, and Charles Roster, centennial director of publicity (right), bid farewell to the Keyes quadruplets (Mary, Mona, Leota,
and Roberta) and Baylor University President Pat M. Neff, as they embark by
train on a centennial publicity trip to visit the Dionne quintuplets in Callander,
Ontario. (Courtesy Dale Miller)

An amused Amon G. Carter, second from left, watches as New York City Mayor
Fiorello H. La Guardia waves greetings with official centennial ten-gallon hat
to arriving members of the Texas Centennial Press Train. Members of the University
of Texas Longhorn Band are in the background. (Courtesy Amon G. Carter
Museum, Fort Worth)

Portrait of a Texas Centennial Rangerette. (Courtesy Dallas Historical Society)

Texas Centennial "Bluebonnet Girl" models a bluebonnet-inspired fashion created especially for the 1936 celebration. (Courtesy Dallas Historical Society)

licity department provided the flags. During the intermission, as the lieutenant governor extended his centennial invitation over the National Broadcasting Company network, members of a bonded distribution agency passed out 25,000 copies of the *Texas Centennial Review* to the Sugar Bowl crowd. And in a pseudobiblical switch, the Texas Christians devoured the Louisiana Tigers, 3 to 2.

In the wake of the New Year's Day bowl games and the national publicity they afforded, advertising board member Gen. John A. Hulen restated publicly two underlying objectives, as he perceived them, of the centennial celebrations; neither included history nor patriotism. They were, first, to attract "ambitious, energetic men and their families to Texas," and, second, "to provide convincing evidence to out-of-state money that in helping develop Texas, it can have assurance that dividends will be earned." Then citing the national publicity recently accorded Texas football teams, Hulen concluded, "People in the North and East who weren't fully acquainted with Texas are having their eyes and interests sharpened."[8]

While Hulen obviously had his detractors, he nevertheless pinpointed one significant fact of the centennial era — the nation in the mid-1930s was not fully acquainted with Texas. To many of the millions who had never visited the Lone Star State, Texas existed in their imaginations as a primitive frontier area occupied largely by Indians, longhorn cattle, illiterate cowboys, and wealthy ranchers. The fictional Texas narratives found in films, radio, books, and magazines had conveyed to the uninitiated essentially a romantic myth; the reality just wouldn't play in Peoria. Thus, in merchandising their wares to the outside world, the centennial publicists simply added their professional touch to the Texas mystique. The process appeared quite simple: exploit the myth and the nation will be drawn to Texas to discover the reality. The state's cultural icons therefore became part and parcel of their promotional baggage. Combined, they merged into an eclectic logo that symbolized Texas — ten-gallon hats, six-shooters, high-heeled boots, Texas Rangers, bluebonnets, and sex. The Texas Centennial Rangerettes, wherever they may roam, began life in 1935 as the ubiquitous offspring of the traveling centennial salesmen.

For the first time in the state's history, its agents developed a na-

[8]*Dallas Morning News*, January 2, 1936.

tional publicity campaign, funded by a legislative appropriation and based on its colorful history, romantic myths, and cultural symbols. From that time forward those symbols would suggest only one place —Texas! Roster had articulated this concept to his first employee: ". . . we will have to build up a background for the whole Centennial idea, and this we will have to do by colorful, romantic and historical stories."[9] During the five months that preceded the central exposition's June 6 opening, Roster, Miller, Tucker, and Watson led their teams of hucksters across the state and across the nation, extolling the wonders of Texas and its centennial and always bearing the symbolic accouterments of the Lone Star State. Most of their efforts yielded positive results; some brought honorable recognition to the state, while others bordered on the bizarre. Yet all commanded attention and contributed toward their ultimate objective—selling Texas and the centennial to the nation. In the process America began another westward migration and rediscovered Texas.

The New Year's Day football classics launched the final phase of the centennial publicity push and set the pattern for the ensuing campaigns. The artifacts and traditions of Texas culture became the metaphor for Texas' message to the nation. They came in widely varying but recognizable forms, all calculated to focus the nation's attention on Texas. None was more familiar than the ten-gallon hat; it became the symbol of all things Texan. Every major department store in the state dispersed these at varying prices, all bearing the official Texas centennial logo. On the eve of the Rose Bowl game the A. Harris Company of Dallas advertised "a real Texas ten gallon hat" made of "first quality fur felt that will stand the most unusual California weather"and priced at $4.85. Everybody who was anybody in 1936 received a complimentary centennial hat, including movie stars, politicians, and even Shetland ponies.[10] Roster scored another publicity scoop by persuading "Admiral" Ginger Rogers to pose in the ladies' version of the centennial hat, manufactured by the Knox Hat firm. "This 'Scoop' is one of the [publicity] department's projects," Roster wrote Governor Allred. "I feel certain that the Knox people will want

[9]Charles Roster to William P. Elliott, August 27, 1935, State Archives.
[10]Peruna, Southern Methodist University's diminutive mascot, wore a specially designed ten-gallon hat at the Rose Bowl game.

to send one to the wives of a few of our good friends. So, would you please ascertain from Mrs. Allred her hat size and the color of felt she prefers." The response: size twenty-three and white.[11]

The Willard Hat Company of Dallas supplied official centennial hats to the publicity department at $16.50 per dozen, and wherever departmental personnel traveled, a supply of the complimentary chapeaus was sure to follow. A supplementary order of hats was airmailed to Elithe Hamilton Beal after she disposed of her initial supply at the National Education Association meeting in Saint Louis. Radio director Merle Tucker ordered $10 hats for movie celebrities John Boles and Shirley Temple, while Roster ordered the same priced hats for Senators Tom Connally, George McGill, Warren F. Austin, and Morris Sheppard, for Congressmen Sol Bloom, Joseph Byrne, and Joseph W. Martin, Jr., and for Vice-President John Nance Garner. Lieutenant Governor Woodul sent a collection of the centennial hats to Congressman Morgan Sanders and all members of the Ways and Means Committee.

Granting honorary memberships in Texas institutions became a national pastime, and to many out-of-state dignitaries this became a symbol of great pride and prestige. Second only to Ginger Rogers's admiralty, commissions as honorary Texas Centennial Rangers topped the preferred list. Each commission bore the state seal and the governor's signature. Roster, who developed the Ranger stunt, mailed the blank commissions en masse to the governor for his signature. (Governors were not as busy in 1936.) Ranger commissions, however, were usually limited to prominent individuals to whom the presentation would be a newsworthy event; New York City Mayor Fiorello H. LaGuardia, for example, was a guaranteed newsmaker. On January 24, 1936, Texas Congressman Maury Maverick, representing Governor Allred, presented "the little flower" his commission as captain in the Texas Centennial Rangers in a New York City Hall ceremony. The presentation included the governor's invitation to visit the exposition. In addition to the commission, exposition General Manager W. A. Webb sent the mayor a roadrunner, the native Texas bird. It arrived in a box bearing the warning "Don't open the cage; this bird runs like hell." The mayor sent the roadrunner to the Central Park Zoo.[12]

[11]Charles Roster to Gov. James V. Allred, February 17, 1936, State Archives.
[12]*Dallas Morning News*, January 25, 1936.

In developing new publicity angles for the centennial, Roster's staff transformed the state flower, the bluebonnet, into a national symbol of haute couture. *Vogue* magazine designed the "Blue Bonnet gown," using bluebonnet blue as the basic fashion color. On March 25, the Texas Centennial Commission of Control hosted a style show for prominent fashion designers and writers in New York's Waldorf-Astoria Hotel to introduce the new fashion color. "Bluebonnet Blue was recognized officially Wednesday as a dominating color for spring and summer fashions," reported the *Dallas Morning News*. "[The event] raised the modest bluebonnet to heights it never had known." The Texas theme dominated the style show; Louise Massey and the Westerners performed "Bluebonnet Blues," while composer Peter DeRose ("Deep Purple") and his wife May Singhi Breen introduced their original composition, "Texas Star."[13]

The Texas Centennial Rangerettes remain one of the supreme publicity creations of the centennial era. They emerged as an unlikely composite guaranteed to attract national attention: beautiful girls clad in western regalia — ten-gallon hats, colorful bandanas, plaid shirts, riding breeches (and sometimes cowboy chaps), Justin boots, and spurs.[14] The Rangerette company, serving as the exposition's official hostesses, consisted of approximately twenty-five young ladies — the staff size fluctuated — who were selected for their individual beauty and charm. Most were beauty contest winners, as was Dallasite Mable Rooks Anderson, who, according to journalist Al Harting, "originated the Rangerette concept, named the group and was the first to be chosen." Bill Langley, staff photographer for the exposition's publicity department, has also been cited as the "entrepreneur behind this phenomenal worldwide publicity for Dallas." Although the priority right remains blurred, both Anderson and Langley performed key roles in creating and operating this unique organization.[15]

The Rangerette company was organized in December 1935, with Mable Rooks and LaVea Kilman as co-captains. (Exposition General Manager W. A. Webb signed their commissions.) As the senior members of the company, and married, they emerged as the Rangerette's

[13]Ibid., March 27, 1936.
[14]Since women's jeans were unavailable in 1936, the Rangerettes wore British-style jodhpur pants. The Justin boots had to be purchased in Fort Worth.
[15]Al Harting, "Centennial Fever," *Westward* (*Dallas Times Herald* Sunday Magazine Supplement), July 13, 1969, pp. 18–19.

"road company," Governor Allred's personal emissaries to publicize the central exposition. For their first publicity stunt they flew to Philadelphia to decorate the grave of George Mifflin Dallas, the former vice-president of the United States, in whose honor some claim the city and county were named. Arriving at the Philadelphia airport dressed in their Rangerette uniforms, they were surprised at the press and radio coverage accorded their arrival. For the first time they discovered they were celebrities. "There was a lot of publicity about us going on these trips," Kilman explained, "and everywhere we landed there were always a lot of people to see us. We *were* celebrities."[16]

During the pre-exposition era, life for the two Rangerettes became a whirlwind adventure. They were virtually mobbed by a fascinated crowd at the Kansas City airport, and they rode in the pace car at the Indianapolis 500 Race. A Washington, D.C., visit marked the high point of their publicity travels. Kilman recalled that a tall young man from Texas named Lyndon Johnson, then an administrative assistant to Texas Congressman Richard M. Kleberg, chauffeured them around Washington with a police escort to deliver centennial invitations to President Roosevelt, Vice-President Garner, Congressman Sam Rayburn, and Federal Bureau of Investigation Director J. Edgar Hoover. A half-century later a former associate explained, with some practical justification, "The girls played well in Washington."

Once the exposition opened, Dallas became the regular "beat" for Rooks, Kilman, and the other members of the corps. One Rangerette was assigned to each visiting celebrity. Kilman's assignments read like a 1936 celebrity hall of fame: film stars Robert Taylor, Jeannette McDonald, Clark Gable (to whom she presented his Ranger's commission), symphony conductor Leopold Stokowski, and pugilist Max Baer, upon whose knees she and Rooks posed simultaneously. Chief photographer Bill Langley was never far away with his Speed Graphic camera; celebrities and Rangerettes were proven newsmakers. He also photographed them riding Brahma bulls, snuggling lion cubs, petting baby chickens, and holding bull frogs by their hind legs. Whatever they did, absurd or otherwise, the Rangerettes fulfilled their mission in life — they gained publicity for Texas and the centennial.

Although the Rangerettes received no salary (only uniforms and travel expenses were provided), there were marginal benefits. Posing

[16]Interview with LaVea Kilman, Dallas, Texas, September 9, 1982.

with celebrities provided invaluable public exposure to those seeking careers in modeling and in motion pictures. Kilman, after two Hollywood screen tests and an offer to appear on the London stage, chose instead a life of domesticity in Dallas, as did Mable Rooks. A half-century later, however, Rooks viewed her centennial experience with mixed emotions; the Rangerette corps had established a precedent which others were destined to follow. She complained that Kilgore (Texas) College "swiped our Rangerette name for its drill team. Our Rangerettes are a part of history and Kilgore didn't even ask our permission."[17] From a historical perspective, she was essentially correct. After 1936, the face of America at play would never be the same; a new image had been struck. Not only did this group of colorful young women gain widespread publicity for Texas and its centennial celebrations, but for generations to come they set the pattern for color and pageantry. At most festive occasions where bands march and crowds gather, hybrid descendants of the 1936 Texas Centennial Rangerettes can still be observed performing their celebrated public rituals.

Not all publicity projects employed the Texas mystique. Some even involved stunts that, while being newsworthy in 1936, appear ludicrous or downright bizarre a half-century later. One such stunt involved the internationally famous Dionne quintuplets. On May 28, 1934, in a log house near Callander, Ontario, a twenty-five-year-old farm wife gave birth to the world's only known surviving set of identical quintuplets. The chubby, dimpled moppets became the darlings of North America, if not the world. For two years their photographs appeared almost weekly in magazines and newspapers. In searching for opportunities to publicize the Texas Centennial, Roster and his publicity associates reasoned somewhat logically that if the quintuplets could garner that much international publicity on their own, a tie-in stunt with real Texas quadruplets should take the country by storm. History proved him correct. Roster, however, faced one problem. The well-known Keyes quadruplets—Mary, Mona, Leota, and Roberta—then attending Baylor University, had been born in Hollis, Oklahoma.[18] But for the moment that was overlooked. On May 8, 1936, the state publicity department launched the Keyes quadru-

---

[17]Harting, "Centennial Fever," p. 19.

[18]Another Hollis, Oklahoma, native, former University of Texas at Austin football coach Darrell Royal, also gained some degree of fame in Texas.

plets on a ten-day publicity trip to Canada and the Northeast, accompanied by Pat M. Neff, president of Baylor University and former governor of Texas.

At North Bay, Ontario, their initial destination, it was the Keyes, not the Dionnes, that commanded attention. The Texas (or Oklahoma) quadruplets arrived bearing gifts, while three representatives of the Pendleton Dudley agency orchestrated the presentation for the accompanying press corps. For the five most publicized children in the world, their equally famous physician, Dr. Allan Roy Dafoe, accepted dolls, dresses, sombreros, and serapes, plus five postdated four-year scholarships to Baylor University. Flashbulbs popped again as the quadruplets presented the diminutive Dr. Dafoe, wearing his ill-fitting sombrero and serape, with his invitation to attend the Texas centennial. The Pendleton Dudley agency reported to Roster that a three-page story, "Dr. Dafoe and Quints to Receive Keyes of Texas," along with glossy prints, had been sent to 450 daily newspapers throughout the country.[19]

And the trip had only begun. With the agency staff in charge, the entourage continued on to New York where the Keyes sisters appeared on the Fred Allen NBC radio program, "Town Hall Tonight," to extol the glories of the Texas centennial. The only blight on an otherwise successful publicity binge occurred in Passaic, New Jersey, where the physician of the Kasper quadruplets would allow "neither the [Texas] 'quads' nor ordinary people" to visit those well-publicized infants. The Keyes sisters nevertheless received for their effort four keys to that city. Continuing on to Washington they had breakfast with Vice-President and Mrs. Garner, attended a luncheon as guests of the Texas congressional delegation, participated in another radio broadcast, and attended a party hosted by Texas Senator Tom Connally.

The Keyes quadruplets' 5,000-mile excursion had well served the centennial cause; the publicity department's clipping files contain the results of publicity stuntery at its very best. Clippings (estimated at more than four thousand) from forty-five states (only North Carolina, New Hampshire, and Vermont are not represented), Cuba, and Canada (Manitoba, Ontario, Saskatchewan, Alberta, New Brunswick, and Nova Scotia) are all devoted to the Keyes stunt. Neff and the Keyes, however, received mixed reviews from the eastern press. The *Boston*

---

[19]Centennial Collection, Texas State Archives.

Herald (May 11) described Neff as "an interesting study in haberdashery with his stiff white shirt, flowing black hat and sack coat." The *New York Sun* (undated) was even less complimentary, referring to the Baylor coeds as "buxom 20-years olds." The *St. Louis Globe-Dispatch* attempted to view the matter in its proper perspective. According to this important mid-American daily, the stunt, however ludicrous, could possibly reap the intended benefits; "the invitation to the children will also be an invitation to all of Ontario, and it is not beyond reason that a lot of Canadians will be found passing through the Dallas turnstiles during the forthcoming celebrations. . . . The invitation, not its acceptance or rejection is the thing of interest."[20] Roster and Miller no doubt agreed.

The Texas Press Association, in conjunction with the state publicity department, staged the greatest publicity stunt of the centennial era — the Texas Centennial Press Train. The route of this promotional special included the nation's capital, the Northeast, the Middle West, and all the major population centers except southern California. With the exception of the central exposition itself, no event promoted during the centennial year had a greater national impact than the Texas Centennial Press Train. This event also brought Lowry Martin back into the centennial picture.

In early April Martin and Roster began assembling a blue-ribbon passenger list; Martin solicited newspaper publishers and advertising executives, while Roster contacted business and political leaders. Roster discovered early on that Governor Allred's participation appeared unlikely. With his reelection campaign just weeks away, isolated criticism of his centennial travels had forced him to reject the initial invitations. Since the governor was the Texas centennial's primary booster, his presence on the train seemed essential to the project's success. Roster began a one-man campaign to persuade the governor to join the tour. On April 8, 1936, he wrote the governor's secretary, Pat Moreland, explaining that "the trip would make him a national figure and . . . his presence would help us gain radio time in many cities. . . . Would you please do what you can to have him re-consider?"[21]

<hr/>

[20] *Saint Louis Globe-Democrat*, May 1, 1936.

[21] Charles Roster to Pat Moreland, April 8, 1936, State Archives. Governor Allred was already a national figure: he had received public commendation from President Roosevelt for his cooperation in the national recovery program, and the National Junior Chamber of Commerce had named him Outstanding Young Man in America in 1935.

He also urged L. W. Kemp of the Advisory Board of Texas Historians to intercede in the matter. Kemp agreed, and on April 10, he telegraphed the governor: "In my honest opinion the speech you made in California [at the Rose Bowl game] did more to advertise the Texas Centennial than any other event. Unless the governor of Texas is on the special centennial train much valued publicity for the centennial will be lost."[22] The governor ultimately bowed to the pressure. On April 26, he and some 125 prominent Texans, including 32 members of the University of Texas Longhorn Band, Texas Ranger Capt. Leonard Pack, and Pack's horse Texas, embarked on the Texas Centennial Press Train for a ten-day, seventeen-city tour to promote the Texas centennial.[23]

Miller, who worked closely with Governor Allred throughout the centennial celebrations, understood Roster's insistence that the governor accompany the tour. "Jimmy Allred . . . was the ideal governor to go on a train of that kind," Miller explained. "He was young, attractive, cheerful, dynamic, and of course, was our number-one exposure everywhere. . . . He was the one that every city wanted, they wanted the governor . . . he just charmed everybody. So, he was more or less the titular head of the train." While the governor may have been the symbolic leader of the tour, R. L. Thornton remained the chief of operations. And to any suggestion Miller offered, the response was usually the same, "Execute! Execute!"[24] Miller and Tucker had preceded the train by some three weeks, making preliminary arrangements for the tour's arrival. Wearing their official Texas centennial ten-gallon hats, they unexpectedly made news wherever they appeared. "We found it very, very exciting," Miller recalled. "There was a great curiosity about Texas. *Everybody wanted to turn out and see what Texans looked like.*"[25] Miller soon realized they were riding the crest of the romantic Texas myth as people clamored to accommodate the visiting Texans. That local enthusiasm is reflected in Miller's periodic telegraph reports to the Dallas publicity office:

[22]L. W. Kemp to Gov. James V. Allred, April 10, 1936, State Archives.

[23]The itinerary included Little Rock, Memphis, Nashville, Louisville, Cincinnati, Charlottesville, Richmond, Philadelphia, Washington, D.C., New York, Albany, Buffalo, Cleveland, Detroit, Chicago, St. Louis, and Kansas City. Captain Pack was also chief of the Texas Centennial Exposition Police Force. A section of the baggage coach was provided for his horse.

[24]Interview with Dale Miller, Austin, Texas, July 21, 1978.

[25]Ibid.

April 9, 1936. Memphis and Nashville enthusiastic over train. Band will parade through Memphis followed by dinner at Peabody Hotel with Chamber of Commerce. Splendid radio show arranged at WMAC 9:30 to 10:00 featuring band and Allred. In Nashville Governor McAlister, Chamber of Commerce, and booster club will meet train and parade to WSM for gala radio reception in studio auditorium and broadcast between 7:30 and 8:00 featuring band, both governors, and other prominent members of party. Fine press cooperation.

April 10, 1936. Rousing reception awaits train in Louisville. Band and party met by Governor A. B. Chandler and Mayor Neville Miller and parade to swanky Pendennis Club for mint julep recep[tion]. Radio program featuring both governors and band arranged.

April 14, 1936. Virginia swings into line with Governor Perry meeting train in Charlottesville and accompanying party to Richmond. Reception in Paramount Theatre . . . and probably regional network broadcasting.

April 16, 1936. Opinion freely expressed here [New York City] that no similar enterprise ever commanded as wide attention in radio circles or elicited greater cooperation. . . . Metropolitan newspapers joined press of other leading cities in evincing considerable interest in train and Centennial, and New York's millions began reading today of forthcoming visit of Texas party.[26]

John Henry Kavanaugh, Austin businessman and former University of Texas Longhorn Band member, recalled the excitement he witnessed as a student traveling on the Press Train: "We were always met at the station by a mayor or a governor, and a host of dignitaries wherever we went." A parade from the train station launched the local reception. "We made quite a show," Kavanaugh recalled. "The parade was the big thing, Texas flags [waving], a cowboy and a Texas Ranger [Capt. Leonard Pack], Texas dignitaries, the governor leading the parade, and the band coming along. Even we were excited."[27]

Wherever they went they told the Texas story to eager listeners. Each host city seemed to try to outdo the others in its generosity. The nation's capital was no exception. A delegation of Texas officialdom —Vice-President Garner, Senators Tom Connally and Morris Shep-

[26]Telegrams, Dale Miller to Publicity Office, State Archives.
[27]Interview with John Henry Kavanaugh, Austin, Texas, July 30, 1982.

pard, and the Texas congressional delegation — were waiting at Union Station for the Centennial Press Train's 7:00 P.M. arrival.[28] Official cars of the vice-president and Postmaster General James A. Farley carried the host committee and the train officials up Pennsylvania Avenue to the Raleigh Hotel. Later that night NBC originated a live network broadcast of the National Press Club banquet in which the Texans, on behalf of the centennial, saluted the nation. The following morning President Roosevelt greeted the Texas entourage in the White House Oval Office. Those who participated in the tour recall this as the trip's emotional high point. Miller's recollections were vivid: "We all met at the White House [and] . . . were taken individually [some 125 people including the band members] down the line so he [President Roosevelt] could shake each of our hands and have something pleasant to say. . . . He remained seated at his desk. . . . His charm was almost unbelievable. . . . He would take the time to speak to everybody and ask them something about themselves."[29]

The press train traveled next to New York, where the visiting Texans took the town by storm. They became the twenty-four-hour hit of the season. According to one journalist, "Each Texan, if he wore his ten-gallon hat, was a cynosure (center of attraction) on the streets of New York, whose bigness can't compare with that of Texas in acreage and headgear. Each was stared at respectfully by a popeyed group as though they had just dropped in from another planet."[30] The Texans literally stopped the show. A circus in Madison Square Garden was halted three minutes while Joe Leonard, a member of the Gainesville Community Circus, commissioned equestrienne Dorothy Herbert a Texas Centennial Rangerette and flopped a ten-gallon hat on her head. The following morning the entourage visited the New York Stock Exchange, where the dignified members "gave vent to Indian hoops and cowboy yells. . . . It was the only place the trippers were outshouted." Manhattan bid its farewell to the Lone Star visitors on the steps of the City Hall. Mayor Fiorello LaGuardia greeted Governor Allred on the steps of that famous landmark while the eighty-five piece Governor's Island band played a new composition, "The Texas Centennial March." During the special remote broadcast, according

[28] The Longhorn Band was forbidden to perform in Union Station because officials feared the vibration would shatter the large glass panels.

[29] Miller interview, July 21, 1978.

[30] *Dallas Morning News*, May 2, 1936.

to one reporter, "the dynamic little mayor . . . had the situation well in hand before someone slipped on his head a Texas ten-gallon hat that reached almost to his chin."[31]

On to Albany, Buffalo, Cleveland, Detroit, and Chicago — nothing was too good for Texas in 1936, and everyone seemed to be trying to prove it. At Chicago, Col. Frank Knox, publisher of the *Daily News*, and Charles Swift, chairman of the board of Swift & Company, entertained the visitors, and Mayor Edward J. Kelly presented the keys of the city to six-year-old Jimmy Allred, Jr., son of the governor.[32] Members of the Chicago Board of Trade accorded the visitors the ultimate consideration by halting work on the world's biggest grain mart for five minutes. At Kansas City, where the Missouri-Kansas Bankers' Association played host to the Texas entourage, the spotlight belonged to Captain Pack and Governor Allred. Captain Pack rode his horse, Texas, into the new municipal auditorium, sending gasps through the audience as his horse skidded precariously on the waxed floor, but they applauded at the sight of an honest-to-goodness Texas Ranger wearing .45-caliber six-shooters on each hip.[33] After the University of Texas Longhorn Band played "The Eyes of Texas," Governor Allred mounted the rostrum wearing his ten-gallon hat and cowboy boots to tell the financiers of the glories of Texas and its forthcoming celebrations. Later that day an airline gave the guests complimentary flights over the city.

According to the train officials' evaluation, the ten-day, seventeen-city tour of the Texas Centennial Press Train had been an unqualified success. R. L. Thornton, returning to Dallas early on business, reported that the exposition had been sold "to the people of the North and East and they will be here 10,000,000 strong. . . . The people of Dallas have no conception of the interest the East is taking in the Centennial. . . . Everyone wants to know about our fair. *People recognize us by our hats*, stopped us on the streets to ply questions and every Texan's interviewer invariably ended by saying, 'I'll be there.'"[34] The governor was equally enthusiastic about the tour's impact. "Our reception in New York alone was worth many times more than the cost of the

[31] Ibid.

[32] Governor Allred remained with the train throughout the tour.

[33] Pack had previously ridden his horse into the lobby of the posh Book-Cadillac Hotel in Detroit. The management had appeared less than enthusiastic.

[34] *Dallas Morning News*, May 5, 1936 (emphasis added).

trip," he stated. "I believe we have made the North, East, and Midwest Centennial conscious."[35]

A state publicity department news release, although tainted with boosterism, attempted to evaluate the trip within the broad scope of history. "It was freely declared," the statement read, "that no state has ever been the beneficiary of so much favorable publicity in such a brief space of time." The Texans received favorable press coverage in nine of the nation's most populous states and in the District of Columbia and made more than twenty-four radio broadcasts, seven over regional and national networks. In addition, the touring Texans met with governors of all states and mayors of all cities along the route. Texas Governor Allred was clearly the star of the tour; his thirty-nine addresses were heard by millions. According to an unidentified "eminent economist," the ten-day tour of the press special "was worth $100,000,000 in ultimate benefits to Texas."[36]

Unquestionably, the trip, as well as the other promotional campaigns, had achieved its purpose—to "sell" Texas and its centennial to the nation on a scale never before attempted. But whatever appealing messages the Texans addressed to the host cities—colorful celebrations, a world's fair, and the untapped economic resources of the Great Southwest—it was the romantic Texas mystique and the attendant cultural symbols that grabbed the nation's attention and ignited the on-going ovations. This was clearly visible to one journalist attempting to interpret the out-of-state image of the Lone Star visitors who wrote that Texans "must be a couple of inches more than six feet tall to live up to the popular conception outside the state."[37]

[35] Ibid., May 7, 1936.
[36] "Centennial Train Worth $100,000,000 to Texas in Eventful Trip East," undated press release, Department of Information, Dallas, Texas Centennial Collection, State Archives.
[37] *Dallas Morning News*, May 7, 1936.

11

MESSAGE FROM SAN ANTONIO:
PATRIOTISM WAS A LOW PRIORITY

While Charles Roster and his publicity staff toured the nation promoting the Texas centennial, many Texas communities had already begun celebrating the long-awaited event. The centennial year marked the culmination of a great ground swell of patriotic fervor that had been building up over the preceding decade. Programmed historical awareness had become part and parcel of public preparation for each step that led to 1936. Since 1924, the centennial had become one of the state's most discussed topics and the most anticipated event.[1] Excepting national tragedies, probably no event in the state's history touched the lives of so many people, both children and adults, as did the Texas centennial. Despite the carnival-like atmosphere that ultimately colored some phases of the celebration, the Texas centennial was truly a grass roots movement, marking the high point of ethnocentrism in Texas.

The publicity department's field services staff, working county by county, had aided local citizen groups in giving their celebrations a historical perspective. In towns and villages throughout the state there would be approximately 240 memorial dedications, fairs, fiestas, parades, festivals, pageants, and reunions to mark the centennial. Each would bear some degree of historical relevance; many would also attempt to focus national attention on the unrecognized resources of the Lone Star State.

Local celebrations fell within two general categories, those mandated by Senate Bill No. 22 (creating the permanent Texas Centennial Commission), and those planned independently by local committees. The state-mandated celebrations marking Texas Independence Day (March 2), the fall of the Alamo (March 6), and the Battle of

---

[1]During 1936, 144 Texas newspapers published 173 special editions. The Texas centennial was the sole topic of most of these special editions. Texas Newspaper Collection, Barker Texas History Center, University of Texas at Austin.

San Jacinto (April 2) represented the major commemorative events of the centennial year. Essentially historic in nature, these celebrations were attended by tens of thousands of citizens whose sole purpose was to pay homage to the patriots who helped win Texas' independence from Mexico. And while these celebrations received well-planned and widely disseminated news coverage, local commercialism was noticeably absent. The overriding mood remained one of pious devotion. Journalist Harry Benge Crozier noted the seriousness that Texans accorded the anniversary of Texas' independence: "The eyes of Texas are turned this week on four shrines of history [the Alamo, Gonzales, Huntsville, and Washington-on-the-Brazos], sacred to all Texans. These seven days contain the one hundredth anniversary of the darkest hours of crisis in the struggle for freedom and [the people] are to be commended for the dignified and appropriate manner in which they will observe these Centennial celebrations."[2]

The citizens of Gonzales launched the week-long Texas independence day celebration with two ceremonies, one in San Antonio and another in Gonzales. On Sunday night, March 1, they dedicated a monument in the Alamo courtyard to the thirty-two Gonzales citizens who answered Col. William Barret Travis's appeal for help. On the previous day in Gonzales, Karl Crowley, Solicitor General of the United States Post Office Department, sold Lieut. Gov. Walter Woodul the first official three-cent centennial postage stamp, scheduled to go on sale there on March 2, 1936. The state publicity department arranged for radio and motion picture newsreel coverage of the sale and Woodul's subsequent address. The stamp sale attracted international interest among stamp collectors. On March 5, Roger Busfield, periodicals division head, telegraphed the stamp editor of the *Times-Union* in Albany, New York: "Gonzales — First Day Covers cancellations totaled 261,000. Even million Texas Centennial stamps sold first day. That was first day allotment. Still about 80,000 covers to be hand cancelled."[3]

Governor Allred remained ever visible, delivering the major addresses at every centennial observance his schedule would permit. On March 2 he performed double duty, appearing at two celebrations marking the hundredth anniversary of the Texas Declaration of Independence. Accompanied by Wisconsin Gov. Philip La Follette, Allred

[2]*Dallas Morning News*, March 1, 1936.
[3]Roger Busfield to *Times-Union*, March 5, 1936, Centennial Collection, State Archives.

traveled first to Brenham, Texas, for the Washington-on-the-Brazos
ceremony, where they met a throng of "several thousand pilgrims [who]
made their way to the shrine on the banks of the Brazos River to honor
Sam Houston and others who formed an empire." At the Washington-
on-the-Brazos speakers' platform, Governor Allred and his party joined
the descendants of the original signers of Texas' most cherished document. Before them lay the original Texas Declaration of Independence,
protected in a glass case, on the same table where it had been signed
a century before. In their addresses, Governor Allred urged the people of Texas to rededicate themselves to the causes the Texans fought
for one hundred years ago, while Governor La Follette proclaimed
that Sam Houston and his ideals "belong to our entire nation. . . .
Let General Houston inspire you to do great things."[4] As the governors spoke in Texas, the Congress in Washington took a brief recess
to hear Sen. Tom Connally speak on the significance of the anniversary; then in the House of Representatives Congressman Fritz Lanham of Fort Worth emphasized the peculiarly American achievement
in the settlement of Texas.

The dedication of the restored Steamboat House, the home in
which Sam Houston died, highlighted the Huntsville ceremony the
same day. That observance began at eleven o'clock in the morning
with the traditional procession from the Sam Houston State College
campus to the general's grave, where Temple Houston Morrow, Sam
Houston's grandson, read portions of the Texas Declaration of Independence; Gov. Hill McAlister of Tennessee, Houston's home state,
delivered the graveside address. Governors Allred and La Follette arrived from Washington-on-the-Brazos in time to participate in the
three-hour-long afternoon dedication ceremony. Some six thousand
spectators had gathered before the speakers' platform, which had been
erected in front of the old Sam Houston home, which stood in its
original setting. Governors Allred, La Follette, and McAlister joined
two former Texas governors, William P. Hobby and Pat M. Neff, for
the dedication. Hobby served as master of ceremonies as Governor
Allred accepted the Steamboat House as a state historic shrine. Portions of the Huntsville ceremony were broadcast over a nationwide
radio network.

On Friday, March 5, one day less than a century, the Alamo was

[4]*Dallas Morning News*, March 3, 1936.

literally stormed again, this time by a friendly army estimated at more than twelve thousand people. Special trains, buses, and automobile caravans transported thousands of citizens, school groups, public officials, church dignitaries, and ranking military officers and their troops to participate in a day-long ceremony marking the fall of this shrine of Texas independence. Tributes to Col. William Barret Travis's immortal band came from the nation's capital, twenty-one states, and several foreign countries. President Roosevelt telegraphed: "These intrepid men became deathless by dying in the cause of human freedom and what seemed like a military defeat became a victory for the principles of liberty." Governor Allred delivered the roll call of Texas heroes, while Governor McAlister of Tennessee, who sponsored the ceremonial flag from the state that produced many early Texans, challenged the audience to heed the wisdom of the fallen soldier's silent "words echoing against battle scarred walls of the former mission-fortress." Governor Allred concluded that the Alamo defense was not useless, as some claimed; he believed "there would have been no San Jacinto victory and no Texas had not the Alamo defenders held the line while Texas prepared."[5]

Three weeks later, on March 27, Governor Allred attended another official state centennial celebration at Goliad. During the religious observance, the Rev. Emanuel B. Ladvina, Bishop of Corpus Christi, officiated at a mass attended by some ten thousand persons, who later witnessed a colorful parade and the dedication of a historical marker at the La Bahía Mission.

An estimated one hundred thousand persons from throughout Texas gathered on the remote field of Saint Hyacinth on April 21 to celebrate the final event of the Texas Revolution. It was on that palmetto flat one hundred years before that a band of 910 Texans defeated 1,360 Mexican troops, winning Texas independence and helping alter the course of United States history.[6] Appropriately, religion and history comprised the dual theme of the day-long memorial service. The Catholics of Texas conducted a morning military field mass, the largest religious spectacle ever held in the South. Pope Pius XI cabled blessings from the Vatican. The official party consisted of thirty bish-

[5]Ibid., March 6, 1936.
[6]Measured by its results, the Battle of San Jacinto was one of the most decisive battles of the world. Events touched off by this encounter added almost one-third of the present area of the United States.

ops, Governor Allred, Secretary of Commerce Daniel C. Roper, Justices of the Supreme Court of Texas, Houston Mayor Oscar F. Holcombe, and other city, county, and state officials.

This was the largest single historical celebration of the centennial year. The early arrivals entered the battleground before dawn, and by midmorning incoming traffic had slowed to a virtual standstill. More than one hundred officers patrolled the access routes, while an airplane circled overhead radioing messages about developing traffic congestion. Governor Allred and other dignitaries traveled down the ship channel to the battleground on the destroyer *Schenck* and the Coast Guard cutter *Saranac*. Taking their place on the speakers' rostrum, they witnessed the colorful, mile-long procession preceding the mass. The blue uniforms of sailors and marines, the many colored robes of the clergy, all led toward the color spectacle of the day—a Texas flag formed by 1,586 school girls, 61 outlining the ribbon at the head of the staff and 49 forming the staff. During the service the girls forming the flag reversed their caps and hoods, changing the formation into a United States flag. After the sermon, a 300-voice male choir accompanied by a pipe organ performed the "Kyrie Eleison," concluding the historic field mass.

The Sons and Daughters of the Republic of Texas arranged the afternoon ceremonies. In what was probably his most historically perceptive and emotionally stirring address of the centennial year, Governor Allred reviewed the fifty eventful days from the signing of the Texas Declaration of Independence on March 2, 1836, to the bloody eighteen-minute Battle of San Jacinto. His dramatic conclusion was long remembered by those who endured the sweltering April afternoon:

Then suddenly, upon the calm and oddly sorted air, was borne the thin and treble courting song. . . . "Will you come to the bower? . . . Will you come to the bower?" And Texas in its pride and courage came, not for a rendezvous with love, but one with death, or victory. Then someone raised the war cry. . . . "Remember the Alamo! Remember La Bahia!" The dream of Antonio Lopez de Santa Anna . . . forever was destroyed.

The decisiveness of San Jacinto cannot be the geographical limits of the free Republic it secured or the sovereign State which took its place. Its import lies in the finality of the decree that Texas should be no buffer State, forever torn by war between two uncompromising factions. That the citizens of the United States and the citizens of Mexico could lie down by night as they have done for nearly a century, each on his own side of an unfortified frontier, a river which either might ford in the dark, yet is respected as the extremest limit of national control.[7]

One week later contractors broke ground for construction of the San Jacinto Battlefield memorial.[8]

The final local historical celebration specified in Senate Bill No. 22 was held on October 16 and 17 in Nacogdoches. The local centennial committee, in conjunction with Stephen F. Austin State College, presented a historical pageant celebrating Nacogdoches history and the restoration of the Old Stone Fort on the college campus as a museum of East Texas history. All of these mandated centennial year observances are significant both in what was proclaimed and in the importance the people attached to those particular moments in history. The 1936 celebrations marked the high tide of the patriotic impulse in Texas; that pinnacle would never again be attained. A half-century later these dates pass virtually unnoticed. The Texas legislature designates no official holidays corresponding to important milestones in Texas history.[9]

The mandated observances constituted only a small portion of the local celebrations that continued throughout the centennial year. There is no exact count, but published accounts suggest that they totaled approximately 240. In the six-month period between March 1 and August 31, the state publicity department reported 138 local celebrations. And while most events followed a centennial theme, many were related economically to some local resource: the Plainview Panhandle-Plains Dairy Show, Raymondville Onion Show, Jacksonville National Tomato Show, Port Aransas Tarpon Rodeo, Mount Pleasant Milk Festival, Weatherford Fruit and Melon Exposition, Henderson East Texas Oil Jubilee, and the Tyler Rose Festival. The Crystal City Spinach Festival and the Uvalde First Annual Honey Bee Festival, two events not

---

[7] *Dallas Morning News*, April 22, 1936.

[8] On April 21, 1937, Claude D. Teer, chairman of the State Board of Control, presided at the cornerstone laying; Jesse H. Jones delivered the main address. The structure was not completed until 1939.

[9] Official state holidays authorized by the Sixty-Ninth Legislature are New Year's Day, George Washington's Birthday, Memorial Day, Independence Day (July 4), Columbus Day, Veterans' Day, Thanksgiving, and Christmas. Yom Kippur may be taken in lieu of one of the other designated state holidays.

Nacogdoches celebrates the Texas Centennial in a parade down Main Street. (Courtesy Ralph W. Steen Library, Special Collections Department, Stephen F. Austin State University)

Dedication of the reconstructed Old Stone Fort, Nacogdoches. (Courtesy Ralph W. Steen Library, Special Collections Department, Stephen F. Austin State University)

At the March 2 centennial celebration of the signing of the Texas Declaration of Independence at Washington-on-the-Brazos, Gov. James V. Allred presents Alabama-Coushatta Indian Chief Ti-ca-i-che with a Texas flag, while Philip La Follette, governor of Wisconsin, looks on. (Courtesy Star of the Republic Museum)

Legionnaire M. B. Holleman explains the six flags of Texas to Governors Allred and La Follette at Washington-on-the-Brazos ceremonies. (Courtesy Star of the Republic Museum)

Huntsville centennial ceremonies on Texas Independence Day began with a traditional procession to Oakwood Cemetery, the site of Sam Houston's grave, where Temple Houston Morrow, Houston's grandson, read from the Texas Declaration of Independence. The Pompeo Coppini memorial shows in right background. (Courtesy Sam Houston State University Library Special Collections)

Thousands line Polk Street in Amarillo to witness the Fourth of July Centennial Parade. (Courtesy Panhandle-Plains Historical Museum, Canyon)

appearing on any official calendar of events, are significant because the state publicity department cooperated in these local centennial activities specifically to gain national publicity. Patriotic journalist Harry Benge Crozier would have found little at these celebrations that was either "dignified" or "appropriate."

Charles Roster developed a tie-in between the comic strip character Popeye and the Crystal City Spinach Festival. Cartoonist Segar, creator of the Thimble Theater comic strip, devoted one issue to the festival and Popeye's well-known addiction to the "green gold." In turn, the local sponsors proclaimed Popeye honorary mayor of Crystal City; Olive Oyl, his girl friend, queen of the festival; and Wimpy, who was equally addicted to hamburgers, city meat inspector. Crystal City mayor and "Spinach King" Bruce Holsomback cooperated in a second phase of the stunt, agreeing to deliver a planeload of spinach (three bushels according to another report) to Segar and Popeye at a New York press conference. Holsomback also carried with him a deed to Crystal City's entire spinach crop to ensure Popeye a permanent supply. That portion of the stunt, however, turned sour. Since Holsomback's airline reservation was subject to space available, he was removed from the plane en route to New York.[10]

Melissa Castle, director of research and cachets, developed the cachet program in cooperation with Solicitor General Karl Crowley. Crowley agreed to extend cachet privileges to Texas towns sponsoring centennial celebrations. This program developed wide interest; thirty-seven communities submitted designs carrying out the centennial motif. One of the more unusual cachets, a honey bee, commemorating the First Annual Honey Bee Festival, was applied to three thousand letters on the front porch of Vice-President Garner's residence in Uvalde. The event drew thousands of Southwest Texans to "this tree-shaded little village . . . to pay homage to a Queen Bee . . . Miss Wilma Russell." The regal one was attended by several duchesses and nine princesses representing "the shrubs from which the honey supply is gained by the millions of bees in this country."[11] Apparently the centennial publicity philosophy was, no matter how bizarre the stunt, if it gets national attention, do it.

Fiesta de San Jacinto, popularly known as the Battle of Flowers,

[10]Telegrams dated April 16, 18, and 19, 1936, State Archives.
[11]Melissa Castle's undated report, State Archives.

is San Antonio's annual observance of the Battle of San Jacinto. The climax of the week-long celebration is the Battle of Flowers parade. On April 25, some 150,000 spectators watched as the three-hour, seven-mile-long entourage — sixty bands, various military ground units, and historical floats — made its way toward the Alamo, while eighteen Army Air Corps planes saluted the spectacle below. At the Alamo Plaza reviewing stand, Governor and Mrs. Allred (dressed in bluebonnet blue) and a host of dignitaries "left their conveyances . . . and ascended the reviewing stand . . . [while] thousands of flowers were thrown toward the Alamo by passing parades."[12]

The centennial Battle of Flowers was far more peaceful than another battle which had engaged the Alamo City since September, 1935. At least two factions (or was it three? could have been four) had been locked in a verbal struggle over distribution of San Antonio's $400,000 federal allotment to fund centennial projects. The participants varied from month to month, but some prominent names surfaced during the ensuing controversy: Vice-President John Nance Garner, Secretary of State Cordell Hull, Secretary of Commerce Daniel C. Roper, Secretary of Agriculture Henry A. Wallace, Congressman Maury Maverick, and various city, state, and centennial officials. As the drama unfolded, the rhetoric emphasized the ongoing conflict between patriotism and commercialism. Indeed, the San Antonio debacle differed little from that which occurred in Houston in 1934, and in various other Texas communities where the absence of strong urban leadership opened the way for a political power struggle. In every case the availability of state and federal money provided the necessary incentive.

San Antonio's nine-month debate raised a number of questions: what local committee had the authority to represent the citizens of San Antonio before the United States Texas Centennial Commission? was it necessary for San Antonio to pass a local bond issue to qualify for the $400,000 federal centennial allotment already committed? what role did politics play in the committees' recommendations? and whatever happened to the $150,000 federal allocation for a memorial stadium? State Rep. Oscar F. Chastain of Eastland, probably unknowingly, cited the philosophical basis for all of the debate, conflict, and confusion when, on November 2, 1934, he told the House of Repre-

---

[12]*San Antonio Express*, April 25, 1936. The traditional Friday afternoon Battle of Flowers was so named because occupants of decorated vehicles once pelted each other with flowers.

sentatives "there isn't enough patriotism in San Antonio to bury a dead soldier."[13]

The somewhat dubious matter of a $500,000 bond issue shifted the debate from the committee chambers to a public forum when E. J. Altgelt, an assistant federal commissioner and San Antonio realtor, told the group of centennial supporters that "we pledged San Antonio to that [$500,000] bond issue and we will lose the $400,000 [government allocation] if it doesn't go over!" Altgelt added that he had submitted a signed pledge during the Washington hearings when "it became obvious that San Antonio would not get federal money otherwise." Altgelt stated further that San Antonio not only was pledged to raise $500,000 by a bond issue, but also was obligated to produce a lavish historical pageant. The following day, however, Altgelt executed an about-face in the bond matter. "We didn't guarantee a bond issue," Altgelt said in an exchange with Congressman [Maury] Maverick. "We said we would ask for a bond issue, because I think one should be asked."[14] The verbal exchange with Maverick had political overtones. Altgelt, a San Antonio businessman, a member of the Committee of Eleven (a subgroup of the 160-member San Antonio Centennial Commission), and a political protégé of R. W. Morrison, stood poles apart from Maverick and his liberal political following. In addition, Maverick and many other citizens opposed a historical pageant, favoring instead more permanent centennial memorials. "Parades [and pageants] are swell," Maverick stated, "but after they're over, what have you got? . . . Our best bet is to spend money on permanent improvements, especially on our historical missions and buildings."[15]

When communications between Maverick and Altgelt broke down, the congressman turned to the nation's capital for some answers. Secretary of Agriculture and United States Texas Centennial Commissioner Henry A. Wallace explained to the San Antonio congressman that when the commission made the $400,000 allocation, it was their understanding that the citizens of San Antonio would raise additional funds through a bond issue. Altgelt's demand that the local centennial committee contribute $1,200 to help finance a publicity campaign to pass the bond issue drew another verbal fusillade — two, in

---

[13] *Dallas Morning News*, November 3, 1934.
[14] *San Antonio Light*, September 25, 1935.
[15] Ibid.

fact, the same day — from Maverick. He first complained to Secretary of State Cordell Hull (also a commission member) about what he considered the federal government's attempt "to blackmail the citizens of San Antonio to pass a bond issue to get Federal money" when the allocation had already been made. That "is to me somewhat disgusting." He complained further that the federal commission "did not require Austin, Fort Worth, or Houston to pass a bond issue in reference to the allocation."[16]

The open hostilities between Maverick and Altgelt, and Mayor C. K. Quinn's indecision in the bond matter, must have indicated to the federal commissioners that no local group spoke for the entire community on centennial matters. In the meantime W. B. Yeager, executive director of the United States Commission, proposed to Secretary Roper that a federally appointed local centennial advisory committee recommend the distribution of the federal allotment in San Antonio. (Similar committees had already been appointed in Dallas and Houston.) Secretary Roper agreed, and on October 26, 1935, Commissioner General Thomas announced the appointment of eight San Antonio citizens to advise him on spending federal funds in San Antonio's centennial celebration. The committee consisted of Claude V. Birkhead, chairman; Judge J. S. Brooks, vice-chairman; and members Clara Driscoll Sevier, Judge C. A. Goeth, L. J. Hart, Col. W. B. Tuttle, Lytle Gosling, and Ernest J. Altgelt.[17] With the exception of Mrs. Sevier, these were all prominent members of the San Antonio business community and political allies of Morrison. This was a clear-cut defeat for Maury Maverick, whose response was predictable.[18] "Wish to enter vigorous protest appointment of Committee [in] San Antonio for expenditure of federal funds for centennial without local recommendations," he telegraphed Secretary Hull. Maverick explained that he considered the present committee entirely satisfactory, and

[16]Maury Maverick to Cordell Hull, September 26, 1935, 811.607 Texas Centennial/39. Maverick's statement was essentially correct. However, Fort Worth and Dallas both passed centennial bond issues prior to the federal allocation.

[17]Undated and unidentified newspaper clipping, Centennial Collection, DRT Library.

[18]In Maverick's 1936 reelection campaign, R. W. Morrison, utilities magnate and member of the Federal Reserve Board, reportedly expressed a willingness to spend as much as $150,000 to defeat Maverick and claimed to have spent tens of thousands in support of his opponent in the July primary. For further information, see Richard B. Henderson, *Maury Maverick: A Political Biography* (Austin: University of Texas Press, 1970), p. 122.

"outside influence should not dictate to the citizens of San Antonio how federal funds should be expended."[19]

The appointment of the Birkhead committee obviously placed the authority of the original centennial committee in jeopardy. Nevertheless, on November 4 Harry Hertzberg, chairman of that committee, submitted his report to Yeager and to Secretary Hull. The major projects included a memorial to the heroes of the Alamo (the Cenotaph), $100,000; restoration of Mission San José, $50,000; purchase of property adjacent to the Spanish Governor's Palace (containing the foundations of the original structure), $25,000; a peace memorial in Washington Square, exemplifying the friendship between the citizens of Mexico and the United States, $25,000; a memorial mall honoring the pioneers of Texas, and a Trail Drivers memorial patio adjacent to the Witte Memorial Museum, $50,000; purchase of the General Cos house on Villita Street, $25,000; funds for "the proper observation of San Jacinto Day," $25,000; and advertisements for statewide pilgrimages to the Alamo, $25,000.[20]

Mrs. Clara Driscoll Sevier's refusal to serve on the Birkhead committee further polarized the Alamo City's already highly charged political atmosphere. In late November, Hertzberg called a joint meeting of the various centennial committees in an attempt to determine their jurisdictional perimeters. His effort met with mixed results. Judge Goeth, a member of the Birkhead committee, the Committee of Twenty-One, and chairman of the citywide 160-member centennial committee, said he saw no reason why all the committees could not work in unison. A majority of the members agreed, passing a resolution to that effect. Maverick disagreed, claiming that Thomas was without authority to make the appointments. Judge Goeth's appeal for intercommittee cooperation, however, went unheeded. The Birkhead committee's efforts were deliberate, secretive, and wholly self-centered, according other San Antonio centennial committees no voice in its considerations.

Little was heard of that committee's activities during the early months of 1936, but by April news began to leak. Many of San An-

[19]Maverick to Hull, October 26, 1935, 811.607, Texas Centennial/64.
[20]Harry Hertzberg to W. B. Yeager and Cordell Hull, November 4, 1935, 811.607, Texas Centennial/74.

tonio's citizens did not like what they heard; patriotism was receiving a low priority. A majority of the Birkhead committee had broken ranks, allocating $305,000 of the $400,000 federal funding for an athletic stadium, while the minority favored $250,000 for the Alamo and nothing for the stadium.[21] While this controversy was still in the rumor stage, opposing sides began to form. The *San Antonio Express* supported the stadium proposal because it "not only would encourage local athletics and bring 'big time' football" and other sporting events to the city but would provide a setting for cultural activities as well.[22] The Daughters of the Republic of Texas understandably opposed the stadium allocation and questioned the economic reality of "big time" sports in San Antonio. Mrs. Leita Small, custodian of the Alamo, cited the recent financial failure of the Pittsburgh Pirates San Antonio training camp. She pointed out that local businessmen had to make up the deficit when the gate receipts fell short of the $25,000 guarantee.[23]

On April 4, Claude Birkhead mailed the committee's recommendations to Washington without publicly divulging its contents. On April 14, the report was announced in Washington; all local interests were served. After adding $29,000 to the original $400,000 San Antonio allocation, the commission assigned the Alamo $75,000; San José Mission, $2,000; a memorial stadium, $150,000; the Alamo Cenotaph, $100,000; other memorials, $84,000.[24] Although Maverick ridiculed the stadium assignment as "mere commercialism and entirely inappropriate," he refused to take sides between the two sets of recommendations submitted by the Birkhead committee. (The Hertzberg committee's report was never considered.) During the meeting Vice-President Garner questioned both Maverick and Thomas on the local support accorded the centennial celebration; both agreed it had been practically nil. Thomas explained that "what little support there is in San Antonio comes from the women." Under further questioning Thomas admitted "he could not recall the name of a single San An-

[21] This was not an original idea. In an earlier discussion of the proposed $500,000 bond election, Albert Steves, Sr., chairman of the Executive Committee of Eleven selected from the 160-member centennial committee, had recommended a $130,000 stadium in San Jacinto Park. R. W. Morrison also supported that program.
[22] *San Antonio Express*, April 1, 1936.
[23] Undated and unidentified newspaper clipping, Centennial Collection, DRT Library.
[24] Yeager to Hull, May 8, 1936, 811.607, Texas Centennial/131.

tonio individual who had contributed a cent to the Centennial. Maverick agreed not a cent had been contributed."[25]

The prolonged and agonizing ordeal to determine how San Antonio would celebrate the centennial was nearing an end. By the end of 1936, restoration work had begun at both the Alamo and the San José Mission, and shortly thereafter sculptors were selected for the memorials approved in the Birkhead report.[26] The Cenotaph and stadium projects were less easily expedited. The State Board of Control considered four different designs for the Alamo memorial before one was selected; choosing the sculptor became another volatile issue. The players in this drama were even more diverse than those who debated the federal allocation. In an attempt to keep politics out of the selection process, Lieutenant Governor Woodul appointed a committee to select another committee to give advice on sculptors. Former Governor Pat M. Neff chaired the second committee, whose members were Sam Gideon, professor of architecture at the University of Texas, Austin; Mrs. Harold Abrams, Dallas; Sam F. Ziegler, professor of fine arts, Texas Christian University, Fort Worth; and Peter Mansbendel, an Austin artist and wood carver. The committee prepared two lists of recommended sculptors for all centennial projects, a primary list of twenty-one leading American sculptors for projects costing $14,500 and above, and a secondary list of twenty-four sculptors for the less expensive projects.

This process appeared valid until the Texas legislature became unofficially involved; then ethnocentrism in Texas reached another high water mark. On February 3, 1937, thirty-seven members of the Texas legislature addressed a letter to Vice-President Garner, Governor Allred, Lieutenant Governor Woodul, Jesse Jones, Claude Teer (chairman of the State Board of Control), and John Singleton (chief of the Centennial Division, Board of Control). Frank E. Mann of Harris County signed the letter, which stated in part:

Native Texas Sculptors are not being accorded the right and fair and open competition with alien and non-resident sculptors in connection with our Texas Centennial monuments. . . . As an example of the policy . . . we cite the recent private conference held in San

[25] *Dallas Morning News*, April 18, 1936.
[26] Land purchases, repairs, and plaques at the Alamo totaled $245,598.86. For an analysis of Alamo expenditures, see King, *Report of Texas Centennial*, p. 58.

Antonio to select a sculptor to execute bronzed [sic] for the $100,000 Alamo Cenotaph. All Taxes [sic] sculptors were eliminated from that competition before it even began. A majority; [sic] if not all, of the four sculptors, invited to the private conference had never seen the Alamo before. Half of them were alien-born [sic] residents of New York, and all four had to come here from New York.[27]

The letter undoubtedly had its desired effect. On June 8, 1937, Claude Teer announced that Pompeo Coppini had been chosen to execute the Cenotaph. (The selection committee had placed Coppini on its secondary list.) The Italian-born longtime San Antonio resident had made his reputation "in an age when a sculptor was judged on his ability to render an acceptable likeness. . . . In terms of human form Coppini was a strict constructionist."[28] When J. Frank Dobie, a member of the Advisory Board of Texas Historians, learned of Coppini's selection, he was furious. He objected to the Cenotaph ("a monument to the Alamo [was like] lighting a candle in order to illuminate the sun"), to Coppini's work ("litter[ing] up Texas with his monstrosities in the name of sculpture"), and the method of selection ("John Singleton . . . knows about as much about art and sculpting as a hog knows about a side saddle").[29] Despite Dobie's much-publicized protestations, the sixty-foot-tall Cenotaph was formally unveiled on September 15, 1939. On viewing the finished work, the great Texas folklorist compared it to a grain elevator, saying "the picturesque poses of Crockett et al. . . . looked as though they came to the Alamo to have their picture taken."[30]

The final action by the federal commission did little to resolve the stadium issue; the location touched off another heated debate. The Birkhead committee recommended that the city purchase a site near Concepción Battlefield; it was subsequently rejected, as were locations identified as the Highway 66 site, the Exposition Park site, and the Saint Mary's University site. At a meeting on June 16, 1936, the centennial committee considered a tract of land in Highland Park at the intersection of Pine and Piedmont streets; after that the San

[27]Frank E. Mann to centennial officials, February 3, 1937, State Archives.

[28]Stephen Harrigan, "Coppini the Great," *Texas Monthly*, October, 1984, p. 142.

[29]*San Antonio Light*, November 19, 1939; Harrigan, "Coppini," p. 229; *San Antonio Light*, undated clipping, Centennial Collection, DRT Library.

[30]Harrigan, "Coppini," p. 231.

Antonio memorial stadium simply peters out in history, as do the records of the Birkhead committee. Undoubtedly something dramatic occurred in the interim. Subsequent accounting records cite no $150,000 stadium expenditure but do contain two items totaling $157,735 not found in the federal commission's original assignments: improvements to the Sunken Garden Amphitheater in Brackenridge Park, $59,457, and construction of the Memorial Building to Rangers, Pioneers, and Trail Drivers, $98,278.[31] Thus, the controversial stadium fades into history.

Despite the negative remarks of Commissioner General Cullen F. Thomas, Congressman Maury Maverick, or State Rep. Oscar F. Chastain about San Antonio's commitment to the centennial celebration, things are often other than what they seem. What appeared to be a victory for commercialism can now be credited to patriotism.

[31] King, *Report of Texas Centennial*, p. 135. San Antonio's major stadium is Alamo Stadium. This facility, dedicated on September 20, 1940, was funded jointly by a San Antonio Independent School District bond issue and a Works Progress Administration grant. The total cost was almost $500,000.

12

ARCHITECTS, ARTISTS, MURALISTS, AND SCULPTORS

uring the early months of 1936, as various Texas communities began celebrating the centennial year, a new city began to emerge from the 185 acres that had been Dallas's Fair Park. The speed with which the transformation was occurring suggested strokes of magic. While men, mules, and machines performed their mundane tasks, the geometric images that George Dahl and his staff set down on their drawing boards were being converted into the dramatic skyline of a world exposition. It was appropriately termed the "Magic City."

Fair Park became Mecca for a new wave of exposition immigration. From the East Coast, the West Coast, and the Midwest came exposition veterans — exhibitors, concessionaires, architects, designers, contractors, builders, painters, sculptors, and muralists — all seeking a role in the unfolding Dallas drama. To the Dallas business community which was helping fund the big show, they were the harbingers of an anticipated economic windfall that would infuse new life into the Dallas business community and ultimately the entire state. For both the employers and the prospective employees, Fair Park represented the promised land of the 1930s.

While the exposition was under construction, Dahl's office on the second floor of the Administration Building became the gateway to June 6. As centennial architect and chief of the technical division, Dahl exercised total control over exposition design. All visible structures required his final approval; "from the largest towering building to the smallest hot dog or peanut stand, from the millions of feet of utilities buried underground to the smallest statue or decoration to be seen, all visible details have been subject to the approval or rejection of the architect in charge," observed one contemporary journalist. "Even exhibitors' signs have been subject to this control."[1] This

[1]*Dallas Morning News*, Souvenir Edition, June 7, 1936. Enforcing the exposition sign

approval process was essential for the exposition's stylistic uniformity and integrity.

Centennial architects worked closely with Paul Massmann's exhibits and sales staff. Once an exhibitor leased an area, that organization submitted a tentative sketch for Dahl's approval or revision. "George had the whole picture to think about," Donald Nelson explained, "so all architectural plans had to be approved by George's office. We did freehand sketches of almost every building at the exposition. Other architects then picked them up and followed through on them."[2] In many cases Dahl's staff members moonlighted, working part-time with exhibitors in developing plans for their facilities. Nelson, for example, designed the Federal Building, the Hall of Negro Life, the Gulf Oil Company's radio studio, and consulted with the General Motors staff in the conversion of the Fair Park Auditorium (now Fair Park Music Hall). Even Dahl found time to help design the "Streets of Paris" concession and the Hall of Religion. Some internationally recognized architects also received centennial commissions. The Ford Motor Company engaged Albert Kahn to design the $2.25 million Ford Centennial Building, while William Lascaze designed the Magnolia Petroleum Company's exhibit hall (later the Margo Jones Theater).

The five-member Dallas Park Board was responsible for developing the permanent Fair Park civic complex. To ensure that this group of buildings would be completed on schedule, "Catfish" chairman Jim Dan Sullivan made each board member personally responsible for a building in the complex. "Jim Dan Sullivan was the driving force behind the Park Board," recalled Barry L. Bishop, former *Dallas Morning News* city hall reporter. "He rode herd on that group like a trail boss and made darn certain that Dallas's portion of the centennial construction was completed on time. Jim Dan seemed to be trying to prove that the 'Catfish Council' had something to offer the City of Dallas besides controversy." Bishop requested that "when the his-

---

ordinance produced at least one personal confrontation. When George Dahl ordered a flashing neon sign removed from the "Midget Village," a Mr. Rogers of the Doufour and Rogers show firm demanded that the sign be replaced. Dahl refused, and Rogers threatened to kill him. As the two men clashed, an assistant called an exposition security officer who removed Rogers from the architect's office. Rogers returned later that day (at General Manager W. A. Webb's insistence) and apologized to Dahl. "Every year for about the next five years," Dahl recalled, "I used to get a Christmas card from Rogers." Dahl interview, April 6, 1978.

[2] Telephone interview with Donald Nelson, Dallas, Texas, August 13, 1985.

tory of the Texas centennial is written, don't leave out Jim Dan Sullivan. He helped make it happen."[3]

But to make it happen, the park board had to turn to George Dahl. The centennial architect recalled later that the board had appointed an association of local architects to develop the art museum, but as the deadline approached for letting the contract, they had never been able to agree on a design. The day before the board was scheduled to approve the plans, Dahl received an emergency telephone call from park board member Robert Shields. "We haven't got a damn thing yet and we got to make a decision," he told Dahl. "What can you do about it?" After working all night he had the answer to Shields's question. "I finally rolled it up and gave it to him at seven o'clock the next morning," Dahl explained. "'It may not be any great achievement,'" he told Shields, "'but this is it; you can present this to your . . . board for action.' That's how the fine arts museum was done."[4]

The exposition construction program proved to be a great professional windfall for Dallas architects as well as the business community. Some local architects "who had previously been forced to consider a broom closet a major commission," wrote architecture critic David Dillon, "suddenly found themselves working on monumental civic buildings, in many cases for the only times in their careers."[5] Credit for their sudden prosperity was due in part to Dahl's years of work as the centennial's unpaid architectural consultant. According to contemporary reports, his romantic exposition renderings were key factors in generating interest in the celebration, as well as winning the central exposition for Dallas. It was also Dahl's idea to farm out the various commissions to local architects in order to complete the project on time. Logically, Dahl's professional colleagues should have credited him, at least partially, for their good fortune. Such was not the case. Nelson explained later that jealousy, not generosity, was a dominant trait in the creative world of architectural prima donnas. More specifically, most Dallas architects did not like George Dahl. The reason: "George was successful."[6]

In Dahl's earliest delineations of the proposed exposition, the state building (Hall of State) formed the centerpiece of the physical lay-

[3]Interview with Barry L. Bishop, Austin, Texas, May 23, 1985.
[4]Dahl interview, April 6, 1978.
[5]Dallas Morning News, August 11, 1985.
[6]Nelson interview, August 13, 1985.

out. This structure represented Texas' major financial investment in the celebration ($1.2 million) and was conceived as a permanent memorial to Texas patriots. The commission for the state building meant both professional prestige and financial rewards for the fortunate architect. Consequently, the state's major firms clamored for the assignment; Dahl thought it should be his. But the State Board of Control, not the centennial corporation, exercised total control over this expenditure, and therein lay Dahl's downfall.

He, Nelson, and the centennial architectural staff had drafted a preliminary design for the state building, and the Board of Control had accepted it. Dahl was elated. "We had complete cooperation from everyone involved [Claude Teer and John Singleton]," Nelson recalled. "In fact, we were about ten days into working drawings when we got word from Austin that the state building would go to another architect." The board unexpectedly reassigned the project to a San Antonio firm, Adams and Adams, headed by Carleton Adams, "The wisest of the politician-architects. . . . He had experience with the Board of Control." Adams and a consortium of ten Dallas firms received the commission by convincing the board "that those ten architects would do a better job than George Dahl," Nelson explained. "And the odd thing about it is, not one of them, including Ralph Bryan, who headed the design [group], . . . felt they could do it."[7] Although disappointed, Dahl remained philosophical in defeat. "I guess human nature comes out sooner or later," he said. "I did run into a number of incidents by the local architects here. They hadn't done one thing to help the exposition along, [but] . . . they wanted to pick the fruits and benefits whenever they could."[8] "George took it very well," Nelson recalled. "I never heard him say a derogatory word about any of those people. He just wanted to get the job done on time." That, unfortunately, did not happen. When the exposition opened on June 6, the Hall of State was the only major unfinished structure; it was finally dedicated on September 6, 1936, three months behind schedule. Although rejected, Dahl still attempted to expedite the project. He offered the consortium all of his tracings and sketches, but they rejected everything. According to Nelson, "It was an example of George's greatness. But I did see a tear from time to time." After think-

[7]Ibid., April 5, 1978.
[8]Dahl interview, April 6, 1978.

ing silently for several moments, Nelson attempted to summarize the
entire Hall of State matter, "What a mess that turned out to be."[9]

Despite Dahl's one great disappointment, he would achieve his ultimate goal; the exposition would open on schedule. It was a monumental achievement. His staff approved the design of all exposition
structures while supervising the construction of forty-five separate
buildings. In addition, they had total responsibility — both design and
supervision — for the construction of twenty-six permanent structures,
all completed within a ten-month period. That record would probably never again be equaled in a peacetime operation.

As the major exhibit buildings neared completion, Dahl and Nelson began to consider the exterior decorations — murals, friezes, bas-
reliefs, and sculpture. Ironically, they were to select a roster of mostly
foreign-born artists to execute the visual interpretation of the Texas
experience. And doubly ironic, these artists had achieved their repu-
tations in a secondary craft; they functioned primarily in the field
of building ornamentation, creating architectural appendages instead
of pursuing their art primarily as artists. Dahl and Nelson "brought
in people who really were not known in the art world at all," explained
Dallas artist Jerry Bywaters. "[They were] known in the exposition
world as designers for exposition buildings."[10] They were, nevertheless, recognized practitioners with good training and wide professional
experience.

Dahl and Nelson had met a number of these graphic artists while
studying in Europe. "Dahl's men were from the Rome school," Nelson explained. "I had met mine with the Paris school."[11] Dahl engaged
Carlo Ciampaglia, also a *Prix de Rome* winner, to direct a crew of
muralists who worked primarily on the exteriors of the temporary
buildings. Nelson recommended Pierre Bourdelle, son of the famed
French sculptor Antonio Bourdelle, to supervise another group of art-

[9]Nelson interview, August 13, 1985. Donald Barthelme, a member of the consortium,
claims he was called in on the project late and in the space of a weekend, reportedly working from Donald Nelson's earlier sketches, completed the design that was approved by the
Board of Control. Barthelme is also credited with arranging the names of Texas heroes
on the front of the building in such an order that the first letter of each name partially
spells his name: Burleson, Archer, Rusk, Travis, Hogg, etc. For more on the design of the
Hall of State, see *The Dallas Downtown News*, December 4, 1978, and Frank Carter Adams,
State of Texas Building (Austin: Steck Co., 1937).

[10]Interview with Jerry Bywaters, Dallas, Texas, February 23, 1978.

[11]Nelson interview, April 5, 1978.

ists who executed murals, sgraffitos, and bas-reliefs. Raoul Josset was one of fifteen European sculptors recruited by the Northwestern Terra Cotta Company in 1926 to help introduce contemporary European design in American pottery products. José Martin (pronounced Martan´), his fellow countryman, joined him later in Chicago. They both worked at the Chicago Century of Progress with Nelson, who recruited them for the centennial project. Other staff members included Juan B. Larrinaga, a West Coast "colorist and delineator" who had worked on the 1915 Panama-Pacific Exposition in San Francisco and the 1935 California Pacific International Exposition in San Diego and had done scene designs for a number of Hollywood films; Julian E. Garnsey, a Harvard- and Paris-trained muralist; Norwegian-born Eugene Gilboe, who had executed murals and decorative designs in theaters, office buildings, and more recently, decorated the ceiling of the new University of Texas Library in Austin; and the well-known sculptor, Lawrence Tenny Stevens. Their arrival in Dallas created a two-fold impact on the local artists. The economic windfall was welcome indeed; some fifty local artists and sculptors were engaged to aid in the exposition decoration. But unlike their architectural colleagues, the Texas artists were not accorded the same professional freedom. Instead they worked largely as journeyman assistants. The ensuing bitterness had a strangely familiar ring; the center of the disagreement again centered on the Hall of State — shades of Claude Teer, John Singleton, and the State Board of Control.

During the early 1930s, a vital colony of Dallas artists established a school of painting that reflected their regional experience. Regionalism in art had gained critical respectability during the interwar period, and the successes of Thomas Hart Benton, Grant Wood, and John Stuart Curry encouraged many young American painters to turn their backs on Europe and seek inspiration in a familiar setting. Benton, speaking in Dallas in 1935, articulated an abiding credo for that new generation of Texas painters: "Art cannot be imported. It has to grow. Keep your plant and water it."[12] Jerry Bywaters, whose painting Benton praised specifically, accepted the great Missouri painter's challenge. He became the leader of a movement that a half-century later would be praised nationally as Lone Star Regionalism.

[12]Rick Stewart, *Lone Star Regionalism: The Dallas Nine and Their Circle* (Dallas: Dallas Museum of Art, 1985), p. 43.

A 1927 art graduate of Southern Methodist University, Bywaters had studied in New York, Europe, and Mexico before returning to Dallas in 1932 to establish himself as an artist. His professional mission was to interpret Texas life as he believed only a native could — the land, the people, farm life, drought, the hardships of tenancy, the tragedy of the Depression. This *was* the Texas experience of the 1930s, and Bywaters and his colleagues wanted to tell the story of Texas to its people through art. The emerging Texas centennial exposition offered an unprecedented opportunity to fulfill that objective. They believed they could, better than anyone else, interpret the Texas experience.

Although the engagement of the professional exposition decorators disappointed Bywaters' group, there remained one great prize of the exposition: the mural in the great hall of the state building, depicting one hundred years of Texas history. This commission meant both money and professional prestige; Bywaters believed his group was entitled to both. The Dallas Nine, as they came to be known — Alexandre Hogue, Thomas J. Stell, Jr., Everett Spruce, William Lester, Otis Dozier, Harry Carnohan, Perry Nichols, John Douglas, and Bywaters[13] — had neither a commission nor encouragement. But they embarked on a voluntary program to demonstrate to John Singleton and the State Board of Control that they possessed the professional stature to execute the murals in the state building.

Bywaters and his group divided the history of Texas into ten periods, with each artist researching and preparing sketches for a visual interpretation of one period. Once the sketches were complete, Bywaters began trying to arrange a showing for Singleton and members of the Board of Control. This was never accomplished. Carleton Adams made an appointment for Singleton to view the sketches while attending an architect's conference in Dallas, but Singleton failed to keep that appointment. "They never gave us a chance to show [our work]," Bywaters recalled years later. "They kept saying that they wanted to meet with us, but we never had a meeting." While waiting to see Singleton following the Dallas conference, Bywaters "saw

---

[13]The work of this group of artists comprised a major exhibit shown in the Dallas Museum of Art a half-century later: "Lone Star Regionalism: The Dallas Nine and Their Circle, 1928–1945." This exhibit, which opened on February 5, 1985, attests to the enduring quality of their art.

[Eugene] Savage [a nationally known muralist from New York] come out of another architect's office and [I] found out the next day that they had [already] signed the contract with him."[14]

Bywaters was both disappointed and mad — disappointed because, following six months of preparation by nine competent artists, their work was never considered for the $30,000 commission, and mad because an outsider, totally unfamiliar with the state's history, traditions, and culture, was given the commission based solely on his reputation. In deep frustration, he wrote Benton speculating on the Board of Control's rationale in engaging Eugene Savage, "but they chose him and are quite willing for some of Savage's students to do all the work."[15]

Savage's casual regard for historical authenticity was later confirmed. When Dr. Herbert Gambrell, director of the Hall of State, went to view the completed mural, he told Savage that Anson Jones, the most important figure in the annexation scene, had been omitted. When Gambrell provided Savage a photograph of the last president of the Republic of Texas, the artist commented, "Well, I never heard of him." The following day Savage returned the photograph and invited Gambrell to view the revised mural. "If you look at it closely," Gambrell explained, "he has Anson Jones right in front of this group of people — painted him in just the night before it was finished."[16]

While Bywaters and his group could never justify the board selecting Savage without first seeing a sketch of the proposed mural, they could, nevertheless, rationalize their rejection. They were, in the perception of the Board of Control, an unknown quantity. Savage, on the other hand, was an established muralist who had received important commissions for other exposition buildings. But the Hall of

[14]Bywaters interview, February 23, 1978. Eugene Savage possessed good credentials, however. He was professor of painting at Yale University and a member of the Federal Commission of Fine Arts. In addition, he had just completed murals for the new library at Columbia University and the Sterling Library at Yale.

[15]Jerry Bywaters to Thomas Hart Benton, February 29, 1936, Jerry Bywaters Research Collection on American Art and Architecture, Fine Arts Library, Southern Methodist University. Bywaters was essentially correct. Savage engaged two Dallas artists, Reveau Bassett and Buchanan Winn, Jr., nonmembers of the Dallas Nine; Leoni Das Lynn of Houston; and William Smith of Austin, who executed much of the mural.

[16]Interview with Dr. Herbert Gambrell, Dallas, Texas, October 20, 1977.

State was not just another exposition building; it was a permanent memorial to Texas heroes and therefore merited an in-depth visual interpretation which Savage did not capture. Bywaters concluded:

> I think we would have gotten a lot more real bite . . . into the history [as well as] a great deal of character of the country itself and the people. . . . In a sense, Savage's painting belonged more outside along with Bourdelle's things. . . . They're all adopted from the past, and in a weaker strain. . . . They completely lacked individualism. They had a kind of fantasy about them which goes along with the exposition as being something unreal. . . . So in that sense, they were all right. But it was an opportunity, I think, to use the talent of the area to better advantage and for a longer staying quality.[17]

The unanimous acclaim accorded the Dallas Nine some fifty years later further substantiates Bywaters' belief in their art's staying quality. Conversely, his experience revealed a basic American assumption that foreign art in all its forms is superior to any domestic product. The Dallas Nine also saw that political connections can yield enormous personal rewards.[18]

Against the background of these personal dramas, various exhibit units were making advance preparations for opening day, still months away. The *Centennial News* reported in November that Robert B. Harshe, director of the Art Institute of Chicago, had begun assembling the art collection, representing American painters, French moderns, and Old Masters, to be exhibited in the new Dallas Museum of Fine Arts on the exposition grounds. The exposition corpora-

---

[17]Bywaters interview, February 23, 1978.

[18]The selection of artists, sculptors, and their work evolved as an ongoing matter of controversy throughout the centennial era. The Commission of Control rejected sculptor William Zorach's model of a memorial to pioneer women to be erected on the campus of Texas State College for Women at Denton. The image of a bare-breasted mother nursing a child prompted historian L. W. Kemp to remark: "History does not record that [Stephen F.] Austin founded a nudist colony." A more sedate version was selected. The erection of a statue of Buffalo Bill (Col. William F. Cody) was delayed more than a month when the Daughters of the Confederacy filed suit, charging that Colonel Cody was a Union spy and therefore an unfit subject to display at the Central Exposition. During the controversy Amon Carter offered to exhibit the piece at the Fort Worth exposition. Both Carter and the Daughters lost. After the statue was placed in front of the Dallas Museum of Fine Arts on the exposition grounds, publicity-wise Rangerettes placed a rose wreath at the foot of the controversial statue.

tion appropriated $100,000 for gathering, installing, and insuring the $10 million collection. In late February a jury was also appointed to select one hundred examples of Texas art for the centennial show. In early January Dudley Dobie, a former history teacher, embarked on a statewide historical artifacts survey, gathering data on material to be exhibited in the Hall of State.

Even before the contract was let for the Dallas Museum of Natural History, a field crew had begun collecting specimens for the centennial exhibit. The antelope group was taken near Sterling City, while the mule deer were shot near Kent. An official of the State Game, Fish, and Oyster Commission accompanied the crew to assist in locating and bagging the game. By early December, museum curator F. W. Miller had begun designing the exhibit that would incorporate the new specimens. But the most dramatic evidence of progress occurred on February 12, when the old main gates of the fairgrounds were demolished to make way for the new $35,000 entryway. As the twin concrete towers fell, the city lost a symbol of its history. Several American presidents had passed between the twin gate towers, as had thousands of American troops en route to the war in Europe in 1918.

With the construction program well under way, the exposition management apparently began to reevaluate the thrust of the celebration and endeavored to achieve a more equitable balance between patriotic and commercial interests. Earlier, former exposition executive, Otto Herold had negotiated with motion picture director Cecil B. DeMille about producing a historical pageant in Dallas. Albert Steves, Sr., chairman of the San Antonio Centennial Committee, pronounced this "a clear cut case of bad faith," as San Antonio had also been considering a historical pageant under DeMille's direction. Steves requested that the federal commission "indicate to him [Herold] the necessity of entirely reconsidering the matter."[19] Executive Secretary Yeager disagreed, informing Steves that the matter did not fall within the province of the federal commission. Dallas proceeded without DeMille's services to develop plans for a $150,000 outdoor spectacle depicting four hundred years of Texas history. By mid-January, 1936, researchers were already collecting authentic properties — longhorn

[19] Albert Steves, Sr., to the United States Texas Centennial Commission, September 11, 1935, 811.607 Texas Centennial/ (additional data illegible).

Transportation and Petroleu
Building Nos. 1&2
1-15-3
P.O.B. Montgomery
Builders, Engineers, Con

Construction of the 1936 Texas Centennial Exposition, the largest peacetime project in the state's history, was completed in record time. Framework of the Transportation and Petroleum Building on the Esplanade of State was in place by
January 15, 1936. (Courtesy State Fair of Texas)

The Varied Industries, Electrical, and Communications complex was nearing completion when this picture was taken, on March 18. Work had not yet begun on the central lagoon. (Courtesy State Fair of Texas)

Artists and sculptors who worked on the 1936 Texas Centennial Exposition. Bottom row, left to right: Pierre Biza, José Martin, Raoul Josset, H. H. Ewing, George L. Dahl (Centennial Architect and Technical Director), Hector Serbaroli, E. L. Amundson, Eugene Gilboe, Lloyd Wallace, Carlo Ciampaglia, Lois Lignell, Gozo Kawamura, Pierre Bourdelle, J. E. Greer, Jack Hubbell, Julian E. Garnsey, G. M. Houston, and A. J. Speh; middle row: Mac Johnson, Perry Nichols, Thomas Stell, and Kreigh Collins; top row: Lawrence Tenny Stevens, Ray Siggins, George Stevens, Harry Carnohan, and John Douglass. (Courtesy Jerry Bywaters Research Collection on American Art and Architecture, Southern Methodist University, Dallas)

Lawrence Tenny Stevens, left, inspects the work of José Martin and two uniden-tified craftsmen on the sculpture *Confederate*, for exhibit on the Esplanade of State at the Dallas exposition. This twenty-foot statue in cast stone was one of six heroic figures representing the six flags under which Texas has been ruled. (Courtesy Jerry Bywaters Research Collection on American Art and Architec-ture, Southern Methodist University, Dallas)

The entrance to Humble Oil Company's Hall of Texas History, still under construction. Exterior art deco frieze depicts the occurrence, exploration, and production of petroleum in Texas. (Courtesy Texas/Dallas History and Archives Division, Dallas Public Library)

The Texas Centennial Exposition opening day parade moves up Main Street in Dallas toward Exposition grounds. (Courtesy Charles Kavanaugh Collection)

Dignitaries at the dedication of the Texas Centennial Exposition on opening day. Left to right: U.S. Secretary of Commerce Daniel C. Roper; Texas Gov. James V. Allred; Fred F. Florence, exposition executive; W. B. Yeager, executive secretary, United States Texas Centennial Commission; and R. L. Thornton, exposition executive. (Courtesy Dallas Historical Society)

Nathan Adams in later years. Adams, with R. L. Thornton and Fred F. Florence, formed the bankers' triumvirate that led the drive to bring the 1936 Texas Centennial Exposition to Dallas. (Courtesy Texas/Dallas History and Archives Division, Dallas Public Library)

Lowry Martin, initial guiding spirit of the Texas centennial movement, in later years at his desk at the *Corsicana Daily Sun* office. (Courtesy *Corsicana Daily Sun*)

Parry Avenue entrance to the 1936 Texas Centennial Exposition. The eighty-five-foot pylon designed by architect George Dahl is topped with a gold star representing the lone star of Texas; James Buchanan Winn, Jr., designed the sculptural frieze. (Courtesy Dallas Historical Society)

The *Spirit of the Centennial* art and sculpture at the entrance of the Centennial Exposition Administration Building. Celebrated model, actress, and singer Georgia Carroll (later wife of orchestra leader Kay Kyser) posed for the statue, designed by Raoul Josset and executed by Dallas sculptor José Martin. Carlo Ciampaglia designed the rear mural. This building now houses the Fair Park maintenance office. (Author's collection)

Esplanade of State looking east from Parry Avenue entrance toward Hall of State. The Federal Building tower is seen in right background. Six porticos, each containing a 20-foot-high statue representing one of the six flags of Texas, face the 700-foot-long central reflecting pool. In 1986, the Esplanade was restored to its original splendor. (Author's collection)

Esplanade of State at night. Building facades were illuminated in constantly changing colors while underwater projectors focused on jets of water and the bases of fountains along the Esplanade. (Author's collection)

The 1.2 million-dollar Hall of State (originally the State of Texas building), funded by the Texas legislature as a memorial to the heroes of Texas history, was the Centennial Exposition's most imposing structure. Considered by many to be one of the finest examples of art deco architecture in the nation, the hall now houses the Dallas Historical Society. (Author's collection)

The Hall of State contains a rich trove of sculpture and murals documenting the Texas experience; the West Texas Room mural by Texas artist Tom Lea focuses on cattle culture. (Courtesy Charles Kavanaugh Collection)

Twenty-four search lights mounted behind the Hall of State pierce the night sky over the Centennial Exposition. (Courtesy Texas/Dallas History and Archives Division, Dallas Public Library)

President Franklin D. Roosevelt's special train stops in Austin en route to the Texas Centennial Exposition in Dallas. Standing on the rear platform are Jesse H. Jones, Mrs. Roosevelt, Gov. James V. Allred, University of Texas President H. Y. Benedict, the president, and Austin Mayor Tom Miller. (Courtesy Austin History Center, Austin Public Library, A07071)

Jesse H. Jones, chairman of the Reconstruction Finance Corporation, and Dallas banker and Centennial Exposition executive Fred F. Florence await President Franklin Roosevelt's arrival at Union Station, Dallas. Florence is wearing a Texas centennial medallion identifying him as an exposition executive. (Courtesy Texas/ Dallas History and Archives Division, Dallas Public Library)

Secret Service agents stand guard as two Indians in native dress present gifts to
President Roosevelt, seated next to Mrs. Roosevelt and Governor Allred, as they
enter the Cotton Bowl for a presidential address, on June 12, 1936. (Courtesy Texas/
Dallas History and Archives Division, Dallas Public Library)

President Roosevelt's motorcade enters the Cotton Bowl for an address to the nation from the Texas Centennial Exposition. Military units stand at attention before a bunting-draped speakers' platform. (Courtesy Texas/Dallas History and Archives Division, Dallas Public Library)

President Roosevelt addresses the nation from the Cotton Bowl at the Texas Centennial Exposition. R. L. Thornton, Dallas banker and exposition executive, and Mrs. Roosevelt, in hat, are seated directly behind the president. The Federal Building tower is visible in the background. (Courtesy Texas/Dallas History and Archives Division, Dallas Public Library)

cattle, buffaloes, a stagecoach, ox teams, covered wagons, and Spanish armor — for a two-hour open-air drama, *The Cavalcade of Texas.* In a vein of somewhat lesser historical importance, the Dallas City Council voted to accept officially the name "Cotton Bowl" for the renovated 45,000-seat sports facility on the exposition grounds.

The rapidly changing face of old Fair Park continued to whet the spectators' imagination. On Sunday, February 23, more than fifty thousand North Texas citizens took advantage of the springlike weather to get a preview of the $25 million world's fair. When General Manager W. A. Webb announced the final open house for Sunday, March 29, more than eighty thousand people visited the site. Between noon and sundown an estimated thirty thousand automobiles clogged the streets near the exposition grounds; a Dallas police official described the traffic as the heaviest ever witnessed in that city. Even before centennial construction could be completed, a Dallas journalist reported, "attracted by Nation-wide Centennial advertising, early vacationists are pouring into the State. License numbers [plates] of nearly every State in the Union may be seen on downtown streets. Hotels have been crowded and restaurants likewise have been doing unusually heavy business." In the same article on March 8 Ray Foley, the exposition's works director, reported that construction was still ahead of schedule, with more than five thousand people employed. He predicted that these numbers would increase markedly as private exhibitors began their individual building programs.[20]

Even journalists, sometimes jaded by their professional commitment to report the news objectively, if not unemotionally, appeared to have caught the patriotic spirit of the centennial movement. A case in point is centennial devotee Harry Benge Crozier's account, not of the building program but of "the suddenly stirred interest and marveling comments of visitors. . . . Incredulousness is lost in the light of convincing evidence of actuality. The observant visitor to the Centennial Exposition these March days can sense and vision the things that are to be before June 6. There is faith now where doubt lingered. . . . Out at Centennial Park they are telling visitors: 'The story can be told. We'll hold open house for the world on June 6. Be sure and attend the Centennial. You won't be here for the next one.'"[21]

[20]*Dallas Morning News*, March 8, 1936.
[21]Ibid., March 16, 1936.

13

WHERE THE WEST REALLY BEGINS

Meanwhile, thirty miles to the west, the sounds of economic prosperity reverberating from Dallas's old Fair Park had awakened a slumbering giant. Fort Worth had remained a minor player in the centennial sweepstakes until early in 1936. Its civic leaders, namely Amon Carter and the Fort Worth Chamber of Commerce, elected not to compete for the central exposition in 1934, planning instead a major memorial to the livestock industry. When the state Centennial Commission of Control arbitrarily allocated $250,000 for that purpose a year later, members of the Advisory Board of Texas Historians threatened to resign. At issue was not purpose but protocol. The matter was resolved later when the federal commission assigned that amount for the Fort Worth celebration, and the state's money was reallocated.

The $250,000 federal allocation fell far short of the city's needs. In June, 1935, a local committee of businessmen, bankers, and stock show officials submitted to the Fort Worth City Council their plan for an unofficial centennial celebration. They wanted to expand the physical plant of the annual Southwestern Exposition and Fat Stock Show, construct a municipal auditorium, and add a summer entertainment package to siphon off visitors attending the Central Exposition in Dallas. The council agreed to support the measure and applied for a Public Works Administration loan-grant to finance the building program. The request specified $150,000 for the site, $1,376,378 for construction, and $68,819 for contingencies. Structures included a $532,378 coliseum and auditorium, a $200,000 agriculture and general exhibit building, a $160,000 cattle exhibit building, an $80,000 horse show building, plus a number of smaller facilities. Adjoining the auditorium and coliseum was a memorial tower to be dedicated to the late actor-humorist Will Rogers, a close friend of Carter. According to Carter's biographer, Jerry Flemmons, this caused some interim problems, prompting "terrible-tongued Harold Ickes, FDR's interior secretary and PWA director, to snap, 'I can't understand why a memorial to Will Rogers should be built in Fort Worth just because he was Carter's friend.'"[1] Carter had other prominent friends, many in the Roosevelt-Garner administration, which undoubtedly helped facilitate the application's approval. Ickes finally waived his objections, and the city council accepted the PWA loan-grant on January 2, 1936.

The Fort Worth grant was for 45 percent of the project's cost, not to exceed $725,727, and a $637,000 loan. To qualify for the PWA funds, the city had to place in the construction account interim funds derived from two bond issues, one for $687,500 and a later one for $250,000.[2] After considerable debate over the site for the proposed complex, the city purchased a 135-acre tract for $150,000, plus one month's interest of $500 and the 1935 taxes.[3] The site was located on a bald prairie west of downtown Fort Worth and across the Trinity River. It had once been part of Camp Bowie, a World War I training facility.

The PWA funding solved some problems but created others. A permanent stock show and auditorium facility near downtown Fort Worth was assured, but the debate over site selection delayed the beginning of construction until March 17. If Fort Worth was to benefit from the summer centennial visitors, city leaders would have to revise their timetable. The original plan was to stage a livestock and frontier days exposition dramatizing the history of the cattle industry. To launch this program the Fort Worth group, incorporated as the Texas Centennial Livestock and Frontier Days Exposition, leased 22.6 acres of the Camp Bowie site from the city, for one hundred dollars a year, to construct temporary buildings for the frontier exposition. Originally the show was scheduled to run from August 1 to December 1, and entertainment was considered a diversionary attraction for those who tired of the rodeo, livestock, and frontier exhibits. Both plans were destined for change.

---

[1] Jerry Flemmons, *Amon: The Life of Amon Carter, Sr. of Texas* (Austin: Jenkins Publishing Co., 1978), p. 299.

[2] For a detailed analysis of the city-federal centennial financial transactions, see Lois Gray, "History of the Fort Worth Frontier Centennial," Master's thesis, Texas Christian University, 1938.

[3] Ibid., p. 62. The city council also agreed to erect a cattle exhibit building at the northside stockyards site.

William Monnig, a local merchant, council member, and president of the corporation, announced that the site would include a reproduction of a typical frontier town with a dance hall, bar, general store, museum of pioneer relics, and other amusement attractions. He believed that "if properly staged," this unofficial exposition would "provide the color, romance, and action to make the Frontier Centennial the most appealing and entertaining of all Centennial celebrations." He projected attendance at two million, yielding a gross revenue of $2 million; half that income, he believed, would produce an operating profit. Monnig appointed two hundred women and about the same number of men to help develop an entertainment package that would lure a portion of the Dallas visitors to Fort Worth.[4]

The women took the lead in planning the exposition. Lacking experience, talent, and Dallas's multimillion-dollar budget, their initial efforts contained the seeds of artistic and financial disaster. According to Flemmons, they "began to fashion a ragamuffin reprint of Dallas' show, a religio-historic extravaganza replete with homemade parts — Boy Scouts painted as fierce Indians, a reproduction of frontier Fort Worth, jelly and baking contests . . . and an amphitheater in which to present a dramatic gala featuring alternating church choirs. Amon [Carter] gawd-damned the dullness of it all, and determined to find a remedy."[5] With Dallas setting the pace in the competition for the nation's entertainment dollars, both Monnig and Carter realized that in order to offer any viable alternative, they had to look for their salvation elsewhere. What occurred during those frantic days of early March, 1936, has been partially blurred by time, but one fact remains abundantly clear — the two civic leaders did indeed find their salvation.

Although the initial negotiations were conducted in secret, such caution was unnecessary. Few people in Fort Worth knew either Rufus LeMaire or Billy Rose. Carter, in desperation, had contacted LeMaire, casting director for Metro-Goldwyn-Mayer Studios and a Fort Worth native, who recommended Rose to resurrect the floundering frontier exposition. According to LeMaire, Rose initially declined to consider the proposition or even go to Fort Worth for a conference. Either Carter or the casting director — or probably both — persisted, and on

[4]*Fort Worth Star-Telegram*, January 11, 1936.
[5]Flemmons, *Amon*, p. 301.

March 6, LeMaire and Rose arrived in Fort Worth by plane, LeMaire reportedly to visit relatives and Rose en route from California to New York. That night the two were Carter's guests at the Fort Worth Club, and after lengthy discussions Rose's now-legendary deal was made: $1,000 a day for one hundred days to produce the Fort Worth Frontier Exposition. Big bucks at any time, but unheard of in Texas during the 1930s.[6] Carter was elated; he felt he had outmaneuvered Dallas in the competition for the national spotlight. Standing before a bank of radio microphones and newsreel cameras, he announced at the annual fat stock show: "You think Dallas invented Texas just because they built a bigger centennial than any other city. But we are going to put on a show of our own and teach those dudes over there where the West *really* begins."[7]

Following the contract signing on March 7, Rose inspected the exposition site, indicated his general satisfaction with the layout, and embarked for New York. While there he took page ads in *Billboard* and *Variety*, inviting concessionaires to contact him about acts for the forthcoming show. Rose's ad copy further fueled the flames of the Dallas-Fort Worth intercity feud. He alluded to the central exposition (not by name) in the March 14 issue of *Billboard* as "a pale carbon copy of the Chicago World's Fair," and in *Variety* he originated the now-classic slogan that did, in fact, define the essential differences between the two expositions: "For education go to Dallas, for entertainment, come to Fort Worth." (Rose would claim later that that slogan alone was worth his $100,000 fee.)

The Dallas sponsors were understandably concerned. Arthur L. Kramer, a Dallas business executive and member of the state centennial advertising board, complained to Monnig: "I deem it important to now bring the matter officially to your attention, because the Dallas exposition has the right to demand that no other city in Texas refer to it either directly or by implication in any advertisement or pub-

[6]Although Rose's salary was never announced officially, the $100,000 figure is probably valid. In *Wine, Women, and Words* (New York: Simon and Schuster, 1948), Rose states: "Carter told me the job had to be done in a hundred days and asked what I wanted for my services. Taking a deep breath, I said, 'a hundred thousand dollars.' The city fathers conferred for all of three minutes and agreed" (p. 19). When the corporation repeated the exposition in 1937, James M. North negotiated with Rose for $50,000 to produce the shows and $50,000 for supervising the entire operation. This was to be paid in installments. Carter Archives.

[7]Newsreel rerun, KXAS-TV, Fort Worth, June 4, 1981.

licity relating to a competitive attraction. It becomes our responsibility to protect this right, and I shall appreciate it if you will consider this letter as an official request that any further references of the type indicated by [sic] promptly discontinued."[8] Monnig read the letter, discussed it with his board, and concluded that Kramer was "unduly disturbed." He cited their consensus that the two expositions were noncompetitive and should complement each other. He expressed surprise that after Fort Worth announced the frontier theme, Dallas was planning a rodeo, and after Fort Worth engaged Billy Rose, "the central exposition planned an enlargement of its entertainment features and duplication, to some extent at least, of what we had planned." Monnig concluded that he felt Kramer's phrase, "the right to demand," was ill-advised, and the board further reserved the right to publicize the Frontier Exposition "in the manner best calculated . . . to achieve the desired ends."[9]

Rose continued to espouse his cause, and for a non-Texan he did some mighty big talking. He claimed the Fort Worth show would make *Jumbo*, his current New York hit attraction, look like a peep show. His plans included a three-ring circus, a livestock show, a frontier city, and a swimming pool one hundred yards square. For headliners, "I'll get Shirley Temple, Mae West, Guy Lombardo, Jack Benny," he promised. "I'll get 1,000 beautiful girls for the Frontier Follies. I'll have a Texas pageant to be called 'The Fall of the Alamo,' 'The Battle of San Jacinto' or some other Texas name. And I'll have 2,000 Indians and 1,000 cowboys — and guess who wins."[10] He reportedly attempted to charter the airship *Hindenburg* to fly one hundred showgirls from New York to Fort Worth and offered the beleaguered Ethiopian Emperor Haile Selassie $100,000 to appear in the show with his lions. In addition, Rose claimed to be negotiating with Fred Astaire and Ginger Rogers, the popular film dance team, to appear in the "Follies," whatever that was. In pursing his goals, he never allowed bad taste to interfere with business. Rose telegraphed Mrs. Wallis Warfield Simpson, the woman for whom Edward VIII gave up his crown, offering her $25,000 a week for a four-week engagement at the frontier exposition. Predictably, he received no response but instead relished the headlines he obtained by making the offer.

[8]Arthur L. Kramer to William Monnig, March 19, 1936, Carter Archives.
[9]William Monnig to Arthur L. Kramer, undated, Carter Archives.
[10]*Fort Worth Star-Telegram*, March 10, 1936.

Rose fulfilled none of these claims. Nor did he expect to; he was stalling for time. If the Fort Worth citizens thought they were getting nothing but big talk for $1,000 a day, time proved them wrong. William Samuel Rosenberg (Billy Rose), as it turned out, was the right man at the right time. Although the diminutive five-foot-two New Yorker had produced the successful *Jumbo*, he was by no means a show business colossus in 1936 (Vice-President Garner described him as a "pursley-gutted little feller"). He had achieved moderate success as a song writer—"Barney Google," "That Old Gang of Mine," and "You've Got to See Mama Every Night or You Can't See Mama at All" — and less as a Metro-Goldwyn-Mayer script writer— $1,000 a week and not a word on film. He had produced *Crazy Quilt*, a highly successful revue, and *Sweet and Low*, a stage musical, and he became a successful nightclub entrepreneur with Casino de Paree and Billy Rose's Music Hall. His latest claim to show business fame, however, was *Jumbo*, a musicalized circus starring comedian Jimmy Durante, tenor John Raitt, Paul Whiteman's orchestra, and a white elephant named Rosie. The show opened at the New York Hippodrome Theater in the fall of 1935, cost $250,000 to stage, and played to approximately 1.5 million people. Although successful, Rose was no theater immortal and was scarcely known outside Manhattan. Were the truth known, he probably was not as difficult a "catch" as LeMaire had indicated. Other than his congenital flair for the gaudy, the grand, and the spectacular, probably his greatest asset in 1936 (or was it a personal liability?) was his wife, the famous comedienne Fanny Brice. "Rose was desperate, even neurotic, to shed the 'Mr. Brice' title," wrote Flemmons, "and in Fort Worth he moved out of his wife's shadow."[11] It would be on that sunbaked hillock at the corner of West Lancaster Street and University Drive that Billy Rose would ultimately establish himself as the preeminent theatrical impresario. With uncharacteristic modesty he admitted later: "Amon Carter, Jimmy North, William Monnig and the rest of the Centennial Committee bought the dream-dust I was peddling and gave me a free and helping hand."[12]

The Rose and Carter partnership brought together the ultimate in divergent individuals: the tall and the short, the lean and the fat, the cosmopolite and the man of the West; one wore pinstripe suits

[11] Flemmons, *Amon*, p. 302.
[12] Fort Worth *News-Tribune*, February 10, 1978.

and spats, the other ten-gallon hats and cowboy boots. They were alike in only one respect: during the summer of 1936 they were mutually committed to making Fort Worth the entertainment capital of the nation. They succeeded, and the partnership grew into a lasting friendship.

Amon Carter was fifty-six years old when Rufus LeMaire introduced him to Billy Rose. For Carter that meeting marked another milestone in his personal crusade to promote Fort Worth. By that time he had acquired all the necessary tools — the *Fort Worth Star-Telegram;* WBAP, that city's first and most powerful radio station; independent wealth; community respect; an ebullient personality; and a world-wide network of prominent and influential friends. His biographer claimed that probably no other man in the nation's history knew so many of the high and mighty. He entertained presidents, European royalty, cabinet officers, corporate executives, movie stars, and sports celebrities at his Shady Oaks Ranch. And all cherished his personal gifts, regional tokens of their friendship — boots, ten-gallon hats, nickel-plated six-shooters, silver belt buckles, and Texas-size steaks.[13] Although the gregarious Carter relished people —"Carter loved crowds like a pickpocket"— Flemmons placed the publisher's social life within the context of his great design: "Famous guests were all part of Amon's great conspiracy to promote Fort Worth into a national prominence."[14]

In 1936, the Fort Worth Frontier Centennial Exposition became the centerpiece of Carter's master plan. He made no bones about it; this celebration would have nothing to do with patriotism and Texas' century of progress. The Fort Worth business community for whom Carter spoke was creating an entertainment package for one purpose only — to switch the nation's economic spotlight to Fort Worth, and Dallas be damned. Carter may not have invented the Dallas–Fort Worth rivalry, but he certainly elevated it to unprecedented heights.[15] Single-handedly, he proved himself a worthy match for the Dallas

[13]Harry L. Hopkins, Works Progress administrator, received a choice portion of a grand champion steer. "At $1.40 per pound on the hoof, it certainly made a very expensive meal," he wrote Carter. "I have never tasted better beef." Hopkins to Carter, April 20, 1936, Carter Archives.

[14]Flemmons, *Amon,* p. 220. Amon Carter was influential in bringing to Fort Worth American Airlines, the Santa Fe maintenance shops and freight terminal, Carswell Air Force Base, and Consolidated Aircraft (later General Dynamics), which established the world's largest bomber plant there during World War II.

[15]When attending luncheons in Dallas, Carter invariably carried his own sack lunch

triumvirate. Thornton, Adams, and Florence promoted Dallas as a business enterprise; with Carter promotion was a way of life that seemingly grew into a normal bodily function. There was no alternative; he and Fort Worth were synonymous.

By March 13 (a Friday), Rose was back in Fort Worth preparing to stage the Frontier Exposition. He established his office in the downtown Sinclair Building and began assembling a staff and contacting performers for the various shows.[16] The process that Rose used in Fort Worth ultimately vaulted him to fame: he engaged the most creative talent in show business, demanded the impossible, and accepted the best they could produce. That is how Billy Rose became a legend. His first order of business was to telegraph John Murray Anderson in London, where he was designing a production of *Jumbo*. He ordered Anderson to return to Fort Worth at once and begin work on the exposition. A man of vast experience, with a flair for the spectacular, Anderson had directed twenty-eight musical comedies and revues in the United States and Europe. His credits included the *Ziegfeld Follies* of 1934 and 1935 and Paul Whiteman's *The King of Jazz*, the first all-color motion picture.

Rose's staff selections also reflected an accent on youth. For his stage and architectural designer, he chose Albert Johnson, a twenty-six-year-old veteran with ten years' experience in the American theater. A protégé of Norman Bel Geddes, Johnson designed all the buildings, concessions, and sets for the entire exposition. Serving concurrently as art director of the Radio City Music Hall, Johnson had to design six shows weeks in advance in order to accept the Fort Worth assignment. To compose the original music for the exposition, Rose chose twenty-one-year-old Dana Suesse. She arrived in Fort Worth with at least three popular hits to her credit: "You Ought to Be in Pictures," "Whistling in the Dark," and "My Silent Love." In addition, the Boston Symphony Orchestra had performed her "Jazz Nocturne." She wrote the

---

and a thermos of Fort Worth drinking water. He and R. L. Thornton were actually good friends and worked together on many projects.

[16] In negotiating performers' contracts, Rose displayed rare skill in cutting costs. Fort Worth musician Woods Moore was present as Rose bargained with a husband and wife team who had a bird act that Rose wanted. "He got 'em down to a ridiculous figure," Moore recalled. "And as they walked out of the door, he [Rose] says, 'And don't forget, *you* feed 'em!'" Interview with Woods Moore, Fort Worth, February 24, 1978. It was also reported that Rose demanded an additional booking fee for himself for each act he engaged for the Fort Worth shows.

music for three separate shows at the Frontier Exposition and produced her most enduring composition, "The Night is Young and You are Beautiful" (Rose and Irving Kahal wrote the lyrics). Twenty-four-year-old Raoul Pène du Bois, son of the renowned painter, designed all the costumes for the exposition shows; he had also worked on both the *Follies* and the Radio City Music Hall revues. Robert Alton, still in his early thirties, created and directed the dances for what evolved as the Casa Mañana revue. His credits included the *Ziegfeld Follies*, *Life Begins at 8:40*, and *Anything Goes*, and he had worked with Rose in staging the Casino de Paree revue. In choosing his professional collaborators, Rose exhibited rare discretion; seldom in the history of the American musical theater had a more capable and experienced staff been assembled to produce a show.

Rose's ongoing verbal assault with names of filmdom's superstars — Dick Powell, Mae West, Shirley Temple, Fred Astaire, and Ginger Rogers — was nothing more than show-business ballyhoo; it held the public's interest while he formulated plans for the exposition. In announcing his production staff, Ross revealed that the summer show would feature spectacular showmanship and the eye-stunning pageantry of Broadway, Paris, and London (Las Vegas was still a desert village), all rolled up on one West Texas hillside. Superstars are lost in pageantry; none were chosen. The ghosts of P. T. Barnum and Flo Ziegfeld dogged Rose's every footstep.

By mid-April a general entertainment format began to emerge: a cafe-theater revue, a pageant of frontier life, a Gay Nineties cabaret, and *Jumbo*. Instead of a two-week performance of New York's *Jumbo*, as originally announced, Rose elected to restage the show in Fort Worth in a circular building designed by Albert Johnson. He replaced Jimmy Durante with Eddie Foy, Jr., and retained Paul Whiteman and his orchestra, who appeared in the New York production. Whiteman's new contract earned him $7,500 a week for six weeks; an option for an additional six weeks was exercised. Known as the King of Jazz, Whiteman had been a major figure in American popular music for almost two decades.[17] When he arrived in Fort Worth he was at the

---

[17]In 1919 Paul Whiteman introduced an integrated musical style known as symphonic jazz, and in 1924 he conducted the premier performance of George Gershwin's "Rhapsody in Blue." In 1931 he introduced Ferde Grofe's *Grand Canyon Suite*, which was written especially for the Whiteman orchestra.

peak of his popularity, headlining a weekly network radio show sponsored by the Woodbury Soap Company.

The singing star of the yet-unnamed revue, was tenor Everett Marshall, who boasted a wide range of stage, radio, and film credits. Ann Pennington, the featured dancer, had also achieved wide recognition in New York as a *Follies* star. Rose stunned the local establishment when he announced that he had engaged Sally Rand, the sensational nude dancing star of the Century of Progress, to appear at the Frontier Exposition. She would personally operate "Sally Rand's Dude Ranch"—"dude" was later switched to "nude"—and also appear in the cafe-theater revue. The local response was predictable. The ministers' association and the women's clubs shouted their opposition in unison. Rose and Carter were elated; public controversy sells tickets, as does borderline sex. Sally Rand, if not Texanic patriotic, was certainly historic. Helen Gould Beck (the stage name came from a Rand-McNally map), a Quaker farm girl from Missouri, had become the sensation at the Chicago World's Fair when she removed her clothes and danced behind a pair of white feather fans to Debussy's *Clair de Lune.* Although she exposed nothing, she was arrested four times the first day and became an overnight sensation. "I was a tan, blonde, big-bosomed, bubble-butted, sexy female," she explained unnecessarily. "I was outraged that someone could question my sense of artistry and taste. The publicity upset me terribly."[18] Rose and Carter loved it. At last they had something that Dallas couldn't match; there was only one Sally Rand.

While Rose hired stars and built buildings, Carter and Monnig began raising money to pay the bills. They soon discovered that Rose had the easier job. In their enthusiasm to enter Fort Worth in the intercity centennial sweepstakes, Carter and his colleagues had failed to assess the financial support for such an undertaking. (Late-night decisions made at the Fort Worth Club sometimes lacked public accord.) They suddenly found themselves in great financial difficulty that persisted throughout the centennial. In order to receive federal assistance to construct the permanent civic complex, Fort Worth citizens approved two bond issues, but contributions for the entertainment package evolved as an entirely different matter. To fund the $1 million project, the Texas Centennial Livestock and Frontier Days

[18]*Austin American-Statesman*, July 22, 1973.

Exposition — not the city — launched a bond drive to raise money for the interim expenses. They believed that once the show opened, ticket sales would ensure the exposition's solvency. The corporation set the target subscription at $750,000, to be derived from bonds bearing 4 percent interest and secured by a first lien on the show's profits. By March 25, only $350,000 had been sold. These sales were from large purchasers: banks, utilities, oil companies, the stockyards, and packing companies. Monnig continued his appeal for support: "We are asking you to make a loan toward carrying out a project that should bring in large and immediate cash-drawer returns to every businessman, professional man and property owner in Fort Worth. It will give employment to thousands. . . . It will give Fort Worth more valuable publicity than could be obtained in any other way."[19] Sales, however, remained slow.

When Rose revealed the final exposition layout, it was readily apparent that he envisioned a million-dollar operation. The 22.6-acre plan contained eight major structures: the world's largest open-air cafe-theater, Casa Mañana (originally the Casa de Mañana), with seating for 3,800 (which was subsequently increased) and a 130-foot circular stage floating on water; a circular theater seating 3,000, designed especially for the musical circus, *Jumbo*; a covered grandstand seating 3,000 for an outdoor rodeo, wild west show, and pioneer life extravaganza, called *The Last Frontier*; Pioneer Palace, an old-fashioned bar and burlesque show; Sally Rand's Nude Ranch; a carnival; an Indian village; and a pioneer village.

On March 31, the corporation's board of control awarded the Casa Mañana contract to three Fort Worth firms on a cost-plus-ten-percent basis. Monnig estimated the building would cost $100,000 and would be completed by July 1, when the exposition was scheduled to open. He was wrong on all counts. Within two weeks construction was under way on Casa Mañana, the *Jumbo* building, and the *Last Frontier* complex. With the scheduled opening less than two months away, contractors began erecting floodlights for night work, and Henry B. Friedman, one of the exposition contractors, urged the local union to import at least one hundred carpenters to relieve the labor shortage. By May 18, one thousand workers were employed at the exposition site. For the first time in years, Fort Worth was enjoying a labor

---

[19] *Fort Worth Star-Telegram*, March 25, 1936.

shortage. Landscape architect S. Herbert Hare and the city applied jointly to the National Youth Administration for four hundred young people to aid in surface conditioning the exposition site.

Increased employment was gratifying, but somebody would have to pay the bills. Many began wondering, who? The corporation's treasury provided no solution. Its precarious financial position became more acute on May 22, when the city building inspector issued permits totaling $455,000 for five show buildings, all over budget. The week before, James M. North, Jr., editor of the *Star-Telegram* and member of the board of control, reported to Carter on the growing disparity between the corporation's income and projected expenses. It would cost $900,000 to open the exposition, he explained, and bond sales to May 14 totaled only $529,000. He offered Carter two alternatives: find underwriters, or arrange a bank loan. "But if we don't raise this money within the next ten days and keep it coming in," North warned, "it is doubtful if work can be continued and the show opened on July 1."[20] Anticipating the worst, Carter had already been seeking alternatives; a bank loan was the last resort. He wrote Harry L. Hopkins, WPA administrator, on April 12, 1936: "I am making an appeal to you as there should be some [legal] elasticity in an emergency of this kind. So, for the love of Mike lend us a hand."[21] Apparently there was no elasticity. He also pleaded with Mrs. Ben J. Tillar, widow of a Fort Worth real estate investor, for financial aid. The exposition bonds, he assured her, were a sound investment. "I think the show will not only pay off the bonds but that we will make a half-million dollars in profits." He predicted the Frontier Exposition "will bring 15 to 25 million dollars new money to Fort Worth, fill all the hotels [she owned one], apartments, clubs, tourists' camps, and private residences in our city." In addition, this undertaking would make Fort Worth "during the period mentioned . . . [the] amusement center of the United States."[22] Mrs. Tillar's name does not appear on the "Final Centennial Honor Roll."

Carter was more successful in his personal plea to Dan Moran, president of the Continental Oil Company. After considerable hesitancy (his company had already invested heavily at the central exposition),

[20]James M. North to Amon Carter, May 14, 1936, Carter Archives.
[21]Amon Carter to Harry L. Hopkins, April 12, 1936, Carter Archives.
[22]Amon Carter to Mrs. Ben J. Tillar, May 20, 1936, Carter Archives.

Moran purchased $10,000 in exposition bonds. Carter also dispatched a three-page form letter to presidents of major corporations throughout the United States, promoting exhibit space at the Fort Worth exposition. The rejection he received from R. H. Grant of General Motors was representative of most corporate responses; previous commitments at the central exposition precluded their Fort Worth participation.

Unaccustomed to rejection, Carter had never developed a controlled response. Multiple gawd-damns seemed to suffice; these were undoubtedly prolonged when he received North's May 24 financial projections. Within ten days the cost estimate had escalated $100,000; it would cost $1 million to open the show. "We have spent approximately $400,000 to date," North explained. "This week's costs will total $100,000. Next week we will have to have $245,000; the remaining two weeks, $250,000." In concluding his report, North, probably unintentionally, cited the crux of their financial distress. "Practically every item on the original budget — *made out without knowing anything about it* — has changed . . . but little. It has hung around $1,000,000 from the very start," he wrote. "Billy [Rose] said the first day he came in that while *some of the items were ridiculous,* the total was approximately correct and *wondered how we guessed so close.*"[23] This was another instance of the uninitiated invading the unknown, an oft-repeated story throughout the state in 1935 and 1936. Essentially this translated into cost overruns, a term that became popular a half-century later with defense contractors and nuclear power plants. The final costs of Casa Mañana ($224,170), the *Jumbo* building ($152,838), and the casino building ($60,000) all exceeded the original estimates. The final May 24 projections were: total construction (including architects' and contractors' fees), $588,802; equipment (staging and operations), $113,370; and miscellaneous expenses (including scenery, $40,000; costumes, $55,000; advertising, $50,000; and Rose's staff, $92,500), $366,500. Total: $1,068,672.[24]

In spite of the dismal financial outlook, apparently no one considered turning back or retrenching. North and Bert Honea, *Star-Telegram* business manager, had prepared a bare-bones budget that

[23]Author's italics, James M. North to Amon Carter (cover memorandum with "Cost Estimates as of May 24"), May 24, 1936, Carter Archives.
[24]Ibid.

everyone, including Rose, elected to live with. With much well-calculated bluster and ballyhoo, Rose forged ahead toward the July 1 opening day. Publicity and the selection of a supporting cast received high priority. Ned Alvord, Rose's colorful press agent, arrived in Fort Worth on April 13, and the two began developing a $50,000 advertising and publicity campaign. Within three weeks some fifty thousand color brochures were being mailed, filling requests throughout the United States and twenty-four foreign countries. Mayor Van Zandt Jarvis sent forty-eight brochures with his personal invitation to the nation's governors. He explained that a special day was being designated for each. "We are just friendly Western folks," he concluded, "and would be pleased to make your acquaintance."[25] In the Poultry Building at the northside Fat Stock Show facility, Alvord had begun assembling 225,000 pieces of outdoor promotional material for distribution throughout the Southwest. The targets: barn sides, billboards, railroad stations, and store windows. "Those dudes over there" would not go unchallenged.

WBAP, the *Star-Telegram* station, began a series of thirty-minute radio programs on May 1, heralding the approach of the exposition. Carter and the articulate Rose were frequent guests. The exposition publicity also took to the air in other ways. On April 14, Braniff Airways inaugurated its Fort Worth–Chicago service, the Centennial Flyer, and one month later a Stinson trimotored airplane left Meacham Field on a city-by-city aerial tour to New York to publicize the frontier show. The crew dressed appropriately in cowboy boots, cowboy hats, and plaid shirts. Rose took time off from his office routine to conduct Scripps-Howard roving reporter Ernie Pyle on an inspection of the exposition grounds; Pyle was on assignment to write a series on the Fort Worth and Dallas expositions.

Dallas, however, was never very far from Rose's machinations. He also followed Monnig's declaration to Arthur Kramer to promote the Frontier Exposition "in the manner best calculated to achieve the desired ends." Erecting a mammoth outdoor sign directly across the street from the central exposition in Dallas fell within that premise. Rose commissioned William E. Jary, Jr., chief designer for Corn Signs, Inc., in Fort Worth, to prepare the controversial visual message: "WILD & WHOO-PEE; 45 Minutes West; FORT WORTH FRONTIER; In Person; Paul

[25] *Forth Worth Star-Telegram*, May 22, 1936.

Whiteman, Sally Rand, Casa Mañana Revue; Billy Rose, Director General." Dallas complained again, this time to the local building inspector, but to no avail. Jary did, however, conform to an engineer's report, reducing the height 25 feet. The width, however, remained unchanged, extending the entire 130-foot length of the building and standing 60 feet above the ground, the equivalent of a six-story building.

Rose, meanwhile, was preoccupied with production problems. After filling the leading roles in the exposition shows with professional performers, his next problem was selecting a supporting cast. This proved to be a trying experience for the impatient New York producer. The Fort Worth shows marked the first time Rose had worked with amateur performers. To compromise with excellence was unthought of; he remained abrasively steadfast in his demands for quality. In two months of tryouts and auditions — interrupted with verbal abuse, intimidation, and the interminable rehearsals — some rank amateurs became overnight professionals. Rose elected to divide the casting of dancers, showgirls, and showboys about equally between professional performers and local amateurs. (The showgirls and showboys did not dance and recited no lines, but they appeared on stage appropriately costumed in pageantry scenes.) To fill these vacancies he placed an ad in the *Star-Telegraph*, and show business fever became a raging summer malady all over Texas. Hundreds of applicants, mostly young ladies accompanied by their mothers, converged on Fort Worth. Olive and Janice Nicolson of Longview, Texas, accompanied by Mrs. Nicolson, appeared in Rose's Sinclair Building office in late April for an interview. He liked their appearance, and his secretary handed them that much-sought-after slip of paper authorizing them to appear at the Texas Hotel for tryouts. The pressure, the competition, and the tension were frightening, Janice Nicolson Holmes remembered. Dance director Robert Alton, his two assistants, and Rose conducted the tryouts. She explained: "They called up three girls at a time and asked, 'Do a time-step and break. Please kick. Do a turn across the floor. Thank you.' We were given numbers and after a week or 10 days of tryouts, certain ones were called forward, others were told to go home." The Nicolsons received contracts; a pretty young blonde from Weatherford went home. On the third night of tryouts she and her six backup girls, the Martinettes, all dressed in black tuxedos, performed a routine to "Sophisticated Lady." Rose liked the act and offered the leader and some of her troupe spots in the chorus line. She refused, explaining she was auditioning as a featured act. Rose was indignant. "I'm not running an amateur show," he exhorted. "You start in the chorus and if you have anything, you work up!" She didn't, and instead embarked shortly for New York. The rest is theatrical history; her name was Mary Hagman (Martin).[26]

Rose was less discriminating in casting *The Last Frontier*. The nature of the show deemed it so. He put out a call for 200 square dancers (he hired 100), 98 cavalrymen, 110 Indians, 75 cowboys and cowgirls, stagecoach skinners, early settlers, bull whackers, 250 horses, 100 cattle, a double herd of buffalo, and a train of covered wagons. The War Department supplied the cavalrymen, assigning 87 officers and men and ninety-two horses from the Second Dragoons, United States Cavalry, Fort Riley, Kansas, to a temporary post on the exposition grounds. The Indians were procured from various reservations and established a camp near the cavalry post. Selecting the 100 square dancers required some care; he conducted the tryouts and then made a seemingly ludicrous decision. He engaged Russian ballet master Alexander Oumansky to coach the square dancers!

By the end of May, with the casting nearly complete and construction well under way at the exposition site, Rose established a subbase of operations in Monnig's Wholesale Store (the cast called it the warehouse) located at the corner of Main and Houston Streets. The sixth floor was vacant, and Monnig gave Rose the use of the facility, without cost, to start rehearsals and begin cutting and sewing costumes. A call went out for 150 seamstresses, and on May 17, A. M. Blumberg of the Brooks Brothers Costume Company of New York City arrived in Fort Worth to supervise the work. The weather had turned unseasonably warm by the middle of May, and without air conditioning the sixth-floor windows remained open day and night. To the casual passerby came the unmistakable sounds of a musical show in rehearsal — the beat of hundreds of dancing feet, the inevitable practice piano, and the stentorian shouts of an irate producer above it all. With opening night less than two months away, they would never make it. That date would have to be changed.

[26] Janice Nicolson Holmes to Kenneth Ragsdale, February 2, 1978, in personal files. In *My Heart Belongs* (New York: Morrow, 1976), pp. 55–57, Mary Martin states that Rose told her to "tend to the family, the diapers. Stay out of show business."

14

AN EMPIRE ON PARADE

The situation over at Dallas's Fair Park was becoming brighter by the day. Seven thousand men working in three shifts were near completing the seemingly impossible task begun some ten months earlier. The centennial exhibit buildings were all complete, the Hall of Negro Life had been accepted, and the Federal Exhibit Building lacked only the finishing touches. As artists applied the decorative frescoes to the exterior walls of the Varied Industries Building, exhibitors were already installing their displays. All street paving was complete, 75 percent of the midway buildings were under construction, and the 750-foot reflecting basin in the Esplanade of State was practically complete, as was the lagoon in the civic complex. On May 20, George Dahl announced that the construction program was far enough ahead of schedule for the exposition to be open on June 1, if that were necessary. This determination to complete the job on time was reflected on signs placed on every major building: "_____ days until June 6. We shall not fail." With the approach of June came the dreaded spring rains, and still the numbers steadily declined — ten . . . nine . . . eight . . . seven. Amidst the organized confusion the workmen scrambled while the sculptors cast the remaining statues and exhibitors scurried to make the approaching deadline.

The Hall of State, the most expensive and most symbolic structure in the complex, remained the exposition's greatest disappointment. A labor strike had stopped construction; completion remained months away. It was, however, the thousands of nonstrikers who were helping reverse the post-Depression Dallas economy. Building permits exceeded the $4 million mark by late March, 1936, approximating the total for the entire preceding year. One month later that total reached $6,364,490, placing Dallas second in the state to Houston's $8,010,755 in building activity.[1] By late April the weekly centennial payroll

[1]*Dallas Morning News*, April 26, 1936.

reached $300,000. One month later Works Director Ray Foley esti-
mated the work force had grown to ten thousand with a weekly income of $400,000. He predicted a gradual decline after June 15.[2]

Each building completion touched off a chain reaction, both in
Dallas and across the state. When the Park Commission accepted
the Art Museum from the Rife Construction Company, Richard Foster Howard, director of the Dallas Museum of Fine Arts, began making preparations to close the museum's temporary downtown facility
and move to Fair Park. By June 1, gallery assistant Everett Spruce
was busily unpacking material in the new museum. Even the Galveston wharf responded to progress along the exposition midway. As
Dallas oil executive D. Harold Byrd supervised the operation, dock
workers gingerly maneuvered a power crane above the deck of the
Mallory Lines *Medina* to hoist the huge Curtiss Condor twin-engine
biplane onto an adjacent Santa Fe flatcar for transportation to Dallas. The Condor, which still rested on its ski-equipped landing gear,
had served as the flagship on Rear Admiral Richard E. Byrd's recent
South Pole expedition. D. Harold Byrd, cousin of the explorer, sponsored a midway concession, Admiral Byrd's "Little America," featuring the historic aircraft.

With the approach of summer vacation for Texas' million-and-a-
half school children, the tempo of centennial preparations also accelerated. On April 27, State Superintendent of Schools Dr. L. A.
Woods, State Supervisor of Music Nell Parmley, and Centennial School
and Club Director Elithe Hamilton Beal began conducting a series
of statewide rehearsals of more than 125,000 public school students.
The objective was to select a fifty thousand-voice All-Texas Chorus
to perform at the Central Exposition on June 13. From two thousand
to seven thousand students rehearsed at twenty-four sites around the
state to prepare for the concert.[3]

The advance sale of 2 million tickets reflected the wide interest
in the forthcoming exposition. A fifteen-man sales force worked within
the state, and American Express purchased 300,000 tickets for national distribution. Some three weeks before the scheduled June 6 open-

[2]Ibid., May 26, 1936.
[3]While on the statewide tour, Mrs. Beal also publicized Write-A-Letter Week. During
the week of May 11–18, school students, members of women's clubs, and civic organizations were encouraged to write residents in other states telling them of the Texas centennial
celebrations.

ing, few advance tickets remained unsold. (The general admission price was fifty cents for adults and twenty-five cents for children under twelve years of age.) The advance ticket sales, exhibit and concession income, and bond revenue placed the exposition in a strong financial position, at least temporarily. According to Assistant Comptroller A. E. Moyle, exposition income totaled $2.5 million, including $300,000 in ticket sales.[4] By mid-May the exposition management had already assembled a staff of approximately 560 young trainees to work as cashiers, ticket takers, guides, and guards. Initially 176 young women, ages ranging from eighteen to thirty, served as cashiers, while 159 young men served as ticket takers, 144 (mostly recruited from college and university bands) as guides, and between 70 and 80 as guards. The guides initially doubled as musicians in an exposition marching band. The cashiers and ticket takers were assigned to five entrances to the exposition grounds. The staff worked in three shifts; gates were open from 9:00 A.M. until midnight.

The City of Dallas had also begun preparing for the surge of exposition visitors. Expecting an overnight guest population of 150,000 persons, Frank M. Smith, manager of the Centennial Housing Bureau, announced on June 4 that there were more than 50,000 rooms registered with the bureau, and 250 guides stood ready to direct visitors to their accommodations. The twenty-one member Dallas Hotel Association offered 5,917 rooms priced from one dollar to eight dollars for singles and a dollar twenty-five to ten dollars for doubles. Visitors could also choose from 858 rooms in twenty-six nonmember hotels, ranging in price from seventy-five cents to four dollars and fifty cents.[5] Southern Methodist University even opened its unused dormitory facilities to centennial visitors, as only a few rooms in its three dormitories were reserved for summer school students. Twenty-seven tourist camps listed 659 cottages varying in price from $1.00 to $4.50.[6] Some homeowners advertised individually: "A1 — Attractive room you'd appreciate. Radio, fan, ice water; two gentlemen. Ten blocks Centennial; $5 week each"; "Attractive front bedroom, gentlemen only, $3."[7] The Texas Tent City, apparently born out of the need of Depression-era travelers, appeared the least desirable accommo-

[4]*Dallas Morning News*, May 16, 1936.
[5]Directory of Dallas Hotels, Centennial Collection, DHS.
[6]Directory of Tourist Camps, Centennial Collection, DHS.
[7]*Dallas Morning News*, June 13, 1936.

dations—wood framed floors and walls, covered with a tent top. Located at the corner of South Haskell and Fitzhugh Streets, the management proclaimed hotel accommodations, Simmons bed, 4-H headquarters, and police guard. No prices were listed.

Traffic control and visitor courtesy were second only to housing as city priorities. The city council approved an $85,000 expenditure to improve the traffic control system, ordered one-way thoroughfares in the Fair Park area (traffic circled the park clockwise), and eliminated most on-street parking. Dallas civic leader John Stemmons, then a young man just out of college, recognized the need for off-street parking in the exposition area and elected to get in on the anticipated centennial business boom. He leased some land in the park area, established several lighted parking lots, "and hired a bunch of people to be my parking attendants." But the anticipated demand for exposition parking never developed; "we never made enough parking revenue to pay for the uniforms we had for the men."[8] Competition was probably a factor. By the time the fair opened, there were some 40,000 automobile parking spaces within two blocks of the exposition charging from fifteen to twenty-five cents for all-day parking.

Police, hotel attendants, taxi drivers, streetcar conductors, and citizens in general were made acutely aware of the importance of presenting a positive image to the out-of-town visitors. The police department set the pace in late March with "an enforced exodus from Dallas streets of all beggars, moochers, and mendicants." This was the "aftermath of the pre-Centennial clean-up drive which saw the cessation of all forms of gambling, from marble tables to dice games."[9] (The total effectiveness of the "cleanup drive" would be questioned later.) Local newspapers addressed the public image matter editorially. "Both Dallas and Texas has [sic] much to gain by giving guests from distant states a favorable impression of their visits here," wrote the *News* editor. "The goodwill of their visits will become an important factor in the future development of the Lone Star State."[10]

By the end of May, downtown Dallas nightclubs and restaurants had begun to feel the impact of the precentennial invasion. Big-name bands and movie stars illuminated the downtown marquees. Actor

[8]Stemmons interview, May 29, 1978.
[9]*Dallas Morning News*, March 27, 1936.
[10]Ibid., June 12, 1936.

George Raft was advertised as the guest of honor at the grand opening of the French Casino, while Freddy Martin's orchestra opened
the Peacock Terrace summer season (no air conditioning) in the Baker
Hotel on May 29. The opening night dinner-dance cost only $2.50
per person, confirming Fenton Baker's promise of no increased prices
during the centennial. Chez Maurice, "the enchanting sky terrace atop
the Santa Fe Building," entertained its first guests on June 4. Henry
Halstead's orchestra and a six-act floor show headed the bill. The opening night dinner and cover charge was five dollars per person; uniformed attendants parked the customers' cars.

Other downtown restaurants were also enjoying a business resurgence. The Semos brothers, both Greek immigrants, operated the coffee
shop in the Jefferson Hotel across from Union Station. During the
early 1930s, as their business steadily declined and indebtedness
mounted, they confided to their banker, R. L. Thornton, that their
future in Dallas appeared hopeless. Thornton encouraged them to
hang on a little longer. "He had faith in them; he had faith in the
city," recalled Chris Semos, the son and nephew. "If you can imagine
some Greek immigrants who didn't speak English . . . that well, being told by a crusty old banker, 'Have faith. There'll be something
coming to Dallas called a centennial'— he knew what it would do for
Dallas. . . . Sure enough, the centennial did come and . . . they got
out of a Depression's worth of debts in those six months that the centennial was here."[11]

While the late-night revelers celebrated downtown, the around-
the-clock preparations at the fairground gained momentum as the
countdown to opening day continued unabated — six . . . five . . . four.
George Anderson, superintendent of buildings and grounds, issued
cleanup orders on June 1. On the following Thursday he barred all
automobiles from the grounds except delivery trucks. Paul Massmann,
still pushing the exhibitors to complete their displays by June 6, ordered that no work would be permitted on opening day; finishing
touches would have to be applied at night after the crowds had left.
The following night exposition technicians first tested the entire lighting system under a full capacity load. The results were astounding.

[11] Interview with Chris Semos, Dallas, Texas, June 6, 1979. The Semos family later established "The Torch," a well-known Greek restaurant in the Oak Cliff section of Dallas.
State Representative Chris Semos served as chairman of the Texas Sesquicentennial Commission.

"Night visitors who witnessed the first full illumination . . . of the 12,000,000 watt power were awed into silence by its beauty," wrote one journalist. "While 24 search lights of 60,000,000 candle power each cast beams into the air, visible for 25 miles, the grounds presented scenes never before witnessed in this section."[12] The final days of preparation also witnessed the arrival of the permanent military garrison to be stationed at Camp Stephen F. Austin on the exposition grounds. The garrison consisted of army, navy, and marine personnel who participated in daily drills, parades, and official functions.

Just when everything appeared to be progressing so smoothly, pandemonium broke loose on the exposition grounds. A frightened, raging Brahma bull broke loose from Col. W. T. Johnson's Wild West Rodeo pens and charged everything in sight. As workmen and concessionaires ran for cover, six cowpunchers chased after the bull on foot, while Policeman J. C. Dorris pushed ahead on his motorcycle warning the people to flee. The bull and his pursuers left the exposition grounds and headed down Pennsylvania Avenue. When the frightened animal reached a vacant lot between Truck and Fourth Streets, one of the more adept cowboys roped it and ended the unscheduled performance of Colonel Johnson's rodeo. The episode did, however, confirm for many out-of-state concessionaires that Texas was still a part of the wild and woolly West. There was one other minor preopening emergency: the egg-laying contest scheduled to begin on Monday, June 1, was delayed until Tuesday because, according to Poultry Director Walter Burton, more hens entered than were expected.[13]

Three . . . two . . . one! On Thursday, June 4, the final cleanup of the grounds began, and by nightfall, with opening day still one day away, all was in order for the first visitors. On Friday night, June 5, major exhibitors and concessionaires held open house for invited guests. The most sought-after invitation was to the Centennial Club, a private club housed in the replica of the SS *Normandie*. This was also the home of the infamous "Streets of Paris" concession. The Centennial Club occupied three air-conditioned "decks," charged dues of twenty-five dollars, and became *the* place to entertain out-of-town guests during the exposition. On June 5, the club held a dinner dance to preview a dress (or undress) rehearsal of Andre Lasky's French

---

[12] *Dallas Morning News*, June 3, 1936.
[13] *Dallas Morning News*, May 21, June 2, 1936.

Revue. Billed as "Saucy! Spicey! Sophisticated," the revue consisted of "forty-five continental artists, twenty-four glorified Belles Parisiennes and 1,000 sensations." The revue's prime sensation was Mlle. Corrine (actually Corrine Boese from Kaufman, Texas), performing her then-famous apple dance, Dallas's response to Sally Rand's fans and bubbles. Jack Gordon, *Fort Worth Star-Telegram* amusements editor, attended the preview and reported to his readers that "the ladies are posing over there as nekked as the day they were born. . . . [Some] wore panties that would have a hard time hiding a vaccination scar." Gordon speculated on when "the cops will start swooping down and they will have to start pasting butterflies here and there."[14] At Chicago it was three weeks; at Dallas, it was somewhat longer.

If any exposition eve fun-seekers tried to sleep late the following morning, they were rudely awakened at 8:00 A.M., when every factory and train whistle in Dallas blew full blast, signaling that the exposition was about to open. The countdown to June 6 was over. After years of anticipation, some ten months of record-breaking construction, and $5.5 million in local funding, it was inevitable that Dallas would produce an opening celebration commensurate with the occasion — the dedication of the Texas Centennial Central Exposition, the centerpiece of the state's year-long birthday party. For two days thousands of visitors had been pouring into the city. In addition to two special trains, all regularly scheduled trains arriving at Union Station carried extra coaches Friday and Saturday morning, while the fledgling airlines reported capacity loads on most inbound flights. After more than a decade of publicity, everyone wanted to be there for the grand opening. Before leaving Austin, Governor Allred requested that all state departments close Saturday to permit state employees to attend the Dallas festivities. (In 1936, state employees worked on Saturday.)

Promptly at 10:30 A.M., as sixteen Army Air Corps planes roared overhead, the centennial parade began to trek slowly along Main Street toward the exposition site some three miles to the east. Eight motorcycle policemen led the parade, followed by six horsemen presenting the six flags of the state's four-hundred-year history. Gen. John A. Hulen, the grand marshal, rode in the first car, followed by twenty-five Texas Rangers on horseback and the United States Marine Band

---

[14]*Fort Worth Star-Telegram*, June 6, 1936.

(which also played "The Eyes of Texas" and "Dixie"). Governor Allred, his son Jim Boy in cowboy costume, and Dallas County sheriff
Smoot Schmid came next, leading the entourage of dignitaries that
included Secretary of Commerce Daniel C. Roper. These were followed by various units of the nation's armed forces. Twelve hundred
national guardsmen protected the line of march as the three-mile-
long "Empire on Parade" passed before more than 250,000 spectators.
Sam Acheson, dean of the *Dallas Morning News* journalists, captured
the emotional impact of the opening day festivities: "Texas' inimitable
tribute to the great dead who won its freedom . . . swung wide its
gates Saturday before the largest crowd ever gathered in the Southwest. . . . More than 250,000 deliriously carefree persons joined in
making it the greatest occasion in the history of Dallas and the most
notable event in Texas since Sam Houston and his men changed the
course of the New World at San Jacinto."[15]

For those unable to witness the day-long spectacle in person, a bat-
tery of newsreel companies and Dallas radio stations provided in-depth
coverage of the event. Radio station WFAA scheduled six different
time slots of centennial coverage varying in length from fifteen minutes
to more than one hour. Coverage began with an 8:30 A.M. broadcast
from an American Airlines plane in which Gayle Northe, fashion com-
mentator, described scenes from the air and presented greetings from
a planeload of prominent guests, including Governor Allred, R. L.
Thornton, and Dallas Mayor George Sergeant. During the thirty-
minute broadcast from the airliner, the occupants showered Dallas
with fresh gardenias.

The official opening of the exposition, held at high noon at the main
entrance, was also broadcast nationally over the two major networks.
The ceremony was scheduled to last four minutes and fifty seconds,
but unfortunately, it ran overtime. All began well: Governor Allred
inserted a gold and jeweled key into a special ceremonial lock that
opened the gates of the exposition.[16] Then the governor introduced
Secretary Roper, who spoke the cue words, "Texas welcomes the world,"

[15] *Dallas Morning News*, June 7, 1936.
[16] The ceremonial key, designed and manufactured by Dallas jeweler Arthur A. Everts,
was solid gold inlaid with diamonds and precious stones from different countries of the
world. At the close of the exposition Everts placed the key on display in his jewelry store,
where it was stolen in 1952. It was never recovered. When crafted in 1936, it was valued
at $50,000.

which were supposed to activate a sophisticated electronic mechanism to cut a ribbon, the last barrier to the fairgrounds. It didn't work! Art Linkletter, who shared CBS announcing duties with veteran Ted Husing at the main gate ceremony, credits the unexpected disasters of that day for sharpening his communicative skills. Forced to improvise under fire, he remembered aging professionally during the ensuing debacle:

> Two mishaps forced us to ad lib for extended periods of time. . . . The U.S. Marine Band got lost somewhere in Dallas marching toward the gates and showed up an hour late. A tricky technological project in which a message was sent from inside the Fair, around the world by wireless and telegraph, was supposed to come back a few feet from where it was sent . . . activating a cutting device that would shear the ribbon and announce the opening of the Fair. Somehow the message was lost somewhere over the steppes of Russia and we had to improvise, and pretend the message had been received.[17]

With the ribbon sheared manually, the gates to the exposition were at last open. The official party entered the fair grounds accompanied by Madge Houston Thornall, age six, a great-great-granddaughter of Sam Houston, and Louis Randall Bryan III, age ten, a descendant of Moses Austin and a great-nephew of Stephen F. Austin. Following a luncheon at the Centennial Club, Secretary Roper presided at the 5:00 P.M. dedication of the Federal Building, visited the Hall of Negro Life, and at 6:30 P.M. delivered a radio address from the Crystal Ballroom of the Baker Hotel. Roper's speech, "Texas and the Nation," consisted primarily of political platitudes but ended on a surprising note. He appraised the role of blacks in the nation's progress, an experience dramatized in the federally funded Negro Life exhibit hall. "No people in all history can show greater progress in their achievement in seventy-three years than the American Negro," he stated. "This is traceable to their patient, loyal, patriotic attitude toward their country and to their gifts of soul and song."[18] The fall elections were less than six months away.

---

[17]Art Linkletter, Los Angeles, California, to Kenneth B. Ragsdale, July 5, 1979, in possession of author.

[18]*Dallas Morning News,* June 8, 1936.

Special features kept the 117,625 first-day visitors entertained con-
tinuously from noon until midnight. During the afternoon, units of
the Army Air Corps performed aerial acrobatics over the exposition
grounds. A squadron of ground-strafing attack planes swept the fair
grounds at treetop level, followed by a squadron of 200-mile-an-hour
pursuit (fighter) planes that performed simulated combat maneuvers
against a cloudless sky. As night fell over the exposition, the festivities
gained momentum, creating a pageantry of light, action, color, and
sound that held the spectators in awe. A flight of nine Army Air Corps
planes circled the grounds in T-formation, carrying electrical signs
that spelled "TEXAS — 1936." But "the climax of the day came after
8:30 P.M.," Sam Acheson reported, "when the exposition lighting system was brought into play, starting from almost complete darkness
and ending in awe its multi-colored brilliance."[19] The Esplanade of
State, a concourse three hundred feet wide and one thousand feet
long leading to the Hall of State, contained a two-hundred-by-seven-
hundred-foot reflecting basin with concealed light sources that transformed the central fountains into multicolored geysers of magnificent
beauty. Along the main concourses, floodlights illuminated the decorative pylons and bathed the building facades with subtle shades of
blues, greens, reds, and yellows. This was the work of C. M. Cutler,
the lighting consultant for the Century of Progress, whom George
Dahl had engaged to design the Central Exposition lighting system.
Of Cutler's innovative work at Dallas, a contemporary technical journal said: "The lighting at Dallas attracted more publicity than any
other aspect of [the] fair [and] set a new high in several features, including subtle and effective application of color, inspiring murals and
sculpture, and the vivid utilization of a historical theme. . . . Never
before has it been possible to experience so fully the power of skillfully coordinated color, brightness, and luminous pattern, and the
fascination of subtle mobility. Here crowds lingered for long periods,
intrigued and charmed by the breath-taking loveliness of the scene."[20]

At midnight the exposition lights began to dim, and the remainder
of the hundred thousand first-day visitors began making their way
toward the exits. The fair was off to a good start, and Sunday's 87,801
attendance was equally encouraging. Each hour a sixty-foot-high rep-

[19] Ibid., June 7, 1936.
[20] *Magazine of Light*, Exposition Issue, 1936, pp. 2–19.

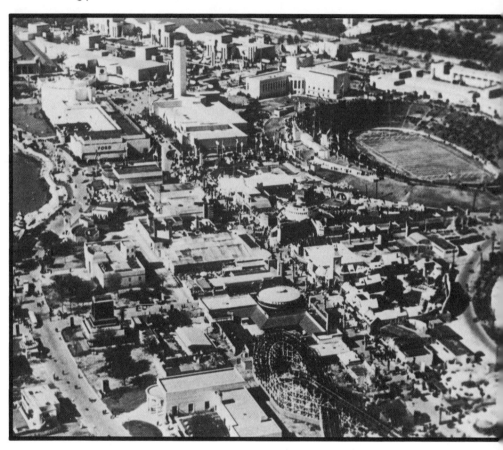

Aerial view of Texas Centennial Exposition, looking northwest. Right foreground, midway and concessions area; left foreground, Hall of Domestic Arts, National Cash Register exhibit, and Aquarium; left background, Ford Building and lagoon; center background, Federal Building and tower, Hall of State behind Cotton Bowl, and Esplanade of State in distance. (Courtesy Charles Kavanaugh Collection)

The Federal Building housed exhibits of some thirty federal departments and agencies at the Dallas exposition. Designed by Dallas architect Donald S. Nelson, the 100-foot tower dominated the exposition skyline. A gold-leaf eagle, designed by Raoul Josset and executed by José Martin, tops the tower. Julian Garnsey is credited with the sculptural frieze depicting the early history of Texas. Now designated the Tower Building, it houses the executive offices of the State Fair of Texas. (Author's collection)

Many exposition visitors witnessed their first live radio broadcast in the glass-enclosed Gulf Studios, which also operated the exposition's public address system. (Courtesy Elithe Hamilton Kirkland)

The Ford Building contained technical exhibits on the construction of that company's automobiles. Like the Gulf Studios, it was a prime example of art deco design; both structures have been demolished. (Courtesy Elithe Hamilton Kirkland)

The Dallas Museum of Fine Arts, erected for the 1936 Texas Centennial Exposition, is the major structure in a permanent civic center funded by the City of Dallas. The building now houses the Southwest Museum of Science and Technology. (Author's collection)

During the 1936 Texas Centennial Exposition, General Motors Corporation converted Fair Park Auditorium into an automobile show room and celebrity bandstand featuring the top orchestras of the Big Band era. The Hall of Negro Life
appears in the left background. An exposition tour bus approaches from the left.
(Courtesy Dallas Historical Society)

Exposition architects maintained the art deco theme throughout the quarter-mile-long midway. Most attractions were both entertaining and informative, with a small measure of "flesh." (Courtesy Dallas Historical Society)

Mechanical dinosaurs attracted visitors to the Sinclair Oil Company's Centennial Exposition exhibit. William E. Shoemaker maintained the internal mechanism. (Courtesy Elithe Hamilton Kirkland)

A National Cash Register replica reported hourly attendance at the Centennial Exposition. (Courtesy Elithe Hamilton Kirkland)

Lines begin forming to purchase tickets for the next performance of *Cavalcade of Texas*, the big hit of the Texas Centennial Exposition. (Courtesy Texas/Dallas History and Archives Division, Dallas Public Library)

A scene from *Cavalcade of Texas* depicting immigration into Texas. (Courtesy Dallas Historical Society)

A replica of the S.S. *Normandie* housed the infamous Streets of Paris, a show-place featuring female nudity and the membership-only Centennial Club. (Courtesy Charles Kavanaugh Collection)

lica of a cash register mounted on top of the National Cash Register company's exhibit recorded the day's attendance. The weekday tally, however, dropped perceptibly: Monday it was 40,322; Tuesday, 29,425; Wednesday, 22,495; and Thursday, 27,109.[21]

Another banner weekend arrived with the president of the United States on Friday, June 12. Nine special trains were scheduled to arrive in Dallas early Friday morning from Missouri, Louisiana, and various points in Texas, carrying exposition visitors to see the president. Facing his first reelection campaign in November, President Roosevelt scheduled a southwestern precampaign swing through Texas, stopping at Houston to visit the San Jacinto Battleground and at San Antonio to see the Alamo. En route to Dallas the special train paused in Austin long enough for the chief executive to flip a switch that touched off a dynamite charge that broke ground for the Texas Memorial Museum.[22]

The president's day in Dallas began with another festive parade up Main Street — the second parade of epic proportion. An estimated half-million people greeted him along the three-mile route to the exposition grounds. "Bands played, guns boomed in salute and crowds yelled a welcome the instant the President and his party [appeared in view]. . . . The streets followed by the presidential parade were solid with masses of humanity. Applause followed the President's car like waves rolling over their heads."[23] President and Mrs. Roosevelt toured the exposition in an automobile, departing only once at the Cotton Bowl, where the president delivered an address that was broadcast nationwide. "I have come here to bear the tribute of the Nation to you on your hundredth birthday; you are a hundred years young!" he began. "This great Centennial Exposition is not for Texans alone — it is for the people of all the other forty-seven states as well," he con-

[21]Attendance Records, Centennial Collection, DHS. All further attendance citations are taken from this document.

[22]On June 1, prior to the president's arrival, the University of Texas launched its six-month-long centennial celebration. By July 30, campuswide exhibits had attracted 90,557 visitors. University students conducted a sale of 1.5 million Texas centennial half-dollars at one dollar each to help fund the Texas Memorial Museum. Extreme security precautions were exercised to ensure the president's safety in Texas. Missouri-Kansas-Texas company track walkers inspected every foot of the track between San Antonio and Dallas. Telephone and telegraph lines were tested, and twenty minutes before the presidential special departed San Antonio, a pilot train bearing the company board chairman and general manager proceeded ahead as added security.

[23]Dallas Morning News, June 13, 1936.

tinued. "I hope that they will take full advantage of it." He alluded to the better times ahead, praised the farmers for their stand against monopoly, defended "the yeomanry of business and industry and agriculture," cited the benefits of the good neighbor policy, and concluded some twenty-six minutes later, "I salute the Empire of Texas."[24] Although the high for the day reached only eighty-nine degrees, the heat on the floor of the Cotton Bowl was oppressive, and during the address a young soldier, standing at attention, fainted. He was rushed out of the arena on a stretcher; throughout the day Mrs. Roosevelt kept inquiring about his condition.[25]

The president's visit drew 101,848 visitors to the exposition on June 12. The following day the National Cash Register recorded 86,301 people through the turnstyles. More than a thousand buses and trucks and thirty-five special trains brought some fifty thousand student members of the "world's largest choir" to perform in the Cotton Bowl. A portion of the program was broadcast nationwide, and again the heat took its toll. As the local announcer introducing the musical selections, Art Linkletter was an eyewitness to another exposition disaster. He later recalled "a program in the Cotton Bowl where 50,000 school children from all over Texas, trained to sing a program of [Texas] songs and billed as the largest choir in the world. During the CBS broadcast of the program in mid-day, I stood on the stage and saw the astonishing and disastrous sight of hundreds of children fainting during the program while alarmed supervisors were leading others out of the Bowl to avoid heat prostration. I think we finished the program with about half the chorus gone, either physically or in person."[26]

Before the program ended, some two hundred firemen (over half of them officially off-duty) and exposition guides milled through the crowd carrying fainting children to the four first aid stations in the Cotton Bowl. When those facilities became overcrowded, the guides established a makeshift infirmary by spreading a tent over the rodeo stalls at one end of the stadium. Estimates vary on the number of casualties; at least 250 were treated at the Exposition Emergency Hos-

[24]Presidential Address, J. Percival Rice Scrapbook, Mrs. J. Percival Rice, Dallas.

[25]L. B. Houston interview, April 3, 1978. Following a luncheon in the Adolphus Hotel's Century Room, Jesse H. Jones, B. J. Toomey, his secretary, and Mr. and Mrs. W. P. Hobby were returning to Houston in a private plane that caught fire in flight and crash-landed in a field in Ellis County. The passengers survived; one of the pilots died later of burns.

[26]Linkletter to Ragsdale, July 5, 1979.

pital during the day. During the emergency many students became separated from their parents or their school groups. John Henry Kavanaugh, one of the exposition guides, recalled he worked until after midnight helping to reunite the various groups.[27]

The second week's midweek attendance (Monday through Thursday) of 151,881 exceeded the preceding midweek attendance by 32,530, and that Friday through Sunday there were 157,608 visitors. A special celebration of Emancipation Day on Friday, June 19, and the dedication of the Hall of Negro Life contributed to the week's attendance. Although the primary focus of the Hall of Negro Life was the advancing role of blacks in American society, racial respect was a goal that remained somewhere in the state's second century. The headline in the *Dallas Morning News* reported the event with a degrading social statement: "Dallas eats cold supper and cotton patches neglected. . . . Mandy wasn't there when Dallas sat down to cold supper Friday night for with Rastus, and thousands of carefree members of her race, she was busy putting in a glorious Juneteenth at the magic Texas Centennial Exposition. . . . [where] hordes of merry makers stormed the purified Midway, its strip shows deleted for the day." The day, nevertheless, was a milestone: the opening of a major exhibit facility at a World's Fair dedicated to black achievements.

The third week, midweek attendance fell below that of the two preceding weeks, and the weekend total dropped to a disappointing 116,457. The heat was undoubtedly a factor. Throughout the week of Sunday, June 14, the temperature hovered around 100 degrees (it seemed much hotter with all the pavement) and reached 105 degrees on June 21. The comparative comfort of the nighttime hours and the beauty of the lighting system attracted most summertime visitors after 6:00 P.M. During the first week of the exposition George Dahl, visiting the exposition at night, met a friend pushing his invalid wife in a wheelchair. As he greeted the couple he noticed the wife was crying. Dahl inquired, "Is there anything I can do for you?" "No," replied the friend, "my wife just thinks it's so beautiful she can't help but — but shed a tear." Almost a half-century later Dahl reflected on that episode — the tender emotional response to a vision of beauty — as one of the genuine rewards for his months of effort to build the exposition. He also confessed his pleasure with his creation: "I'll say

[27]Kavanaugh interview, July 30, 1982.

the same thing that Lord Byron said of Paris, 'In spite of her warts and blemishes, I love her still.'"[28]

The warts and the blemishes were comparatively few and mostly confined to the midway. At the English Village, the Falstaff Tavern remained under construction, and the actors at the Old Globe Theater performed on an unfinished stage. Tony Sarg's Marionette Theater still lacked some of its paraphernalia, and workmen labored around the clock there and at the Old Globe, installing the air conditioning systems. Throughout the first week of the fair, the Museum of Natural History staff worked eighteen-hour shifts installing the wildlife exhibits, while laborers completed laying the rubber tile floor in the museum lobby. The rough concrete in the exhibit halls remained uncovered. And still the people came, fascinated with everything they saw, including the work in progress. Other than the still-under-construction Hall of State, the exposition's one great blemish was the historical pageant, the *Cavalcade of Texas*. Two weeks after the exposition opened the writers were still revising the script.

The *Cavalcade* was an undertaking of almost unbelievable magnitude. Before the old racetrack grandstand spread the "world's largest stage," a plot of ground 300 feet wide and 170 feet deep with fabricated bluffs and mountains that rose from the plains to a height of sixty feet. Spectators sat in the grandstand, which also housed a sophisticated lighting and sound system. The voices of the on-stage actors were not audible, so the dialogue was synchronized with other actors speaking in a sound booth. The script called for eighteen reversible sets mounted on wheels that were switched to tracks on turntables in the wings. These were manually pushed on stage for the four-hundred-year-long saga, whose scenes shifted from galleon to oxart and presidio to mission. Ships moved onto the great stage in real water. During scenery changes, a forty-foot water screen sprayed upward (flooded by colored lights at night) to obscure the action from the spectators' view. Jan Isbelle Fortune, Texas poet and dramatist, wrote the script; David Guion, internationally known Texas composer, wrote the theme song, "Cowboy Love Song"; and Mark Hamilton served as the original director. And therein lay part of the problem.

Cavalcade, the Centennial Corporation's one great acknowledgment of Texas history, appeared doomed from the beginning. Charles

[28]Dahl interview, April 6, 1978.

P. Turner, the corporation's original finance and special events director who launched the $110,000 project, died unexpectedly on March 5, when the show was some three months into production. The *Cavalcade*'s future remained temporarily in doubt until General Manager W. A. Webb placed his assistant, Bill Kittrell, in charge of the production; Kittrell left major responsibility for the staging to Hamilton. Rehearsals continued, but on the eve of the scheduled June 6 opening, the show ran almost four hours long, an impossible length when two shows were scheduled each night. Hamilton refused to cut the show, and during the first week of the exposition Webb replaced him with Blanding Sloan, the lighting director. He also placed A. L. Vollmann in charge of production. The cast rebelled, and it appeared momentarily that the project would have to be scrapped. When Vollmann called a cast meeting in the grandstand to outline his new policies, R. L. Thornton, Webb, and Kittrell joined him at the meeting to evidence their support. During Vollmann's talk, Hamilton arose unexpectedly from a remote section of the grandstand and demanded an explanation for his removal. His appearance was the emotional spark that incited the discontent of his supporters, who "charged the stands. Members of the cast were in full costume and makeup. Women and children cried. Then one hysterical woman screamed 'Remember the Alamo,' and instantly a scene took form which the actors had been attempting for weeks to simulate. The whole affair had its ridiculous aspect as well as near-tragedy implications."[29]

In four days of continuous rehearsals, Vollmann and Sloan cut the show to approximately seventy-five minutes and added a new finale.[30] The show finally opened Sunday night, June 21, with two performances at 8:15 P.M. and 10:00 P.M. John Rosenfield, cognizant of the project's turbulent history, attended the Saturday night preview and reported: "'Cavalcade' was born in agony but apparently is a lusty offspring of the Centennial spirit. . . . There was a little trouble when the Alamo ran off the track but the machinery meshed otherwise."[31]

[29]Undated and unidentified newspaper clipping, R. L. Thornton Scrapbook.

[30]Art Linkletter reported he helped rewrite and coproduce the revised edition of *Cavalcade*. His name, however, does not appear in the program credits. A. L. Vollmann produced *Cavalcade of the Golden West* in 1939 at the San Francisco World's Fair, and Art Linkletter wrote the script. The following year they produced *America! Cavalcade of a Nation*, at the same location.

[31]*Dallas Morning News*, June 21, 1936.

Vollmann had quickly turned a failure into a success. One week after *Cavalcade* opened he wrote a show business friend in Cleveland explaining that his effort had yielded both a popular and financially profitable production:

> The press has been very generous and the people that worked on it in the organization claim it is the finest thing ever done in outdoor show business. . . . We are turning them away for two performances a day . . . and we are getting considerable cash. . . . It pleases the audiences to have re-enactments of historical scenes so we just pour it on. . . . Our expense down here for operating is terrific and I hope to have that in hand in the next 15 days. [The original cast, staff, and crew totaled nearly 260 people.] Mr. Hamilton set it up without any knowledge of cost or operation at about $14,000.00 per week. I am going to bring it down without any noticeable change in the performance to half of that.[32]

The *Cavalcade of Texas* proved to be *the* hit of the exposition. Constant complaints about crowd management (one customer sustained broken ribs while attempting to purchase tickets) seemed not to deter the eager throngs waiting to pay forty cents to see the $250,000 historical pageant (the original budget was $110,000). Between sixty thousand and seventy thousand people a week sat spellbound as the overture ended, the lights dimmed, and a faint spotlight focused on a lone Indian standing atop the mountain in the center of the stage. The prologue began: "Out of the pages of history comes the story of the Cavalcade of Texas, marching onward through four hundred years up the steep peaks of empire. A mighty commonwealth has been robbed out of the vast wilderness of the Southwest." By early September five hundred thousand people had seen *Cavalcade:* this amounted to approximately one out of every six exposition visitors. Between seven thousand and ten thousand saw the show nightly; gross receipts averaged $60,000 weekly. Texas history was a paying proposition. To meet the public demand, the management increased the weekly matinee performances from four to seven on September 1. Unquestionably, the Centennial Corporation had gotten a bargain in Jan Isbelle Fortune's historical creation; she received only eight hundred dollars for the original script.[33]

[32]A. L. Vollmann to Edward Hungeford, June 28, 1936, Centennial Collection, DHS.
[33]*Dallas Morning News*, August 13 and September 1, 1936.

15

A MIGHTY STOREHOUSE OF INFORMATION

djacent to the *Cavalcade* stage and beyond, throughout the 185-acre expanse, spread a new world of ideas, information, and experiences never before encountered by most exposition visitors. It was the fulfillment of Theodore Price's 1923 proposal for "a city not now in existence." Probably unknown to most visitors, that city — labeled the "Magic City" by the press — forecast the world of the future, a world in which science and industry dominated by the ideas of man would determine the shape of things to come. The seeds of midcentury America were sown throughout the 185-acre complex.

Although the leaders of the Texas centennial conceived the celebration within a two-fold concept of patriotism and commercialism, expositions by their very nature transcend such easily defined objectives. President William B. McKinley, addressing the Pan-American Exposition in Buffalo on September 6, 1901 (a few hours before he was fatally wounded by an assassin), viewed expositions within a much broader and more realistic context. He proclaimed them "the time-keepers of progress. They record the world's advancement. They stimulate the energy, enterprise and intellect of the people, and quicken human genius. . . . They broaden and brighten the daily life of the people. They open mighty storehouses of information to the student. Every exposition, great or small, has helped to [take] some onward step"[1] Despite what the Dallas civic leaders may have thought, Billy Rose was essentially correct; Dallas alone offered the educational experience. And while Mlle. Corrinne's apples remained much in evidence, the Central Exposition evolved, exactly as President McKinley proclaimed some thirty-five years before, as a mighty storehouse of information.

[1] Edward Lee Pell, *McKinley and Men of Our Times* (St. Louis: Historical Society of America, 1901), p. 185.

The *Official Guide Book* published on May 15, 1936, listed 130 exhibitors and concessionaires at the exposition, representing every major industry in the United States. At Dallas and the other four major United States expositions held during the 1930s, rapid advances in the fields of science and industry formed the predominant theme.[2] The I. E. Du Pont de Nemours company demonstrated how dye was made from coal, refrigerants from salt, and synthetic camphor from turpentine of the southern pine tree. The Ford Motor Company displayed a stroboscopic light that visually "froze" the high speed crankshaft of a Ford motor to demonstrate the inner working of the powerplant, while General Motors exhibited the forerunner of microwave cooking by frying an egg on a block of ice. In the Hall of Electricity, the Elgin Watch Company erected a model observatory to demonstrate the use of celestial observation in determining the correct time, and the Western Union Company demonstrated the practical application of the electric eye.

In the Travel and Transportation Building, Delta Airlines exhibited a mock-up of the cockpit of Lockheed Electra (not the later accident-prone turboprop Electra). Visitors could sit in the co-pilot's seat and hold the controls while a uniformed airline captain explained the wonders of commercial air travel. A panoramic view through the windshield created the illusion of flight.

Compared to other fields of endeavor, communications represented the greatest degree of progress in 1936 and held the greatest fascination for exposition visitors. When the United States celebrated its centennial in 1876, the telephone represented the latest marvel in communications; at Dallas it was television. A news report of this new communication medium revealed the primitive state of its development: "The demonstration enabled one person to see another person using the other end of the telephone line."[3]

While the scientific exhibits amazed as much as they informed, the social and cultural experience had greater lasting impact on exposition visitors. These were experiences the average individual could more readily comprehend. The Gulf Refining Company's radio studios evolved as one of the exposition's more popular attractions. Art Link-

[2]The other exposition were Chicago, 1933; San Diego, 1935; San Francisco and New York, 1939.
[3]*Dallas Morning News*, July 30, 1936.

letter, the studio's program director, remembered "Texans gathered by the thousands to watch live broadcasts through the windows of our Gulf studios. For most, it was their first opportunity to see a radio broadcast of any kind and when we brought in national stars and big name bands, it was a big thrill."[4]

Seeing celebrities was one of the memorable thrills of the exposition. Most Texans comprised an unsophisticated society in the mid-1930s: 59 percent were rural, only sixteen out of one hundred homes had telephones, fewer still received daily newspapers, and one year later only one out of six homes had a radio. To most people, celebrities were merely names, voices on the radio, images on a motion picture screen; within the frame of reference of most, they probably did not exist as real living human beings. No one had ever seen one, but at the exposition there they were: movie stars, radio personalities, famous people whose names brought immediate identity. From Hollywood came Ginger Rogers (accompanied by an unknown actress named Lucille Ball), June Knight, John Boles, Buddy Rogers, Alan Jones, Robert Taylor, Clark Gable, Lupe Velez, and Gene Autry filming a motion picture, *The Big Show*, on the exposition grounds. Politicians were ever-present, beginning with the president and later the vice-president of the United States.

Popular radio bandleaders and recording stars ranked with movie stars in the 1930s as America's premier celebrities. Most of the more famous appeared at the exposition. Well-known bands were the primary attraction at the General Motors Auditorium, the converted Fair Park Auditorium which served as a combination showroom and celebrity bandstand. The groups, most of whom played two-week engagements, included Jan Garber, the "Idol of the Air Lanes"; Art Kassel and his Kassels in the Air; Herbie Kay; Horace Heidt and his Musical Knights (triple tonguing trumpets were his trademark); Phil Harris; Tommy Tucker; Jimmy Joy, who played two clarinets simultaneously; and Ben Bernie, the "Old Maestro." At other locations on the fairgrounds were the equally famous bands and orchestras of Duke Ellington, Cab Calloway, Isham Jones, Ted Lewis, Tommy Dorsey, and Rudy Vallee. Most performed free, sponsored by some exhibitor. Ligon Smith's orchestra served as the exposition's "house band."

---

[4]Linkletter to Ragsdale, July 5, 1979.

Smith's group, popular with dancers throughout Texas and the Southwest, performed at dances, receptions and celebrity events in both the Amphitheater and the Cotton Bowl. These were the musical celebrities, the teenage idols of the Depression era, who read music, wore matching blazers, and combed their hair with Vitalis and Brilliantine. In the 1930s "longhair" musicians played in string quartets and symphony orchestras.

The exposition's underlying theme of Texas history was reflected in many exhibits. In the Petroleum Building, the Humble Oil and Refining Company's Hall of History interpreted the state's history through a series of fourteen skillfully crafted dioramas, while the state's geology was illustrated on eight huge relief maps built into the floor.[5] The company distributed free copies of *Twice-Told Tales of Texas*, a forty-six-page history of Texas illustrated with photographs of the dioramas. A historian was present to answer visitors' questions. The Hall of State, which did not open until September 5, represented the major trove of historical memorabilia. It was also the exposition's most imposing structure; former governor Pat M. Neff described it "the Westminster Abbey of the Western World." Beyond the great mural and the historical statuary, the visitor could view in the four regional rooms over three thousand artifacts of the state's history. The Central Exposition also had its Alamo, the Texas Ranger Log House featuring a wide range of law enforcement artifacts, and a replica of Judge Roy Bean's saloon, the Jersey Lilly.

For the millions attending the exposition that experience evolved as a revelation and an inspiration. They discovered on every hand that a better and more rewarding lifestyle awaited somewhere beyond the Depression-wracked era in which they were living. As they toured the exhibits and strolled the pedestrian ways, they experienced President McKinley's 1901 pronouncement that expositions "broaden and brighten the daily life of the people." In General Electric's "House of Magic," they saw domestic life of the future served by electricity: modern refrigeration (the ice box was still widely used in the mid-

[5] In 1937, when the exposition was repeated as the Texas and Greater Pan American Exposition, the Mexican Government threatened to withdraw from participation unless certain unidentified dioramas were changed. The changes were made according to that country's wishes. At the close of that exposition the company gave the exhibit to the Texas Memorial Museum in Austin.

1930s), electric cooking, indirect illumination, and a photoelectric cell that automatically opened and closed doors.[6]

Building material firms erected what they predicted would be the homes of the future, incorporating the newest materials and building methods. The Southern Pine Home and the Contemporary House represented two extremes in mid-1930s architecture, folksy charm and the futuristic version of the emerging International style of architecture. Cheaper components subsequently rendered the Masonite House and the Portland Cement House impractical. None of the four structures represented domestic immediacy for most visitors, but all foretold a future in which interior comforts and conveniences would prevail.

The interior comfort that fascinated all exposition visitors was air conditioning. The Texas Centennial Central Exposition was the first air-conditioned world's fair. The climate of the two previous exposition sites, Chicago and San Diego, did not require it (air conditioning was employed sparingly in Chicago in 1933), and the process had not been developed to the point of practicality. But in 1936 it was, and for Dallas it was a necessity. Sustaining massed attendance in enclosed exhibit halls during the Texas summer would have been virtually impossible. Air conditioning, which many experienced for the first time at the exposition, would ultimately change the American way of life. And it was a major factor in boosting summertime exposition attendance. The Dallas attendance had been almost double that of the San Diego exposition for the first seventeen days and not far under Chicago's for the same period. A visitor could traverse approximately five miles of air-conditioned exhibit areas, and almost 75 percent of the midway shows were air-conditioned. Thirty-seven exhibitors required 1,461 tons of air conditioning, and various cooling processes used more than six million gallons of water daily.[7]

In the exposition planners' attempt to present the world of the future, the cultural experience did not go wanting. Visitors had many opportunities to savor the creative works of art, architecture, drama, and folk culture. The new Dallas Museum of Fine Arts exhibit of 750 representative pieces, valued at $10 million, marked another mile-

---

[6]Rural Electrification Administration service did not reach some areas of the state until the late 1930s.

[7]"Air Conditioning Within the Grounds," Centennial Collection, DHS.

stone in southwestern art history. *Art Digest*, dedicating the June, 1936 issue (Texas Centennial Special Number) to the art show, reported: "With the Texas Centennial as a background, the new Dallas Museum of Fine Arts is holding an exhibition that will write a new and important chapter in the annals of American art — an assemblage that takes the visitor not only on a comprehensive tour of the world's art, ancient and modern, but particularly emphasizes the significance of the Southwest. Texas a big . . . and, whether New York knows it or not, that commonwealth and the other states of the Southwest . . . are contributing a vital element to the nation's art."[8]

There was stage drama as well. Many Texans witnessed their first productions of Shakespeare in a replica of the Old Globe Theater, where a professional stock company presented five different plays (four comedies and *Julius Caesar*). Orson Welles restaged *Macbeth* for black actors in Haitian setting in the Amphitheater. The exposition was also the site of the week-long Third National Folk Festival, whose presentations encompassed all the cultures represented by the state's six flags, plus identifiable folk strains from other sections of the nation.

The real star of the exposition remained the physical plant itself. Under George Dahl's counsel and supervision, seventy-seven buildings were either completely remodeled or constructed especially for the exposition (another source places the total at sixty-nine, twenty-one permanent) — all in the modern style. At least two other world expositions in the United States have greatly influenced subsequent architectural trends. The Renaissance Revival facades of the 1893 World's Columbian Exposition in Chicago became a retarding force in the establishment of an organic style of American architecture; Louis Sullivan, who designed the Transportation Building, claimed: "Thus architecture died in the land of the free and the home of the brave. . . . The damage done by the World's Fair will last for a half a century, if not longer."[9] Bertram Grosvenor Goodhue, architect of the Panama-California Exposition held in San Diego in 1915, drew on Spanish Colonial sources for his California Building. His pièce de résistance set the trend for Spanish Colonial Revival architecture; the residual impact may still be seen today throughout the southwestern

[8]*Art Digest*, June, 1936, p. 10.
[9]"Fairs," *Architectural Forum*, September, 1936, p. 177.

United States in decaying railroad stations, residential mansions, and recent taco shops.

George Dahl, on the other hand, drew on a more recent source, the Exposition des Arts Decoratifs held in Paris in 1925. Like his more progressive colleagues, he abandoned historical eclecticism and instead embraced the modern movement. It was a practical as well as an aesthetic decision; the simplicity of modern lines facilitated the crash construction program. Dahl said later he had hoped to create a monument to simplicity. While the Central Exposition architecture bore little relevance to Texas history (except in bas-reliefs and murals), it nevertheless accorded millions of Texans their first opportunity to see good examples of modern architecture. From this experience they gained an awareness of a design concept other than the traditional. The Hall of State, the Federal Building (now the State Fair of Texas administration building), the Ford Building (now demolished), and the redesigned facades facing the Esplanade of State were prime examples of the modern school of architecture. The Magnolia Petroleum Building (later the Margo Jones Theater), designed by William Lescaze, represented one of the early Texas examples of the International style. Although Dahl and his staff did not introduce the modern style to Texas, the exposition complex gave renewed impetus to its application throughout the Southwest. [10]

The amusement section of the exposition occupied a quarter-mile-long strip in the eastern sector of the fairgrounds. Like most of the exhibits, it was, for the most part, both entertaining and informative, if not educational. The $250,000 Black Forest concession, an acre-wide replica of a German village, contained a sixteen-hundred-seat restaurant, an ice show skating rink, a rathskeller, and a shopping center. Other foreign concessions included the English Village, the Old Nuremburg Restaurant, and the City of China. Admiral Richard E. Byrd's (and D. Harold Byrd's) "Little America"; Sing Sing Prison Warden Lewis E. Lawes's "Crime Prevention" show (his *20,000 Years*

[10] Fort Worth's Sinclair Building was built in 1930, and the Texas Highway Department administration building in Austin dates from 1932. The term "art deco," frequently applied to the exposition buildings and decorations, did not come into vogue until 1966. The commemorative exposition "Les Années '25," held at the Musée des Arts Decoratifs in 1966, was the source of the "art deco" designation. The term has subsequently been loosely applied to both art and architecture, especially the field of decorative arts between the two world wars. It refers specifically to art forms that follow a linear style with characteristic preference for shiny surfaces.

in Sing Sing was a best-seller); "The Holy City," a collection of religious art works; and "Life," the story of man, his creation, and reproduction, were typical of the more informative attractions along the midway. The old State Fair roller coaster remained in service, but the fair offered few rides. (At that time world's fair promoters had not developed the amusement park syndrome.) There were, in addition, the usual midway attractions, including flesh!

Foreign settings contributed to the wicked ambiance of the "Streets of Paris" and the competitive "Streets of All Nations," where barebreasted nudity (and most other parts, as well) keynoted the entertainment. Mlle. Corrine, following a legal mix-up, left the "Streets" with her basketball-size apple in hand to appear at the "Nations." She was quickly replaced by "Mona Llesslie," whose forte was diving nude into a flaming pool of water which was extinguished just moments before she singed her dimples. While the spectators reported nothing objectionable about these two midway revues, such could not be said for the peep shows both emporiums offered. An outside barker set the appropriate tone: "Everyone admitted except the youngsters under eighteen and the old men over eighty. The youngsters don't understand it and the old men can't stand it."[11]

In mid-June the "March of Time" released a film report on both the Dallas and Fort Worth expositions. A segment on the purported girl show rivalry suggested that the threat of Billy Rose's extravaganzas caused Dallas to install peep shows and apple dancers. The newsreel showing in a Dallas theater touched off another verbal battle in the intercity rivalry. "Dallas was fully stocked with undraped torsos, to say nothing of limbs, long ere Fort Worth decided to catch on our coattails," retorted the *Dallas Morning News*. "'March of Time,' far from dodging a fight, likes to pick one. The murmurings over the centennial episode is [*sic*] calculated to sell many a ticket."[12]

It appeared that when Billy Rose's show eventually opened, the two cities would attempt to meet one another head-on, undraped, body for body. And that would, indeed, sell many a ticket.

[11] *Eastland Chronicle*, July 17, 1936.
[12] *Dallas Morning News*, June 21, 1936.

16

DALLAS FOR EDUCATION;
FORT WORTH FOR ENTERTAINMENT

Fred S. Benge never met either Billy Rose or Amon Carter, but they knew him well—by reputation. Just three weeks following the opening of the Central Exposition, he became the millionth person to pass through the turnstiles. General Manager W. A. Webb was waiting with a rickshaw to pull him on a much-publicized ride down the Esplanade of State. While Benge celebrated being the local "king for a day," neither Rose nor Carter could view Thursday, June 25, with the same ebullience. The Fort Worth exposition buildings remained unfinished, and grading crews were still pouring concrete on the three major access routes to the exposition site. Just three days before Dallas celebrated its millionth visitor, the directors of the Frontier Centennial decided to delay the opening until July 18. Expense continued to mount, bond sales lagged, and Dallas was getting all the business.

As Rose pressed for the July 18 opening, both Carter and North begged for federal money to keep the Frontier Exposition solvent. (It is important to differentiate between the adjacent permanent civic complex—auditorium, livestock arena, and Will Rogers Memorial Tower—funded by a PWA loan-grant and the temporary Frontier Exposition entertainment park, financed by local bond subscriptions.) Appeals were dispatched to Jesse H. Jones, chairman of the Reconstruction Finance Corporation, and to members of the United States Texas Centennial Commission. North wrote Jones on June 20 that "we are unable to pay off our sub-contractors today and some of them are more or less frantic."[1] Senators Morris Sheppard and Tom Connally also joined in the solicitation for funds, as did Elliott Roosevelt, then living in Fort Worth. Executive Secretary W. B. Yeager stated the federal commission's position: "there are no unallocated funds. . . . I may add that there is some doubt in my mind as to the legality

---

[1]James M. North to Jesse H. Jones, June 20, 1936, Carter Archives.

of expenditures in Fort Worth."[2] Secretary of State Hull, however, gave Carter his only hope for ultimate federal assistance. "W. B. Yeager . . . will confer with the Vice President on August 3rd and the situation will be reviewed most carefully," he wrote. "Please regard this statement as confidential. The above is all that I can say at this time."[3]

When the goverment solicitation failed, Carter turned again to the big corporations. General Motors remained high on his list. Having been rejected previously by R. H. Grant, a GM vice-president, Carter appealed directly to William S. Knudsen, the company president. When Carter persisted, Knudsen called Jack Dineen, who managed the company's Central Exposition facility. Knudsen explained that "Amon Carter is just bleeding for $20,000," and while the company "can't [afford to] give anybody twenty cents," he nevertheless asked Dineen to go to Fort Worth and try to appease Carter. Dineen and Frank Harting, publicity director for the General Motors Dallas exhibit, made several trips to Fort Worth in a vain attempt to placate Carter. He "wined and dined us like princes, he was so desperate to get the money," Harting recalled. Carter again refused to be denied. "So after we had been over there on two or three successive days, Dineen said, 'Look, let's give him the $20,000 and get it over with . . . we can't be running back and forth to Fort Worth every day.'" The following day they met Carter in Rose's office on the exposition grounds and told him that the company would give him the $20,000 in exchange for erecting a small, inconsequential public address system on the exposition grounds. Carter was elated. "He yelled at somebody," Harting recalled, "go get Billy. And Billy Rose ran up a dusty road; I can still see him. He ran sixty miles an hour. . . . He wrote very hurriedly a contract on the back of a piece of music, between General Motors and the Fort Worth Centennial [for] $20,000, three second-hand microphones strung up in the trees. He [Dineen] gave him the $20,000 and they opened. They were at the end of their money bag by the time that happened."[4]

General Motors' $20,000 was not Fort Worth's financial salvation, but it at least staved off the creditors while the sponsors moved ahead toward opening day. In the meantime rehearsals for all the shows con-

[2]W. B. Yeager to Cordell Hull, July 23 and 24, 1936, Carter Archives.
[3]Cordell Hull to Amon Carter, July 24, 1936, Carter Archives.
[4]Interview with Frank Harting, Dallas, Texas, November 4, 1977.

tinued throughout the city. New York arranger Murray Cutter rehearsed the twenty-four piece *Jumbo* band in the Musicians Club in the Medical Arts Building, while pianist Roy Bargy rehearsed the Paul Whiteman Orchestra in a hotel ballroom.[5] Rose divided his time between dance ensemble rehearsals in Monnig's warehouse (where costume fittings continued between numbers) and the *Last Frontier* arena at the exposition site where the exterior numbers were being staged. Construction continued around the clock, and on June 25, as Fred S. Benge was being entertained in Dallas, John Murray Anderson moved all rehearsals to the exposition site. A minor celebration was held at the park on July 4; the Pioneer Palace set up temporary tables and chairs and began serving food for the show casts and construction workers.

Dress rehearsals began on the Casa Mañana stage on July 11, one week before the show opened. That was an experience no member of the cast, crew, or orchestra can ever forget. Rehearsals seemed to go on interminably, day and night, without pause and without consideration of human endurance. Evelyn Gracy (Barkow), a fifteen-year-old Polytechnic High School student and member of the Casa Mañana cast, explained the ordeal of the final dress rehearsals:

> We'd start out in the morning, something like about ten or eleven o'clock, and then we'd get an hour break for lunch, and then we'd rehearse until six . . . then we'd be able to go home and have dinner and change and come back, and sometimes we would leave there the next morning about ten. . . . I do remember their sending for the police or somebody and making John Murray stop the rehearsal because it had been going on all night long. And of course, we had rehearsed all the day before. So he let us go home but we had to be back at rehearsal at eleven, and that went on for almost the last week before the show opened.[6]

---

[5] In mid-July Billy Rose announced that Paul Whiteman would conduct the orchestra for the Casa Mañana Revue, while Hyman Maurice, who formerly conducted the Worth Theater orchestra, would conduct the *Jumbo* orchestra. The Fort Worth musical extravaganzas were a great economic windfall for musicians. When the shows opened, 102 union musicians were working at the exposition. The weekly pay scale varied from fifty-five dollars for *Jumbo* to eighty-five dollars at Casa Mañana. Featured performers in the Paul Whiteman orchestra commanded higher salaries.

[6] Interview with Evelyn Gracy Barkow, Fort Worth, Texas, June 6, 1981.

E. Clyde Whitlock, the *Star-Telegram* music critic, attended a Casa Mañana dress rehearsal and reported that "a grand opera would receive no more scrupulous drill, probably not as much. . . . The lighting crew worked almost three hours, repeating over and over again, without pause, a portion of the show which probably finally will be done in less than five minutes. John Murray Anderson . . . stands before a microphone, talking constantly, for hour after hour, never losing patience or enthusiasm."[7] Anderson gained quality at the cost of great personal sacrifice. Girls fainted while rehearsing dance routines in one hundred degree heat, and Fayee Meyers of McAllen, Texas, fractured an ankle while performing an intricate dance turn. During a night rehearsal another dancer, executing a reverse step, missed the bridge railing over the still-empty lagoon in front of the stage and fell backward five feet to the concrete bottom. She was severely injured and removed from the cast.[8] And they did this for twenty-five dollars a week—after the show opened!

During the final week of rehearsals, as construction continued, the Frontier Exposition site became a flurry of activity; a medley of hammers and saws played amidst the odor of wet paint and turpentine. Throughout the park rushing and shouting men and women worked feverishly to put everything in place for the grand opening on Saturday night. By midweek a small army of new recruits began arriving. They were the ground workers engaged to serve the anticipated three million visitors: waiters and waitressess, parking lot attendants, ticket sellers, cashiers, and bank employees.

Amon Carter was not one to leave anything to chance. On the eve of the grand opening he entertained six hundred editors and publishers from Texas and four adjoining states in the "world's largest outdoor theater-restaurant" before previewing the final dress rehearsal of the Casa Mañana revue. To insure that "those eastern dudes" would also learn about "Broadway on the prairie," an American Airlines

---

[7] *Fort Worth Star-Telegram*, July 12, 1936.

[8] Despite Anderson's demands, he, unlike Billy Rose, was well liked by the cast. "He was a darling man and we all just loved him," recalled Dorothy Bigbee Litrel. "During rehearsal, if he just spoke to you, your day was made." Interview with Dorothy Bigbee Litrel, Fort Worth, Texas, June 5, 1981. Anderson addressed everyone by nicknames of his own choosing: "Eyebrow Sisters," "Winnie the Pooh," "Amarillo," "Amy McPherson," "Mona Lisa," etc.

charter flight bearing some of New York's most prestigious colum-
nists and critics arrived late that afternoon in time for the opening
festivities. Nor was the rest of the nation excluded. That night Carter's radio station, WBAP, originated an hour-long, eighty-five station coast-to-coast broadcast from the exposition site.

Although 1,853,042 visitors had already passed through the Dallas
turnstiles, there was little "those dudes" could do to blunt Amon's
day of glory. The house lights were lowered, Paul Whiteman began
the overture, "Rhapsody in Blue," and the show began. The cast fulfilled John Murray Anderson's greatest expectations. John Rosenfield,
Jr., the *Dallas Morning News* amusements editor and one gifted with
a critical eye and ear, reported "the show beggars description." He
succumbed to the spectacle of "two hundred girls and principals and
sets larger than life [that] fill the 130-foot stage." Rosenfield also liked
"the exciting dance routines, the most delightful and tasteful of costumes and [the] amazing lighting effects." He concluded: "Fort Worth's
Frontier Centennial . . . is a show of immensity, novelty and resource-
fulness. We don't see how it can avoid being a potent attraction within
the state and without."[9]

The New York-based writers were equally enthusiastic. Dan Rogers,
who covered the preview for the United Press, stated that he was "really
lost for words to describe the Casa Mañana spectacle." John Lardner,
reporting for the North American Newspaper Alliance, called it "a
gorgeous show . . . [and] one of the best outdoor dining and amusement places I have ever seen." *Literary Digest's* Whitney Bolton described the open-air night club as a "thrilling and beautiful spectacle."
And John Harkings of the Universal News Service undoubtedly made
Amon Carter proud when he wrote, "[Casa Mañana] is better than
anything of the kind we have in New York."[10] Musicians and enter-
tainers could probably view the outdoor spectacle with a greater ob-
jectivity. Woods Moore, who played in the Whiteman orchestra, pronounced it "the best extravaganza I ever saw. I don't think there has
been anything like it since, anywhere." He had worked in the *Follies*
and the *Vanities*, and Casa Mañana "started where they finished."[11]
Paul Whiteman also pronounced it the greatest show he ever appeared

[9] *Dallas Morning News*, July 18, 1936.
[10] *Fort Worth Star-Telegram*, July 19, 1936.
[11] Interview with Woods Moore, Fort Worth, Texas, February 24, 1978.

in. Thus it seemed that Fort Worth's great competitive gamble with Dallas had at last paid off. And opening day was still a sunrise away.

Carter orchestrated the festivities with a newspaperman's eye for the spectacular. Visiting dignitaries were met at the Texas and Pacific station by a stagecoach which rumbled to the exposition grounds behind a detachment of the Second Cavalry. He also recognized that names make news. President Roosevelt dispatched the following telegram to Carter: "Congratulations on opening the Fort Worth Frontier Centennial. I am sending this opening message by wigwag visual signal from the schooner yacht *Sewanna* to the USS *Potomac*, both in the Atlantic Ocean off the southern end of Nova Scotia, and thence by radio and land wire to you. Best of Luck to you all."[12]

The electrical impulse that sent the telegram also tripped a knife that slashed a ribbon that, in turn, parted a lariat barring the exposition entrance. The waiting throng surged through the main gate, and the last major event of the centennial year was under way. The stagecoach lumbered on down the midway loaded with the notables who took part in the opening ceremony: Governor Allred, Sen. Tom Connally, Elliott Roosevelt, Attorney General William McCraw, and C. R. Smith, president of American Airlines (of which Carter was a major stockholder). Following a mock holdup in the arena of *The Last Frontier*, in which the United States Cavalry rescued the dignitaries, both the governor and the attorney general spoke to the occasion. Their comments were brief; the temperature stood a one hundred degrees in the arena. Following the ceremonies, an estimated 25,000 people paid admission to see the initial performances of the exposition shows. But the opening day belonged to Carter, Rose, and Monnig. They, like their Dallas counterparts, had just pulled off another construction miracle. In less than eighty days an open prairie had been transformed into one of the largest amusement enterprises in the nation. Now they were ready to give "those dudes over at Dallas" a run for the entertainment dollars.

During the summer of 1936, Fort Worth became an entertainment mecca. Rose had told the nation that was where the action was; he provided the entertainment and Carter opened up the town. Jerry Flemmons explained: "Fort Worth was wide open during the centennial. Illegal liquor was served everywhere because Amon had made

---

[12]Telegram from Franklin D. Roosevelt to Amon Carter, July 18, 1936, Carter Archives.

Groundbreaking with silver spades and ten-gallon hats marked the beginning of the Fort Worth Frontier Centennial Exposition on March 10, 1936. Amon G. Carter, left, turns the first soil, while Mayor Van Zandt Jarvis, Uel Stephens (PWA director), and William Monnig (president of the exposition board), left to right, await their turns. (Courtesy University of Texas at Arlington/Fort Worth *Star-Telegram* Photo Collection)

Billy Rose, director general, Fort Worth Frontier Centennial Exposition, presides at a beauty contest to select "Texas Sweetheart No. 1." (Courtesy Fort Worth Public Library)

Amon G. Carter, Fort Worth civic leader, newspaper publisher, and guiding spirit of the Fort Worth Frontier Centennial Exposition. (Courtesy Amon G. Carter Museum, Fort Worth)

Amon G. Carter with actor-humorist Will Rogers. Carter's admiration for the
entertainer led to erection of the Will Rogers Memorial Tower at the exposition
site. (Courtesy Amon G. Carter Museum, Fort Worth)

Controversial sign raised across the street from the main entrance of the Dallas exposition to lure visitors to the Fort Worth Frontier Centennial Exposition. (Courtesy William E. Jary Historical Library, Fort Worth)

Aerial view of the Fort Worth Frontier Centennial Exposition: foreground, main entrance and Sunset Trail concessions; right center, circular *Jumbo* circus building; center, Pioneer Palace (angular building); right background, *Last Frontier* complex; center background, West Texas Chamber of Commerce Building (rectangular building); and left background, Casa Mañana dinner theater. The U.S. 2nd Cavalry unit and Indian campground appear at the upper left. (Author's collection)

The Pioneer Palace, left, and *Jumbo* circus building, rear center, during the final days of Fort Worth exposition construction. The Will Rogers Memorial Tower is visible in the background. (Courtesy University of Texas at Arlington/Fort Worth *Star-Telegram* Photo Collection)

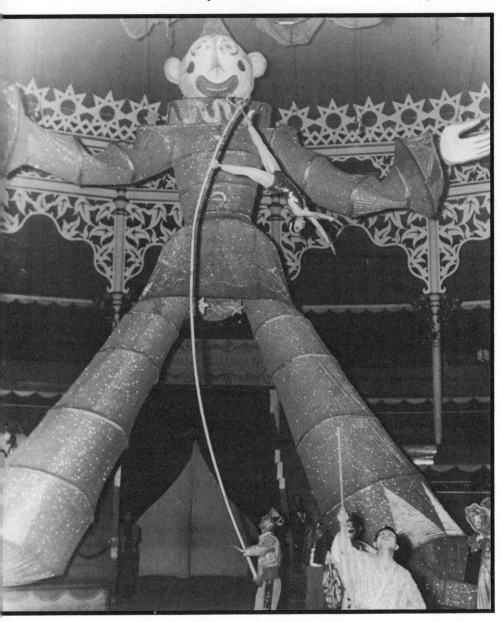

A scene from *Jumbo*, the musical circus produced by Billy Rose at the Fort Worth Frontier Centennial Exposition. It was staged in a traditional circular circus building constructed specifically for this production. (Courtesy University of Texas at Arlington/Fort Worth *Star-Telegram* Photo Collection)

Ben Young's orchestra plays for listeners, in background, and dancers, foreground, in the Pioneer Palace. (Courtesy University of Texas at Arlington/Fort Worth *Star-Telegram* Photo Collection)

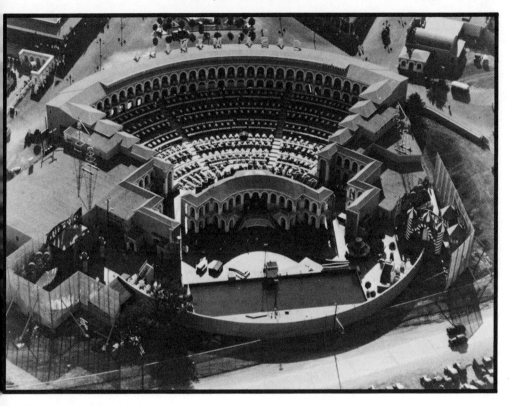

Aerial view of the Casa Mañana, the world's largest outdoor dinner theater, at the 1936 Fort Worth Frontier Centennial Exposition. Various sets are stored on either side of the circular, revolving stage; dressing rooms are at the left. (Courtesy University of Texas at Arlington/Fort Worth *Star-Telegram* Photo Collection)

Exterior of Casa Mañana dinner theater, Fort Worth Frontier Centennial Exposition. (Author's collection)

Paul Whiteman, internationally renowned orchestra leader, arrives at Fort Worth City Hall on horseback as honorary mayor-for-a-day. His escorts are Hub Whiteman, left, nationally known rodeo performer who appeared in *Last Frontier*, and Texas Ranger Kelly Rush. (Courtesy University of Texas at Arlington/Fort Worth *Star-Telegram* Photo Collection)

Sally Rand, dancing star of Fort Worth's Casa Mañana revue and operator of Sally Rand's Nude Ranch, strikes a familiar pose with her fans. (Courtesy Demp Toney)

Sally Rand, famous fan dancer, poses for a publicity photograph with Texas Motor Transportation Association conventioneers in Fort Worth. Being lassoed by Miss Rand are, left to right, Henry E. English, Lufkin; F. G. Dorsey, Houston; and Ted V. Rodgers, Washington, president of the American Trucking Association. (Courtesy University of Texas at Arlington/Fort Worth *Star-Telegram* Photo Collection)

Production number in Casa Mañana revue, Fort Worth Exposition. Dancers performed on a revolving stage overlooking a lagoon. At the end of a performance, the stage moved forward over the lagoon to provide dance space for customers. (Courtesy Fort Worth Public Library)

Closing scene of Casa Mañana revue at 1936 Fort Worth Frontier Centennial Exposition. Everett Marshall and beauty winner Faye Cotton are at stage center. (Courtesy University of Texas at Arlington/Fort Worth *Star-Telegram* Photo Collection)

a deal with the state's Liquor Control Board. . . . Officers agreed to go blind while Fort Worth celebrated."[13] That spelled trouble for Dallas. Hubert Rousell, writing in the *Houston Press*, described the Central Exposition as "the great lemon and strawberry pop fair."[14] Carter was delighted, especially when Fort Worth's midweek attendance remained strong. Heat, however, emerged as the exposition's nagging problem; the temperature reached 104 degrees on July 20. There were necessary adjustments. Opening hours were changed from 11:00 A.M. to 5:00 P.M., and the two nightly performances of the three major shows were set at 8:00 P.M. and 10:00 P.M.

Jumbo, however, evolved as the exposition's ongoing trouble spot. With no air conditioning in the cone-shaped circus building, the temperature sometimes reached 112 degrees. Chorus girls fainted, and Eddie Foy, Jr., who replaced Jimmy Durante in the Fort Worth show, threatened to quit. Band members, who performed out of sight of the audience, stripped to their underwear. John Murray Anderson provided a temporary solution. He cut the show in half, and audiences continued to patronize an abbreviated version of the musical circus.

In spite of the discomforts, visitors were lavish in their praise for the Frontier Exposition. Mr. and Mrs. M. D. Chateen of Milford, Indiana reported they "came expressly to see 'Casa Mañana' and 'Jumbo' and would drive another 1,300 miles to see such a show." The social impact was what impressed Mr. and Mrs. F. J. Wolf of Philadelphia: "We came expecting to see countryfied folks down here in Texas but they're ultramodern." Jorge Sanchez, a Cuban planter, stated after his visit, "This surpasses anything I have seen in Paris, Havana, New York and Buenos Aires."[15] The editor of the *Terrell Tribune* was equally

[13]Flemmons, *Amon*, pp. 325–26. The local law enforcement agencies must have agreed likewise. On September 4, 1936, the Texas Livestock Centennial and Frontier Days, Inc., and John Bogganio negotiated an agreement "that on slot machines and wheels the cost of such is to be amortized, such amortization not to exceed $22,500 and Bogganio to submit itemized bills to sustain such costs." Other concessions held by Bogganio included the Sally Rand Dude [Nude] Ranch, Tango, and the Ziegfeld Milk Bath. Bogganio agreed to settle with the corporation daily on income derived from the slot machines and wheels. Settlements on all other concessions were made "each Saturday for the previous week." Carter Archives.

[14]*Time*, July 8, 1936, p. 13.

[15]Flemmons, *Amon*, p. 291.

impressed: "To put it mildly, Tarrant County's show will, without doubt, prove to be one of the outstanding features of the entire Texas Centennial."[16]

Traffic remained brisk throughout the summer, producing a positive cash flow. On Saturday, August 1, *The Last Frontier* had its largest audience to date, and *Jumbo* played to good crowds at both performances. Casa Mañana remained the exposition's headline attraction. The accounting office reported 4,800 persons at the first performance of the theater-restaurant revue, and hundreds were turned away. What a difference six weeks had made; Carter and North were no longer hounding their friends for money.

Thornton and his colleagues were unable to share Carter's enthusiasm. After the first two weeks of operation, attendance at the Dallas exposition began a normal decline, then gradually fell far below the original projections. On July Fourth, 113,161 people visited the Central Exposition. That was the third and final one-hundred-thousand attendance day. There remained 148 days of operation, and during that time attendance reached fifty thousand on only seventeen days. By the end of the 177-day run, the average daily attendance would total only 35,900. Before the end of June it became apparent that management was faced with one mammoth selling job. They gave it their best shot.

The promotion department planned special days and special events for every conceivable occasion. Special days proved the more lucrative. They were designed to attract kids (five cents admission), Irish, Poles, underprivileged children, hay fever sufferers, homeopaths, the American Legion, blacks, every state in the union, and practically every town in Texas. When the promotion department designated July 20 as San Marcos Day, the local chamber of commerce arranged for a special train ($4.81 round trip) to carry the local citizenry and the Southwest Texas State Teachers College "Bob Cat" Band to Dallas. Civic pride was at stake, the *San Marcos News* claimed. "Brenham, [Texas] for instance sent 1,400 of its citizens up there a week ago. San Marcos ought to have 300 or more. . . . San Marcos folks will be proud to follow the Bob Cats through the Exposition grounds when the parade forms upon the arrival of the special train." Each

[16] *Fort Worth Star-Telegram*, July 24, 1936.

person wore a badge proclaiming: "San Marcos, Texas, Cottonseed Capital of the World."[17]

Special events were staged in the Cotton Bowl and in the Amphitheater to produce double revenue, the gate admission plus the additional charge for the event. The most ambitious of these were the "Queen's Night" beauty revues staged in the Cotton Bowl on four weekends in July.[18] Motion picture stars Robert Taylor, Allan Jones, June Knight, Bob Burns, and Ginger Rogers headlined the event, while regional beauty contest winners competed for a Metro-Goldwyn-Mayer motion picture screen test. The *Dallas Morning News* and the Chrysler Corporation jointly conducted the local elimination contests, and the Hollywood Electrical Pageant Company of Memphis, Tennessee, produced the pageants on a commission agreement. The first event, featuring actor Robert Taylor (he substituted for Jean Harlow) and Rudy Vallee's orchestra, was scheduled for July 4–5 and was expected to launch the series with a great public ovation.[19] That, unfortunately, did not happen. By the second show the sponsor had lost $30,000 and refused to invest further in the project. "The show last night was great," wrote company president R. B. Snowden, Jr., "but the crowd was poor and it just seems that Dallas is not going for the thing."[20] The series ended as scheduled, however, on July 31. A sixteen-year-old blonde, Geraldine Robertson of Lamesa, Texas, won the contest and was never heard of professionally again. Nor was R. B. Snowden, Jr.

Good taste appears not to have been a consideration in scheduling special events at the Central Exposition. The promotion department arranged to stage the wedding of Violet Hilton, a twenty-four-year-old Siamese twin, and James Moore, a twenty-five-year-old Cleveland, Ohio, dancer. For the maid of honor Violet chose, appropriately, her twin sister, Daisy. The publicity department sent out invitations to Texas newspaper editors "to attend the strangest wedding

[17]*San Marcos News*, July 14, 1936.

[18]Offers to stage a bullfight and establish a nudist colony were summarily rejected. Either would have probably attracted a larger audience.

[19]The American Airlines flight bringing actor Robert Taylor to Dallas was delayed in Abilene, Texas. When it was learned that a large crowd of fans and media representatives were awaiting the scheduled stop at Fort Worth's Meacham Field, a private airplane was dispatched to bring Taylor directly to Dallas, flying over Fort Worth. Reportedly, this decision was made to prevent Fort Worth from benefiting from the actor's publicity value.

[20]R. B. Snowden, Jr., to Ed Brown, Special Events, Texas Centennial Central Exposition, July 12, 1936, Centennial Collection, DHS.

ceremony ever performed in Texas." Newspaper ads carried similar copy: "Everybody 25¢. No extra charge for dancing. Doors open at 6 P.M. Come early — get up close to congratulate the bride and groom."[21] There remains no record of the outcome of this event, either domestic or financial, but it is assumed that Texans, even a half-century ago, had the discretion to invest their quarters elsewhere. Some were being invested in Fort Worth. The Frontier Exposition opened concurrently with the Siamese twin's wedding.

Despite subpar attendance, those who visited the Dallas exposition liked what they saw. But most importantly, the price was right. Mr. and Mrs. O. D. DeWitt of Fairview, Oklahoma, spent only $14.50 on their vacation trip to the exposition. Food and fuel en route cost seven dollars; admission, one dollar; tourist camp, two-fifty; parking car, twenty-five cents; plate lunch on the midway, thirty-five cents each; two hamburgers, ten cents each; two hot dogs, same price; and nine bottles of soft drink, five cents each. The only paid admissions were at "Streets of Paris," "Streets of All Nations," "Little America," and the "Midget City," which cost twenty-five cents each; they also spent ten cents each at the "Gorilla Village." At the end of the day the DeWitts counted their money and decided they could spend another day at the fair. They pronounced it the most economical vacation they had ever taken.[22] The influx of out-of-state visitors produced social benefits as well. J. D. Huff of Kansas City, Missouri, said that "a new idea of a Texas vast in resources and culture, as well as size, will be spread through the East by the Centennial." He pronounced it "a wonderful fair, and it is putting Texas on the map. The nation will be given a new idea about the state. I know of one boy in Kansas who had an idea that all Texans wore boots and rode horses before he came to Dallas."[23]

Some Texans viewed the exposition experience within a much broader context. W. A. Smith, writing in the *San Saba News*, stated: "There is a solidity and integrity about it that strikes the guest subconsciously but profitably. To say it is educational is to employ a hackneyed term. . . . It is, in short, modern civilization aggregated and displayed. The crowds of happy people afford in themselves a new

[21] *Dallas Morning News*, July 18, 1936.
[22] Ibid., July 19, 1936.
[23] *Dallas Journal*, July 10, 1936.

feeling of confidence in the Nation's social and civic institutions. There is something at the Centennial for every comer."[24] Frank Harting saw the exposition as a temporary respite from the rigors of the Depression. He, like thousands of others caught up in the carnival atmosphere, remembered "it was fun and there was a spirit about it . . . it seemed that every day was like a holiday. Everybody seemed to be happy."[25]

But Thornton, Florence, and Adams were not happy; nothing seemed to be going right. On the night of July 20, when attendance still had not reached the two million mark, a violent thunderstorm swept the exposition, inflicting $23,250 in damages. Flags and banners accounted for $6,767 of the loss. Lightning struck the *Cavalcade* set, damaging costumes and equipment and forcing cancellation of several performances. The downpour, instead of bringing relief from the heat, intensified it. On July 21 the temperature reached 105 degrees, dropping attendance the following day to 27,179. And on July 24, a delegation of Dallas ministers complained to the ailing W. A. Webb about the immorality at some midway concessions. Webb conducted an investigation, and some of the peep show participants were ordered to cover the areas of complaint.

Webb appeared not to feel well during the conference and was absent from the office most of the remainder of the month. On August 8, he was stricken with a heart attack and died the following day. Associates reported that Webb had been working eighteen hours a day for more than four months. On Tuesday, August 11, exposition activities ceased at ten o'clock as some six thousand fair employees stood with heads bowed for five minutes while the Catholic Mission bells tolled. Governor Allred ordered flags at the state capital flown at half-mast in Webb's memory.

During his final weeks Webb was faced with an abhorrent task. Sluggish attendance forced him to release some employees and reduce the salaries of others who had helped build the great expositions. On July 9, Frank N. Watson, director of promotion, circulated an interoffice memorandum containing Webb's directive. Marked "Confidential — Do Not Give Any Publicity," it stated: "It is with ex-

---

[24] *San Saba News*, undated, clipping file, State Archives.
[25] Harting interview, November 4, 1977.

treme regret that I am obliged to inform you of the seriousness of
our financial conditions and that it is only as the last resort of necessity that we are compelled to make an horizontal reduction in all
salaries of twenty per cent, effective with the present pay roll period,
commencing with the general manager and including the entire staff
on general office pay rolls. I hope this will be only temporary."[26] The
Advisory Board for Advertising acted accordingly. They reduced the
publicity staff gradually over the final four months of operation, from
twenty-six employees to thirteen, effecting a month-by-month budget reduction from $3,647.77 to $2,203.33. The Tracy-Locke-Dawson
agency revised the advertising budget, concentrating on 164 newspapers in eight southern and midwestern states at a cost of $28,544.50.[27]
The results were disappointing. The three-millionth visitor did not
arrive until August 19, and attendance did not reach the four-million
mark until September 17, on a day when only 19,458 visitors passed
through the turnstiles.

When a traffic study revealed that Fort Worth was siphoning off
a major portion of the automobile traffic entering the metroplex area,
the "Catfish Council" interpreted this as a mandate to act. Someone,
still unidentified, called an unofficial council meeting in the board
room of the North Texas Trust Company, with specific instructions
"not to bring the mayor [Sergeant]." At issue, this group believed,
was the future of the Central Exposition. The decision was made;
Police Chief Bob Jones and City Health Officer Dr. J. W. Bass received
the news late that afternoon. "We've got to open up the town," Dr.
Bass was told. "Mr. Thorton [he was not at the meeting] is in a hole
for a lot of money and going in deeper all the time." The solution:
convert Dallas into an "open city" in order to compete with Fort Worth.
That's where the entertainment was; Billy Rose had announced that
to the nation, and Carter had "made arrangements" with the Liquor
Control Board.

The new policy was clearly articulated: open up the bookies, no
more closing bars for illegal liquor sales, and "keep the whores as safe
as possible, . . . keep them in the houses and off the streets." This
evolved as a well-coordinated operation. In less than one month Dr.

---

[26]Frank N. Watson memorandum, July 9, 1936, Centennial Collection, DHS.
[27]Advisory Board for Advertising revised budget, State Archives.

Bass's office had issued 2,400 "health cards" to women purported to be prostitutes. Al Harting, a cub reporter covering activities at the centennial exposition in 1936, confirmed Dallas's new open-city policy: "honest-to-gosh prostitutes prospered in the best — and worst — little whorehouse in Dallas, doing their darndest to make folks feel at home."[28]

The madams who operated the houses along Griffin Street and near the downtown hotels emerged as the key enforcers of the "Catfish law." They would not tolerate anyone without a card from the City Health Department. "The best policemen we had were the whores in the houses . . . because they would turn in a street whore, right quick," Dr. Bass recalled. "If a policeman didn't catch 'em, another prostitute in a house would."[29]

The "Catfish Council" did not invent crime in Dallas. It existed before, during, and after the exposition. Gambling, numbers, slot machines, bookie joints, and illegal marble tables enjoyed a lucrative trade long before the clandestine meeting in the North Texas Trust Company. And while the "Catfish" may have attempted to endow Dallas with a brief convention city reputation, this policy of tolerance and indifference did little to ease Thornton's financial bind.

Meanwhile in Fort Worth, Carter and North were finding partial solutions to their financial problems. Through a readjustment of the San Antonio federal allotment, the United States Commission reassigned $50,000 to the Frontier Exposition. Vice-President Garner explained to Carter that the transaction was "strictly confidential."[30] Early in September the original $250,000 federal allocation for the permanent Fort Worth centennial structures was finally disbursed through the State Board of Control. At that time the Frontier Exposition owed almost $250,000 to a variety of suppliers who had helped build the temporary facilities. The $50,000 enabled the board to resolve about 40 percent of those claims. In addition, North explained to Lieutenant Governor Woodul on August 29 that "the Frontier Centennial itself is doing fine. . . . [It has] taken in enough cash each night, with the exception of the first week, to more than pay [operating]

[28]Bass interview, September 15, 1983; Harting, "Centennial Fever," p. 14. According to contemporary newspaper accounts, it appears that Mayor Sergeant was unaware of the policy change.

[29]Bass interview, September 15, 1983.

[30]John Nance Garner to Amon Carter, August 25, 1936, Carter Archives.

expenses. . . . This week will be our best and cash reserves will probably be 25 percent above the previous week."[31]

Despite North's optimism, Rose closed two money-losers, *Jumbo* and *The Last Frontier*, following the Saturday performances on September 26. The Pioneer Palace and Casa Mañana remained the only fee attractions on the grounds. Protracted rainy weather in early October forced the transfer of the Casa revue to the abandoned *Jumbo* circus building. With seating reduced to 2,100 (later there was food service for 1,100), Rose scheduled three shows a night during the weekends, and still long lines formed before all performances. It was inevitable, however, that the shows could not continue. With the Central Exposition's closing less than a month away, Rose and Carter decided to ring down the curtain on Fort Worth's Broadway-on-the-prairie. The final performances were scheduled on Saturday night, November 14. The last Casa Mañana revue began at ten o'clock; the Pioneer Palace finale was scheduled at eleven-thirty. For most of the Casa audience, it was a nostalgic trip to see once again the sentimental highlights of the show: the "Rhapsody in Blue" overture (Joe Venuti's orchestra played the final performance), Sally Rand's fan dance,[32] Everett Marshall singing "The Night Is Young and You Are Beautiful" to Faye Cotton, and the grand finale featuring the entire cast of some two hundred singers, dancers, and performers. And thus the show was over.

The exodus from Fort Worth had already begun. Paul Whiteman's orchestra had departed for another engagement, and Sally Rand was assembling a cast of Casa Mañana showgirls for a theater tour. Everett Marshall was off to London, and Faye Cotton left shortly for the West Coast and a motion picture contract. Amon Carter was out of the city and missed the final performances. He telegraphed Rose that night at the Fort Worth Club: "It has been an outstanding success. I think in advertising value alone it has been worth to Fort Worth all it cost. I believe in actual business terms it has paid for itself in the visitors it has brought to the city and the money turned into our business channels. I regard it as the biggest and best thing Fort Worth ever has done and no little of the credit goes to you, for without you

---

[31] James M. North to Lieut. Gov. Walter Woodul, August 29, 1936, Carter Archives.

[32] Sally Rand's so-called nude dance was actually a study in feminine beauty, poise, and grace. Viewers explained she would have revealed more wearing a trench coat.

and the magnificent shows you created none of this value could have been obtained."[33] Before leaving for Hollywood on Sunday morning, Rose dictated a brief note to Carter: "No use trying to put in words how I feel about you. . . . As a producer you will pardon me if I envy you. I build shows — Christ!, you built a city."[34]

Labor Day weekend marked the midway point in the Central Exposition's six-month run and the much-delayed dedication of the Hall of State. At eight o'clock on the evening of September 5, Baylor University President Pat M. Neff delivered the dedicatory address, marking the hundredth anniversary of Sam Houston's election as president of the Republic of Texas. Although the three-day attendance totaled 184,366, it was still 243,021 short of the four million mark and more than six million short of the ten million conservatively projected for the fair's entire run. The intense summer heat had undoubtedly been a retardant factor. On August 10, the mercury reached 109.6, an official all-time record for Dallas, and the following day was little better at 107.2 degrees. The autumn rains and cooler weather spurred renewed optimism in the administration building: "With cotton picking soon to be over and stock shows, school programs, football games and other gala affairs to be daily events, it is now believed the total attendance will approximate 10 million."[35] The cooler weather, however, also brought heavy rains; attendance fell below the twenty thousand mark on each of the last six days of September.

With the reopening of the public schools in September, Governor Allred heeded Billy Rose's advice and encouraged all of Texas' 1.5 million school children to "go to Dallas for education." On Friday, September 18, he issued a proclamation declaring two-day class suspensions, by districts, "in recognition of the unprecedented educational advantages offered at the Texas Centennial Exposition."[36] The railroads offered a special rate of one-half cent per mile for school groups, exposition admission was set at twenty-five cents, and the

[33] Amon Carter to Billy Rose, November 14, 1936, Carter Archives.

[34] Billy Rose to Amon Carter, November 14, 1936, Carter Archives. The Fort Worth exposition launched Rose's career as a producer of exposition extravaganzas. He produced various editions of *Aquacade*, a water spectacle, in Cleveland in 1937, at the New York World's Fair in 1939, and at the San Francisco Fair in 1940. Almost 2 million people saw the San Francisco show, which featured Morton Downey, Johnny Weissmuller, and Esther Williams.

[35] *Dallas Morning News*, September 9, 1936.

[36] There was a precedent for this action. In September, 1853, "all the school children

Cavalcade of Texas offered a special student matinee at the same price. A group of 365 students from Pleasant Hill, a Cottle County three-teacher school, was the first to arrive. As not all the students had sufficient money to make the trip, principal Robert L. McKain explained they pooled their finances for admissions and "others brought a dozen eggs, a hunk of bacon, and other food sufficient for the weekend trip to Dallas."[37] Some nine hundred Lamb County citizens, including five hundred school children, chartered an eighteen-coach special train for the two-day school holiday. They also carried their own provisions: — three barbecued steers. Lacking convenient railroad connections, Nacogdoches High School hired the town's nine taxis and assigned eight students to each for the educational excursion to Dallas.

Statistics differ on the number of students attending the exposition during the designated days. Dr. L. A. Woods, state superintendent of schools, placed the count at 275,000. Elithe Hamilton Beal, who coordinated school and club activities, reported only 117,250.[38] Whatever the actual figures were, they contributed little toward the total attendance. The five million mark was reached on October 18, and by early November Harry A. Olmsted, who became general manager following Webb's death, finally accepted the inevitable. He announced the revised attendance projection at 7 million. "If there is anything like a break from the weatherman," he stated, "I know there will be more than a million visitors in the remaining 24 days of the exposition."[39] The weatherman apparently failed to cooperate; the daily attendance continued to fall short of the most conservative estimates.

During the final days, concessionaires began displaying bargain signs, some cutting prices in half, hoping to dispose of their centennial artifacts before closing. And still the weather refused to cooperate. On Sunday morning, November 29, with the temperature standing in the low fifties, a cloudy, rainy day marked the end of the Texas Centennial Central Exposition. At 9:00 A.M. Olmsted entered the main gate, where he was joined by other exposition officials and fair em-

---

in New York City were given a day at the 'Crystal Palace.'" Suzanne Hilton, *Here Today and Gone Tomorrow: The Story of World's Fairs and Expositions* (Philadelphia: Westminster Press, 1978), p. 31.

[37]*Dallas Morning News,* September 27, 1936.

[38]Elithe Hamilton Beal to Frank N. Watson, December 7, 1936, Centennial Collection, DHS.

[39]*Dallas Morning News,* November 8, 1936.

ployees for a ceremonial march through the grounds to inaugurate the final day. At twelve o'clock noon in Studio B, the Gulf Studios broadcast the closing ceremonies over the Texas Quality Network. Ligon Smith's orchestra provided the music, and centennial officials and Sen. Tom Connally spoke. Governor Allred and United States Commissioner Cullen F. Thomas telegraphed their regrets.[40] Art Linkletter concluded the broadcast: "And so, until we greet you from these grounds next June . . . best wishes from all of us at the Centennial."[41]

At 6:15 P.M. the lights along the Esplanade of State were turned on for the last time. The band and troops from Camp Stephen F. Austin formed before the Hall of State for the closing ceremony. Nathan Adams, chairman of the Centennial Corporation board, made a brief address. At 9:30 P.M. a brilliant fireworks display was staged by the lagoon in the Civic Center. Exhibit buildings were closed at 10:00 P.M. with a final program scheduled in the Hall of State. As midnight approached Mayor George Sergeant made his way to the main gate where, at the stroke of twelve, he declared the show to be at an end. The final attendance stood at 6,354,385. Then came the lonely tones of taps from the Camp Stephen F. Austin bugler. Journalist Al Harting witnessed the closing ceremonies: "The walkways, streets and buildings emptied quickly. Gulf Oil's PA system broadcast the song it had played each midnight to signal the end of the day. This time it was the end of a dream. With a cold wind blowing through the park 'Tumbling Tumbleweeds' sounded mournful and appropriate."[42]

The following week another journalist, Barry Bishop, visited the exposition site and composed a nostalgic word picture of the fair's aftermath:

A jilted lover stood alone in South Dallas Sunday shivering under the belated touch of winter and wondering where her admirers . . . had gone so suddenly. . . . Singing pylons were strangely silent and beautiful fountains were dreary in their aridity. . . . On the Esplanade of State leaves fell unnoticed in the dry reflecting basin. And down on the Midway canvas fronts . . . flapped nonchalantly in the

[40]James V. Allred had just been reelected governor for a second term by a landslide vote. His close identification with the centennial celebrations undoubtedly accounted for some of his popularity.
[41]Radio Script, Ligon Smith Collection. The decision had been made to repeat the fair as the Greater Texas and Pan American Exposition, running from June 12 to October 31, 1937.
[42]Al Harting, "Centennial Fever," p. 19.

breeze. . . . Inside the Varied Industries Building . . . workmen worked in semi-darkness completing the work of tearing down displays and packing them for shipping or storage . . . there was no mistake that the Texas Centennial Exposition had closed, for the wrinkles and faded cheeks of old age were showing up rapidly after one week of neglect.[43]

Texas had celebrated its first century. Another one would begin in a few days.

[43] *Dallas Morning News*, December 7, 1936.

EPILOGUE

T he 1936 Texas centennial left in its wake some permanent memorials, a brighter economic outlook, pleasant memories, plus a lot of red ink. World's fairs, in reality, are not supposed to make money; this one didn't.[1] Centennial celebrations — and sesquicentennials, for that matter — are at best amateur media events that muster all spheres of civic and economic interest under a single legislative umbrella. The manifestation of patriotism, however sincere, usually translates into subtle, and often blatantly unsubtle, appeals to tourism and ultimate economic enrichment. Immediate returns are usually sacrificed for long-term profits. Such was the case of the great 1936 birthday party. The Texas Centennial Central Exposition Corporation reported a total income of $3,304,234.86 (including ticket sales of $1,276,362.10) against $6,193,086.86 in expenses, which included $701,715.80 in accounts payable. With only $15,105.83 in cash on hand, the corporation concluded business on November 29, 1936, with a total loss of $2,888,852.00.[2]

The Fort Worth Frontier Centennial exposition, being smaller, fared somewhat better. It too wound up in the loss column, despite some adroit book-juggling and optimistic rationalizations. The total cost of the eighty-day crash-construction program reached $1,509,033.36 — a cost overrun of approximately $300,000. The exposition yielded an operating profit of $289,286.67 on a total attendance of 986,128.

[1] Of forty-three major world expositions held between 1876 and 1975, twenty-six reported a loss. John Allwood, *The Great Exhibitions* (London: Studio Vista, 1977), pp. 180–85. The 1984 New Orleans World's Fair posted an estimated $110 million loss, including approximately $46 million in state-appropriated funds.

[2] This amount would have been far greater had not many bondholders signed agreements of waiver releasing their claim to one-third of the gate receipts. Those who did not sign the agreements received a total of $74,886.82. The exposition concluded with an unpaid balance of $22,536.18 on bond subscriptions totaling $97,600. Report of Examination, Texas Centennial Central Corporation, by Ernst & Ernst, Accountants and Auditors, Dallas, Texas, January 14, 1937. Document in author's possession.

This, however, was more than one million visitors short of the most conservative estimate. The exposition leaders had based this projection on one-third of Dallas's lowest attendance estimate of 6 million. When the operating profit was applied to the $302,438.29 in open accounts, the corporation ended up with a $16,451.01 deficit. This, however, was resolved by a "paper sale" of office furniture and miscellaneous maintenance equipment to the successor corporation, the Frontier Fiesta Association, which operated the amusement park during the summers of 1937, 1938, and 1939. Of the major attractions, only Casa Mañana proved profitable. It showed an operating profit of $145,351.67 on an income of $477,700.55, while all other shows lost money. The Pioneer Palace and *Jumbo* were the biggest losers, posting deficits of $52,594.89 and $23,988.78 respectively.

These profit and loss figures are misleading when taken out of context. The exposition bonds were never redeemed; bond sales, notes in lien of bonds, and loans totaled $1,117,575.00. Corporation president William Monnig explained: "Your board regrets exceedingly the inability of the corporation to redeem these bonds and notes. It is likewise embarrassed by the fact that it borrowed $342,000 upon statements supplied to it, showing that such sum would be sufficient to pay all outstanding costs and leave an operating reserve, as of opening date, of $50,000." Monnig believed, however, "the Fort Worth Frontier Centennial was worth all it cost to Fort Worth, in the advertising it gave to the city, the favorable impression made upon visitors, and the business activity for which it was responsible, estimated at approximately $5,000,000."[3]

Amon Carter's assessment of the exposition's finances differed somewhat from Monnig's. On January 9, 1937, Carter again appealed to Vice-President John N. Garner, as chairman of the federal commission, for additional funds. The show still owed $27,000, and with approximately $7,000 in cash on hand, Carter claimed "another $20,000 would enable us to wipe the slate clean." Knowing that federal funds were restricted to buildings, Carter explained that the $27,000 was owed on buildings, "for materials, supplies and labor. The creditors are mostly small firms, plumbers, electricians, painters, etc.— concerns

[3]Report of the Texas Centennial Livestock and Frontier Days Exposition, Inc., dated March 11, 1936; that date is obviously incorrect and should be March 11, 1937. Lois Gray, "History of Fort Worth Centennial," appendix.

who should not be forced to take this loss and who can hardly afford to do so." Without Garner's help, he could foresee "no way of those people getting paid." While there is no record of Garner's response, it can be assumed it was negative. Disregarding their financial dilemma, Carter, like Monnig, also believed the benefits far exceeded the cost. More conservative than his colleague, he placed the value of civic exposure through advertising, promotion, and the exposition's national prestige at $2.5 million.[4]

Growth benefits spawned by the adjacent expositions, whatever the cost, was the one topic on which both Dallas and Fort Worth leaders could agree. Looking back on the centennial summer, internationally renowned merchant Stanley Marcus remembered the repeated assessments on Dallas business establishments to keep the Centennial Corporation solvent. "They raised the money that way during the summer, [and] kept it alive," he recalled. "And I think that it is probably the best single investment Dallas ever made—that is, if you believe in the theory of growth."[5] John Stemmons, another Dallas civic leader and growth advocate, reviewed the centennial's impact on the city in a broad historical context: "The centennial took us to our first plateau. World War II took us to our second plateau. And there's just no stopping us now. Just look out that window."[6] Robert Cullum, corporate executive of the Cullum Companies, Inc., operator of the Tom Thumb-Page supermarkets, translated the centennial experience in terms of its impact on the Dallas civic leadership. "It melded the business community. Unified them in a way that very few cities have ever enjoyed because the business community built the centennial [exposition]." And in addition, "they took this prairie down here and built a hell of a show and did it with their hands, . . . and meager incomes, and made it a success. And Dallas has been a kind of 'can do' town ever since. In a way that it was not before." Cullum concluded, "Texas has become a pretty serious issue in the country now, you know."[7]

The urban profiles displayed during the centennial era revealed widely varying qualities of leadership that projected, at least in the short term, the civic expectations in Texas' four largest cities. Houston and San Antonio, unlike Dallas, lacked aggressiveness in the com-

[4]Amon Carter to John Nance Garner, January 9, 1937, Carter Archives.
[5]Marcus interview, July 26, 1978.
[6]Stemmons interview, May 29, 1978.
[7]Cullum interview, May 16, 1978.

petition for the central exposition. Although hosting a world class exposition created an immediate financial obligation, it offered great economic benefits in the long term. Yet neither Houston nor San Antonio was organized to gain that advantage. The reasons differ widely. According to C. Stanley Banks, the San Antonio business community enjoyed the luxury of a "built-in economic gold mine"— the multimillion-dollar annual military payroll — and never learned how to "scratch for a dollar."[8] Therefore, the economic benefits of a major exposition meant far less to San Antonio than to Dallas. In addition, the social dynamics of San Antonio, boasting a 1934 population of 231,542, are somewhat misleading. While the Dallas leadership could rely on broad-based community support from some 260,000 citizens, such support existed to a far lesser degree in San Antonio. Bexar County in 1930 was 68 percent minority, and at that time, minorities had little involvement in civic leadership. (That, of course, has changed.)

Houston, on the other hand, was the state's largest city in 1934, with 292,352 inhabitants, and possessed far greater economic wealth. Judge Wharton's warning that "Houston's leadership in this state hangs in the balance" caused relatively little local concern, for the Bayou City was enjoying a rich economic harvest in the petroleum industries. (Even during the centennial exposition construction boom, Houston's annual building permits exceeded those of Dallas.) Another factor undoubtedly contributed to Houston reticence in the exposition matter — Jesse Jones. Although residing in Washington, Jones still wielded considerable influence in his hometown, and he was from the outset unenthusiastic about a world's fair to celebrate the Texas centennial. "It seems to me the day of the world's fair is passed," he stated. "The hoochy-koochy and Midway Plaisance" of former expositions, he reasoned, were now passé.[9] Also, Houston's leadership was never aggressive in developing a diversified industrial economy, which partially accounts for that city's economic dilemma in the mid-1980s. Finally, Houston was never a fair-oriented city; on at least three occasions in the twentieth century, it rejected proposals to host a major exposition.

Without question, Fort Worth during the centennial era was a one-

[8]Interview with C. Stanley Banks, San Antonio, Texas, October 3, 1984.
[9]"The Texas Centennial," reprint of address delivered to Fort Worth Exchange Club, March 31, 1928, Jones Papers.

man town—Amon Carter's. As long as Carter remained active, civic
policies were well defined and the city prospered. He recognized the
benefits of urban boosterism and promoted Fort Worth's version of
the celebration. But with his demise his power was not passed to
waiting hands; there were none. Oscar Monnig, son of William Monnig, explained, "He was the dominant figure here in Fort Worth. In
fact he's been criticized somewhat for being so dominant that when
he died, there was nobody to succeed him. He just pushed everybody
else down."[10] Woods Moore, another Fort Worth businessman, explained Carter's dominance in comparative terms: "Mr. Carter was
like a giant oak tree. Nothing can grow in its shadow."[11]

The Dallas style of cooperative leadership, unique in the state,
helped that city win the central exposition. Following the close of
the successor fair, the Greater Texas & Pan American Exposition of
1937, R. L. Thornton moved to further institutionalize the process.
C. A. Tatum, Jr., a Dallas industrialist and civic leader, explained
that "out of the centennial grew an organization in Dallas called the
Dallas Citizens Council. . . . Mr. Thornton told me that he formed
the [organization] because he got tired of trying to make up a list
of men to call . . . when he had a public problem."[12] Thornton wanted
a body of leaders, "yes and no" men who could address a civic problem and make immediate decisions. The Dallas Citizens Council was
chartered on November 22, 1937; the bylaws limited voting membership to "the Chief Executive officer or President or the top executive
official of a business enterprise transacting business . . . in the metropolitan area." Membership was by invitation only; twenty-two Dallas business executives comprised the original board of directors, which
included all of the centennial exposition leaders.[13]

Following the Dallas expositions of 1936 and 1937, the Citizens Council attracted wide attention, and other cities considered the plan. "I
went to a number of towns [Kansas City, Topeka, Atlanta, Birmingham, and Memphis] to make speeches about the Citizens Council,"

[10]Interview with Oscar Monnig, Fort Worth, Texas, February 22, 1978.
[11]Moore interview, February 24, 1978.
[12]Interview with C. A. Tatum, Jr., Dallas, Texas, July 25, 1978.
[13]*Charter, By-laws of Dallas Citizens Council*, Dallas, Texas, 1978, p. 5. The Dallas
Citizens Council has no relationship whatsoever with the later citizens councils throughout the South that defied integration.

C. A. Tatum, Jr., explained. "They couldn't believe it would work."[14]
And for other cities it didn't; the reasons remain unclear. Most political observers speculate that the Dallas civic environment that spawned
the Citizens Council was indeed unique, as was its initial leadership.
The spirit of R. L. Thornton endures. Under his guidance the council
evolved as an instrument for community service, while at the same
time eliminating the need and the potential for a single individual
achieving a dominant role. Dallas has never had a city "boss."

In a half-century assessment of the Citizens Council, *D Magazine*
reported: "Members were expected to do what was good for Dallas —
not for their own self-interest — with the expectation that as the city
grew, their companies would benefit also. Without the constraints
of law or the demands of holding companies, the Decision Makers
gave generously from their corporate proceeds."[15] The council was
totally nonpartisan in its functioning (it offered independent slates
of candidates in city elections), but it addressed every major issue
facing the city: water resources, transportation, integration, housing, education, hospitals, schools, etc. With the exception of a brief
interim in the 1970s, when the organization lost some of its initial
clout, the Dallas Citizens Council still functions for community betterment, just as Thornton launched it in the centennial's wake.[16] Felix
McKnight, former editor of the *Dallas Times Herald*, reflecting on
the legacy of the centennial era, stated that "you can draw a straight
line from the 1936 Texas Centennial [exposition] to the dedication of
the Dallas–Fort Worth Regional Airport in 1974, with only slight de-
viations in between."[17]

Any evaluation of the centennial's residual impact must consider
the advertising and publicity programs. Through media saturation
the nation's attention was, indeed, turned to the Lone Star State. An
editorial in *Farm & Ranch* magazine called this undertaking "the biggest dividend-paying investment any state has ever made. Extra gaso-
line taxes paid back to the state more than the original investment

[14]Tatum interview, July 25, 1978.

[15]*D Magazine*, October, 1984, p. 80.

[16]The Dallas Citizens Council is not without its critics. The organization has been accused of "benefitting only business and overlooking the poor, the minorities, and the salaried class." A. C. Greene, *Dallas USA* (Austin: Texas Monthly Press, 1984), p. 30.

[17]Interview with Felix McKnight, Dallas, Texas, October 20, 1977.

the first six months of 1936, but that is insignificant as compared with the advertising the state has received which has resulted in new developments in business and industry which will pay dividends throughout the years to come."[18] The Texas Highway Department recorded daily the direct benefits of the advertising campaign. Approximately 45,000 visitors entered Texas each month during the celebrations and traveled an average of 540 miles in the state. Visitors came from every state in the nation, and according to one report "the centennial has been the principal attraction."[19] Frank Watson, director of promotion for the Dallas exposition, reported that out-of-state visitors accounted for only 13 percent of the total gate count during the opening days of the fair, but by August that figure had increased to 21 percent; slightly more than one-fifth of the daily exposition visitors were non-Texans.[20] This statistic gave heart to the exposition sponsors; they believed investors were certain to follow the tourists. Immediately following the exposition's closing, Clyde Wallis of the Dallas Chamber of Commerce reported the chamber was already planning the centennial harvest years. "Just as we are still feeling the effects of the Industrial Dallas, Inc., advertising campaign some years ago," Wallis stated, "so we will continue to benefit for years from the exposition. Many executives of businesses and industry came here who otherwise would not have come, and undoubtedly many of them will come back to establish businesses here."[21]

The tourists also left an immediate mark on the local economy. Small change made the exposition cash registers ring loud and long in 1936. The visitors consumed five million gallons of bottled drinks and like amounts of coffee, tea, and milk, two million donuts, and 204,000 loaves of bread at a cost of approximately $1 million. Transactions in the Dallas business community, however, were recorded in larger denominations. Hotels reported a 35 percent gain in business, while restaurant operators reported their sales up as much as 50 percent. Increases in wholesale sales ranged from 22 to 40 per-

---

[18]"Texas and the Centennial" (editorial), *Farm & Ranch*, October 15, 1936, p. 8. Through August 31, 1936, receipts from the Highway Motor Fuel Tax increased by $4,037,310.08. By August 31, 1937, the two-year increase totaled $9,332,883.23. *Annual Report of the Comptroller of Public Accounts of the State of Texas, 1935, 1936, 1937.*

[19]*Dallas Morning News*, August 7, 1936.

[20]Ibid., August 5, 1936.

[21]Ibid., November 29, 1936.

cent, while the Texas & Pacific Railway Company reported that 1936 traffic rose as much as 35 percent over the previous year.[22] Employment statistics also reflected the centennial year economic resurgence. Traffic at the United States Government Re-employment Service increased nearly threefold. Statewide, that agency found employment for 268,820 people in 1936, as compared to 98,121 the previous year. Employment in Dallas County, however, rose more than 400 percent. In 1936, the Service placed 16,157 persons in new jobs, as compared to 3,666 in 1935. Banks, however, reported the big economic gains. Between March, 1935 and June 30, 1936, one month after the exposition opened, bank deposits increased $30,131,988.12. In a *Dallas Morning News* story, headlined "Centennial Launches Dallas' Greatest Era," a journalist concluded, "The consensus . . . among businessmen generally is that the city has made more history and more progress in the last six months than in all its previous existence."[23]

Departing from statistical data to the realm of speculation and assumption makes valid assessments far more difficult. There can be little doubt, however, that the great media blitz of the mid-1930s helped launch that southward trickle of humanity that a half-century later had reached flood tide, altering the nation's traditional east-west migration pattern. And while there would emerge stronger and far more profound factors to impact the human condition, many discovered the "Sun Belt" long before the term entered the vernacular. World War II, for example, brought to Texas millions of draftees and national guardsmen, who endorsed what the tourists had discovered a few years before. The combination of the two invasions catapulted Texas into the national consciousness as a place with assets. What had once been a hinterland province of "blackeyed peas and turnip greens" was being acknowledged as the promised land of the 1980s. Stanley

---

[22] Ibid.

[23] The economic depression of the time must also be considered a factor. The Census Bureau estimated that for the year ending July 1, 1935, Texas gained 42,000 in population. Also, the westward migration had slowed as the Rocky Mountain and Central States posted population decreases. The great drought of 1934 and 1935 also impacted the national demography. Population increase, however, is an integral part of the state's history. By 1930, the population had reached 5,824,715, a 24.9 percent decade increase, representing 1,161,487 newcomers. The decade of the 1930s brought a 10.1 percent gain or an additional population of 590,109. With a 20 percent growth rate for each of the next three decades, the state population had reached 9,579,677 by 1960. The 1980 population exceeded 14 million, more than double that when the 1936 Texas Centennial Central Exposition opened.

Marcus, that astute observer of the changing scene, recognized this early on. He explained:

> I've frequently said that modern Texas history started with the cele-
> bration of the Texas Centennial, because it was in 1936 . . . that the
> rest of America discovered Texas. The spotlight was thrown on Texas,
> and people from all over the United States came here. It was a hot
> grueling summer, as I recall, but, nonetheless, they liked what they
> saw. I've also said that ever since 1936, we haven't had a peaceful
> weekend . . . because there's been an invasion of people from all
> parts of the world . . . who find their way to Dallas and find their
> way to my office or my home. We — the store [Neiman-Marcus] —
> contributed to the Centennial celebration by staging a very large
> fashion show of international significance. We brought fashion lead-
> ers from all parts of the country to Dallas for the occasion, many
> of whom had never been west of the Hudson [River].[24]

To the hordes in this new invasion, Texas was a great phenomenon.
Many came expecting cowboys, and while they found their token cowboys, they discovered much more — a unique state, though not totally
unlike their own, offering a new and a virtually untapped resource
potential. Many saw Texas and the Great Southwest just as Theodore
Price had predicted, as one of America's last frontiers. Ultimately,
Yankees began collecting Texas dollars in Texas, and vice versa. (William E. Jary, Jr., recalled a Thorntonesque homily from the centennial era: "A Yankee is better than a bale of cotton and twice as easy
to pick.") The process of acculturation accompanied the new invasion. Many of these out-of-state visitors, seeing Texas for the first time,
expressed their praise for the "new Texas"; they found not the "countryfied folks" they had expected, but an "ultramodern" culture. This
changing attitude among non-Texans ultimately created a great cultural
impact on the state, negating the "pride with shame" syndrome and
instilling a new sense of state pride in Texans. "They found people
from the outside coming in saying what people on the inside had been
saying all along," Marcus observed.[25] This outside approval verified,
for those within, that regional self-consciousness was, after all, not
a congenital deformity.

[24]Marcus interview, July 26, 1978.
[25]Ibid.

One visible and enduring asset of the centennial movement is the abundance of memorials, markers, restorations, museums, and civic complexes financed as part of the celebration.[26] These helped sharpen individual awareness of the state's heritage, but when examined state-wide, they also form a permanent historical mosaic that documents for all time the Texas experience. The program of historical aware-ness and preservation launched in 1936 was destined to continue. In 1953 the state legislature created the Texas State Historical Survey Committee (which became the Texas Historical Commission in 1973) to survey, record, preserve, restore, and mark all phases of Texas his-tory. As a result, some four thousand additional historical markers have been erected throughout the state.

These are the residual benefits of the patriotic impulse that helped the centennial movement reach fruition. A half-century later one can only speculate whether Texas would have celebrated its centennial as it did had not Theodore Price inspired the state's media executives and business leaders with the idea of using history to "sell Texas." His-torian Jeffrey Hancock believed that very likely there would have been celebrations, but "the tempo, mood, and motives would perhaps have been different."[27] Furthermore, the Texas centennial was an accident in time, occurring at exactly the right point in history. Five years ear-lier, the Depression would have rendered a world exposition in Dal-las impossible, and five years later would have coincided with World War II.

Texas in the mid-1930s was a state floundering in social, cultural, and economic adolescence, awaiting the maturity of adulthood. The multiple forces that created the statewide celebrations also spurred growth enzymes and ultimately drew the state into the mainstream of the national experience. Yet in the process Texas both won and lost. The patriotic fervor expressed openly during the 1930s is gone for-ever; populations grow faster than cultural traditions.

Communications have also destroyed the once-restrictive barriers that confined a person's loyalty and commitment to his home com-

[26] In *Here Today and Gone Tomorrow*, a book on the major expositions, Suzanne Hil-ton documents the transitory nature of these events. Such was not the case of the 1936 Texas expositions. Civic centers in both Dallas and Forth Worth attest to the foresight of the celebration's planners. Balboa Park in San Diego and HemisFair Plaza in San Antonio are other exceptions.

[27] Hancock, "Preservation of Texas Heritage," pp. 1–2.

munity. The world is now philosophically smaller; personal interests have been dispersed to areas of the world that were once mere names and places in a geography book. A Texan's economic well-being, once limited to a farm, a ranch, a place of business, is now dependent upon what happens halfway around the globe. Today Texans are far more concerned with developments in Iraq, Iran, Kuwait, Taiwan, and Japan than in the latest news from Midland or Kilgore or Port Arthur. The mind and the pocketbook are attracted to where the action is.

The homogeneous makeup of the state's population has also been diluted by wave upon wave of southbound migration. And consequently loyalties have been divided. Interest in the statehouse carnival in Austin is now shared with the human comedies being played out in Columbus, Indianapolis, Lansing, or Springfield. Texans of the 1980s are an entirely different breed. In the half-century since Texas celebrated its centennial, its citizens have elected a Republican governor, approved liquor by the drink, and repealed the state's 122-year-old blue law. Citing this last event as an example of the changing temper of Texas, *Newsweek* reported, "Massive growth and urbanization are taking some of the old-time T out of Texanhood." The measure's sponsor, also recognizing the changing signs of the times, explained, "We're becoming more of a national state than a Southern state." One local pundit observed, "Even 'Bubba' favored repeal."[28]

With all the other factors that have also been at work, one fact remains abundantly clear. The Dallas-Fort Worth Metroplex stands today as a vision projected as half-century ago by Amon G. Carter, Robert L. Thornton, and their urban colleagues. Each in his own way helped launch their respective cities on growth cycles that led to the booming eighties and the economic coming-of-age of the Great Southwest. Were they living today, these two great urban competitors would relish the fruition of their efforts. Nowhere are their differing styles, methods, and personalities reflected more graphically than in the centennial celebrations each directed. Their objectives, however, were identical: stimulating the region's economic growth. To accord the Texas centennial celebrations major credit for all the changes that have occurred during the ensuing half-century would be a gross exaggeration; to ignore it as a factor would be an oversight. Texas had

[28]*Newsweek*, June 17, 1985, p. 20. At the wheel of his dilapidated pickup truck with a can of Lone Star Beer in his hand, "Bubba" has emerged as Texas' redneck "Everyman."

more going for it than a birthday party. Petroleum production, for example, had weakened the Depression's grip on the state and would emerge as a major growth factor for fifty years.

From the vantage point of five decades later, the centennial experience emerges as a barometer of changes that were already occurring in the Lone Star State; the image of Texas at the beginning of the decade bears scant resemblance to that at the end.

One remarkable achievement of the exposition, however, proved less enduring, although perhaps it presaged changes to come. The Hall of Negro Life at the Texas Centennial Exposition marked the first time the black race received such recognition at a world's fair. (The nearest previous approach to this had been the Jamestown Exposition in 1907, when white administrators had supervised a predominantly black staff.) But what began as a successful experiment in race relations ended as a disappointment for the black leaders who promoted and administered the Dallas exhibit. When it was announced that the exposition would continue in 1937 as the Greater Texas and Pan American Exposition, the black leaders assumed that the Hall of Negro Life would be retained as part of that exposition. Such was not the case; it was the only structure demolished immediately. In speculating on the reason for the abrupt change in policy, Jesse O. Thomas, general manager of the Hall of Negro Life, wrote: "Vice President Garner's letter . . . accredits some local citizens with opposing the continuance of Negro Participation. Who they were and what authority they had, what connection they sustained to the Texas Centennial Commission is not clear."[29]

Thus, the mid-1930s emerge as the watershed years in the twentieth-century Texas experience. While many Americans did indeed discover Texas, Texans were also participants in the discovery process. The great infusion and exchange of knowledge stimulated by the statewide observances, especially the central exposition, made Texans more knowledgeable about the world beyond their home communities, while at the same time giving them a better understanding of themselves. This was, in essence, the fulfillment of Cullen Thomas's prediction that the "centennial year should become in our history the year of great awakening. In 1936 Texas should be born again economically, educa-

---

[29] Jesse O. Thomas, *Negro Participation in the Texas Centennial Exposition* (Boston: Christopher Publishing House, 1938), p. 120.

tionally, culturally, patriotically, and spiritually."[30] At the central exposition, the centerpiece of the centennial celebrations, one could also discover the source of President McKinley's proclamation: "They open mighty storehouses of information. . . . Every exposition, great or small, has helped to [take] some onward step."

One aspect of the centennial experience frequently overlooked in a broad-based social and economic assessment is its emotional and psychological impact on the population. Times were difficult, the economy weak, and the statewide celebrations offered a variety of free and inexpensive events that helped enrich the lives of many of the state's citizens. The centennial provided emotional relief from the economic drama of mid-1930s and offered a new vision of hope for the future. Fort Worth advertising executive William E. Jary, Jr., addressed this fundamental topic when he stated: "In the depths of the depression the centennial activities, more than anything else, made Texas get off its ass and stand on its own two feet."[31]

In any analysis of the centennial's ultimate impact the movement's broad-based support must be considered. Every segment of government and society — the state legislature, the federal government, the business community, the media, and above all, the people — pursued all aspects of the centennial with dedication and commitment. Combined, they assured the celebration's success. And for whatever forms that success may have assumed, each group bears a measure of the credit.

Examined in any context, the 1936 Texas centennial and its broad spectrum of experiences — social, cultural, and economic — had helped change the face and mood of Dallas forever, and the residual benefits were not limited to the Metroplex. Somewhere in mid-decade Texas had begun to turn an important corner and was now headed down untrodden paths toward "that new era which lies ahead." The Lone Star State would never be the same. The great 1936 birthday celebration helped deem it so.

---

[30] Telegram, Cullen Thomas to Lowry Martin, July 15, 1934, State Archives.
[31] Interview with William E. Jary, Jr., Fort Worth, Texas, February 19, 1978.

BIBLIOGRAPHY

Correspondence

Aston, James W. Dallas, Tex., April 24, 1980.

Dahl, George L. Dallas, Tex., April 20, 1978; July 13, 1979.

Deakins, Katrine. Fort Worth, Tex., April 25, 1978.

Gambrell, Dr. Herbert. Dallas, Tex., March 13, 1979.

Glasser, Doris. Houston, Tex., August 20, 1984; October 5, 1984.

Green, H. Gordon. Longview, Tex., May 2, 1979; May 30, 1979; June 18, 1979; July 26, 1979.

Holmes, Mrs. Jack T. July 31, 1977; May 2, 1981; May 28, 1981.

Houston, L. B. Dallas, Tex., July 15, 1978.

Jary, William E., Jr. Fort Worth, Tex., April 18, 1979; February 22, 1980; September 19, 1984.

Kirkland, Elithe Hamilton. Coleman, Tex., August 29, 1982; October 26, 1984.

Kreneck, Dr. Tom. Houston, Tex., undated.

Linkletter, Art. Beverly Hills, Cal., July 5, 1979.

Martin, José. Dallas, Tex., undated.

Matthews, Wilbur L. San Antonio, Tex., February 23, 1984.

Miller, Dale. Austin, Tex., July 21, 1978. Washington, D.C., April 4, 1980; April 30, 1980; June 4, 1980; July 8, 1980; August 4, 1980; August 16, 1980; January 30, 1981; March 23, 1983.

Nelson, Donald S. Dallas, Tex., December 28, 1978.

Ortega, Belen. Dallas, Tex., November 19, 1982.

Rice, Mrs. J. Percival. Dallas, Tex., June 6, 1979; June 28, 1979.

Sellers, Linda. Dallas, Tex., September 26, 1984; October 18, 1984; February 11, 1985; April 3, 1985.

Smith, Ligon. Dallas, Tex., October 10, 1978; April 14, 1979.

Tyler, Dr. Ron. Fort Worth, Tex., May 4, 1978; January 4, 1979; October 15, 1984; November 29, 1984.

White, W. D. Dallas, Tex., November 6, 1978.

Wortham, Ethel. Corsicana, Tex., March 16, 1980.

Interviews

Anderson, Hugh H. (Andy). Dallas, Tex., October 19, 1977.
Aston, James W. Dallas, Tex., May 12, 1978.
Banks, C. Stanley. San Antonio, Tex., October 3, 1984.
Barkow, Evelyn Gracy. Fort Worth, Tex., June 6, 1981.
Bass, Dr. J. W. Canton, Tex., September 15, 1983.
Belcher, Virginia. Dallas, Tex., August 1, 1980.
Berry, Clay J. Fort Worth, Tex., February 20, 1978.
Bickley, Alex N. Dallas, Tex., February 23, 1978.
Bishop, Barry Lee. Austin, Tex., April 27, 1978; May 23, 1985.
Bovis, Ann. Telephone interview, June 5, 1979.
Bywaters, Jerry. Dallas, Tex., February 23, 1978.
Campbell, Martin. Dallas, Tex., February 23, 1978.
Crawford, Dr. William M. Fort Worth, Tex., February 21, 1978.
Cullum, Robert B. Dallas, Tex., May 16, 1978.
Dahl, George L. Dallas, Tex., April 6, 1978.
Deakins, Katrine. Fort Worth, Tex., February 24, 1978.
Dobie, Dudley. San Marcos, Tex., May 14, 1979.
Finn, Albert, Jr. Houston, Tex., April 20, 1980.
Ford, O'Neal. San Antonio, Tex., April 13, 1978.
Gallagher, Wayne H. Dallas, Tex., July 26, 1978.
Gambrell, Dr. Herbert. Dallas, Tex., October 20, 1977.
Garrett, Jenkins. Fort Worth, Tex., May 17, 1978.
Garrett, Virginia. Fort Worth, Tex., February 25, 1978.
Ginsburg, Marcus. Fort Worth, Tex., January 29, 1982.
Gordon, Jack. Fort Worth, Tex., February 25, 1979.
Green, H. Gordon. Longview, Tex., June 4, 1979.
Hale, Arthur K. Dallas, Tex., July 26, 1978.
Harris, Fred Red. Texas Judicial Systems Project, Baylor Program for Oral History, Baylor University, Waco.
Harris, Phil. Telephone interview, undated.
Harting, Frank. Dallas, Tex., November 4, 1977.
Herzog, Leo. Austin, Tex., undated.
Holmes, Janice. Fort Worth, Tex., February 20, 1978.
Houston, L. B. Dallas, Tex., April 3, 1978.
Jary, William E., Jr. Fort Worth, Tex., February 19, 1978.
Jones, Bess Harris. Austin, Tex., May 27, 1980.
Kavanaugh, John Henry. Austin, Tex., July 30, 1982.
Kettle, John J. Dallas, Tex., July 25, 1978.
Kilman, LaVea. Dallas, Tex., September 9, 1982.

Kirby, Hal P. Dallas, Tex., April 5, 1978.
Kucera, Henry. Dallas, Tex., April 5, 1978.
Lemens, Sen. Vernon. Austin, Tex., October 11, 1984.
Litrel, Joseph and Dorothy. Fort Worth, Tex., June 5, 1981.
Lovell, James V. Dallas, Tex., July 25, 1978.
McKnight, Felix. Dallas, Tex., October 20, 1977.
McLean, Malcolm and Margaret. Arlington, Tex., April 4, 1978.
Marcus, Stanley, Dallas, Tex., July 26, 1978.
Martin, José C. Dallas, Tex., May 16, 1978.
Martinez, Virginia. Fort Worth, Tex., June 6, 1981.
Matthews, Emily Von Hoven. Fort Worth, Tex., February 24, 1978.
Merrill, James F. Fort Worth, Tex., February 24, 1978.
Miller, Dale. Austin, Tex., July 21, 1978.
Monnig, Oscar. Fort Worth, Tex., February 22, 1978.
Moore, Woods. Fort Worth, Tex., February 24, 1978.
Nelson, Donald S. Dallas, Tex., April 5, 1978; May 24, 1985.
Nichols, Vance. Dallas, Tex., September 9, 1982.
Ortega, Belen. Dallas, Tex., June 6, 1979.
Payne, William. Dallas, Tex., May 15, 1978.
Pool, Robert. Austin, Tex., January 1, 1979.
Rand, Sally. Telephone interview, April 8, 1979.
Rice, Mrs. J. Percival. Dallas, Tex., June 6, 1979.
Rucker, Joe. Dallas, Tex., April 4, 1978.
Semos, Chris V. Dallas, Tex., June 6, 1979.
Smith, A. Maceo. Dallas, Tex., November 3, 1977.
Smith, Leonard. Austin, Tex., July 29, 1982.
Smith, Ligon, Dallas, Tex., October 20, 1977.
Spruce, Everett. Austin, Tex., April 18, 1978.
Stell, Tom. San Antonio, Tex., April 13, 1978.
Stemmons, John. Dallas, Tex., May 29, 1978.
Stewart, James Henry. Dallas, Tex., May 17, 1978.
Swank, Arch, Jr. Dallas, Tex., April 3, 1978.
Tatum, C. A., Jr. Dallas, Tex., July 25, 1978.
Teddlie, Pete. Dallas, Tex., October 20, 1977.
Thornton, R. L., Jr. Dallas, Tex., May 16, 1978.
Walker, Jack. Dallas, Tex., April 6, 1978.
West, Dick. Dallas, Tex., July 26, 1978.
Wheeler, Ronald W., Jr. Commerce, Tex., June 4, 1979.
Williams, Doyle. Fort Worth, Tex., June 5, 1981.
Wilson, James A. Dallas, Tex., April 4, 1978.
Wilson, Robert. Dallas, Tex., April 4, 1978.

Woodward, Lee (Red). Fort Worth, Tex., February 2, 1978.
Wortham, Ethel. Telephone interview, October 14, 1984.
Young, Lucille. Fort Worth, Tex., April 8, 1978.

Public Records and Manuscript Collections

Annual Report of the Comptroller of Public Accounts of the State of Texas,
  1935, 1936, 1937.
General Laws of the State of Texas, Thirty-Ninth Legislature, Regular
  Session, January 13, 1925 to March 19, 1925.
General Laws of the State of Texas, Forty-Second Legislature, Regular
  Session, January 10, 1933 to June 1, 1933.
General and Special Laws of the State of Texas, Forty-Third Legislature,
  Second Called Session, January 29, 1934 to February 27, 1934.
General and Special Laws of the State of Texas, Forty-Fourth Legislature,
  Regular Session, January 8, 1935, to May 11, 1935.
General Records of the Treasury Department Relating to the Texas Cen-
  tennial. Record Group 56. National Archives.
Hearings Before the Committe on Foreign Affairs, House of Representa-
  tives, Seventy-Fourth Congress, First Session, on H.J. Res. 293, May 23,
  1935. Record Group 233. National Achives.
Journal of the Senate of Texas, First Called Session, Forty-Third Legis-
  lature, September 14, 1933, to October 13, 1933.
Journal of the Senate of Texas, Second Called Session, Forty-Third Legis-
  lature, January 29, 1934.
Journal of the Senate of Texas, Fourth Called Session, Forty-Third Legis-
  lature, October 12, 1934, to November 10, 1934.
Journal of the House of Representatives, Regular Session, Forty-Fourth
  Legislature, January 8, 1935, to May 11, 1935.
King, Tom C. *Report of an Examination of the Texas Centennial. A Re-*
  port to Governor W. Lee O'Daniel and the 56th Legislature Dealing
  with the Period from March 24, 1934, to February 28, 1939. Austin:
  Office of the State Auditor and Efficiency Expert, 1939.
Mayes, Will H. "Report of the Secretary of the Texas Centennial Com-
  mission, March 24, 1934 to January 7, 1935." Centennial Collection,
  Texas State Archives.
Records of the Works Progress Administration, Information Division, Historic Shrines File, Texas: San Jacinto Battle Ground. Record Group
  69. National Archives.
Reports of the Advisory Board of Texas Historians to the Commission of
  Control for Texas Centennial Celebrations, Majority and Minority Re-
  ports, October 1, 1935.

Schoen, Harold (ed.). *Monuments Erected by the State of Texas to Commemorate the Centenary of Texas Independence. The Report of the Commission of Control for Texas Centennial Celebrations.* Austin: Commission of Control for Texas Centennial Celebrations, 1938.

State Department Decimal File 811.607, Texas Centennial. Record Group 59. National Archives.

Texas Centennial Collection. Texas State Archives, Austin.

U.S. Department of Commerce. Federal Participation: HemisFair '68. Washington, D.C.: Government Printing Office, 1971.

Manuscript Collections

Amon Carter Museum of Western Art, Fort Worth. Amon G. Carter Archives.

Barker Texas History Center, University of Texas at Austin. J. Frank Dobie Papers. Jesse H. Jones Papers. Texas Newspaper Collection.

Baylor University Library, Waco. Texas Centennial Collection, Texas Collection.

Dallas Historical Society, Dallas. R. L. Thornton Scrapbook, Scrapbook Collection. Texas Centennial Central Exposition Collection.

Dallas Public Library, Dallas. Texas Centennial Collection, Local History Collection.

Daughters of the Republic of Texas Library at the Alamo, San Antonio. Sarah Roach Farnsworth Collection. Texas Centennial Collection.

Fine Arts Library, Southern Methodist University, Dallas. Jerry Bywaters Research Collection on American Art and Architecture.

Fort Worth History Collection, Fort Worth. William E. Jary, Jr., Papers.

Houston Metropolitan Research Center, Houston. George Hill Collection.

Kirkland, Elithe Hamilton, Coleman, Texas. Texas Centennial Collection.

Rankin, James W., Dallas. Texas Centennial Collection.

Rice, Mrs. J. Percival, Dallas. J. Percival Rice Scrapbook.

San Antonio Public Library, San Antonio. Texas Centennial Collection.

Smith, Ligon, Dallas. Personal Papers.

Toney, Demp, Austin. Sally Rand Collection.

Books, Articles, Documents, and Theses

Adams, Frank Carter. *State of Texas Building.* Austin: Steck Co., 1937.

Allwood, John. *The Great Exhibitions.* London: Studio Vista, 1977.

Art Deco. Madison: State Historical Society of Wisconsin, 1973.

Art Deco Design. Austin: University Art Museum, University of Texas at Austin, 1975.

Boswell, John D. "Negro Participation in the 1936 Texas Centennial Exposition." Unpublished term paper, History 389, University of Texas at Austin, 1969.

Bruce, Edward, and Watson Forbes. *Art in Federal Buildings: An Illustrated Record of the Treasury Department's New Program in Painting and Sculpture.* Washington, D.C.: Arkin Federal Buildings, Inc., 1936.

Brunham, Daniel H. "How Chicago Financed Its Exposition." *Review of Reviews* 86 (October 1932): 37–38.

Bywaters, Jerry. *Seventy-Five Years of Art in Dallas: The History of the Dallas Art Association and the Dallas Museum of Fine Arts.* Dallas: Dallas Museum of Fine Arts, 1978.

Catalogue of the Exhibition of Painting, Sculptures, Graphic Arts, Dallas Museum of Fine Arts, June 6 to November 29, 1936. Dallas: Exline-Lowden Co., 1936.

Chariton, Wallace C. *Texas Centennial: The Parade of an Empire.* Plano, Texas: Privately printed, 1969.

Commemorating a Hundred Years of Texas History. Dallas (?): Publicity Committee, Texas Centennial Commission, 1934.

Conrad, Earl. *Billy Rose, Manhattan Primitive.* Cleveland: World Publishing Co., 1968.

Coppini, Pompeo. *From Dawn to Sunset.* San Antonio: Naylor, 1949.

Crunden, Frederick M. "The Scope and Features of the Louisiana Purchase Exposition." *Review of Reviews* 86 (May 1903): 547–56.

D Magazine (October, 1984).

Dahl, George. *Selected Works.* New York: Architectural Catalog Company, 1953.

Dallas 1936. Dallas: A. H. Belo Corp., 1936.

Dallas. Texas Centennial Central Exposition, 1936. The Official Guide Book.

Dealey, Ted. *Diaper Days of Dallas.* Nashville: Abingdon Press, 1966.

"Fairs." *Architectural Forum* 65 (September 1936): 171–89.

Fehrenback, T. R. *Lone Star: A History of Texas and Texans.* New York: Macmillan, 1968.

Flemmons, Jerry. *Amon: The Life of Amon Carter, Sr. of Texas.* Austin: Jenkins Publishing Co., 1978.

Frantz, Joe B. *Texas: A Bicentennial History.* New York: Norton, 1976.

Fuermann, George M. *Reluctant Empire.* Garden City: Doubleday, 1957.

Garrett, Julia Kathryn. *Fort Worth: A Frontier Triumph.* Austin: Encino Press, 1972.

Gillette, Michael L. "The Rise of the NAACP in Texas." *Southwestern Historical Quarterly* 81 (April 1978): 393.

Gottlieb, Polly Rose. *The Nine Lives of Billy Rose*. New York: Crown Publishers, 1968.

Gray, Lois. "History of the Fort Worth Frontier Centennial." Master's thesis, Texas Christian University, 1938.

Green, A. C. *Dallas: The Deciding Years — A Historical Portrait*. Austin: Encino Press, 1973.

———. *Dallas, USA*. Austin: Texas Monthly Press, 1984.

Hancock, Jeffrey Mason. "Preservation of Texas Heritage in the 1936 Texas Centennial." Master's thesis, University of Texas at Austin, 1962.

Harrigan, Stephen. "Coppini the Great." *Texas Monthly*, October 1984, 142–234.

Harting, Al. "Centennial Fever." *Westward* (*Dallas Times Herald* Sunday Magazine Supplement), July 13, 1969, 6–19.

Henderson, Richard B. *Maury Maverick: A Political Biography*. Austin: University of Texas Press, 1970.

Hilton, Suzanne. *Here Today and Gone Tomorrow: The Story of World's Fairs and Expositions*. Philadelphia: Westminster Press, 1978.

Jackson, George. *History of Centennials, Expositions and World's Fairs*. Lincoln: Wekesser-Brinkman, 1939.

James, Jack, and Earl Weller. *Treasure Island: "The Magic City."* San Francisco: Pisani Printing and Publishing Company, 1941.

Johnson, Alva. "Colonel Carter of Cartersville." *The Saturday Evening Post*, November 26, 1938.

Kreneck, Thomas H. "The Letter from Chapultepec." *The Houston Review* 3 (Summer 1981): 268–71.

Macdonald, William. "The California Expositions." *Nation*, October 21, 1915, 490.

MacFarlane, W. G. *The Texas Centennial and Dallas Exposition, 1836–1936*. Chicago: American Autochrome Co., 1936.

Magazine of Light 5, 1936.

Martin, José. "My Good Friend Raoul." Unpublished reminiscences of Martin's professional association with sculptor Raoul Josset. Photocopy in author's files.

Martin, Lowry. "First Authentic Memoirs of Texas Centennial Celebration History." *Texas Press Association Messenger* 12 (January 1937): 24–29.

Martin, Mary. *My Heart Belongs*. New York: Morrow, 1976.

Meinig, Donald William. *Imperial Texas: An Interpretative Essay in Cultural Geography*. Austin: University of Texas Press, 1969.

Murchison, Wayne. "Remembering Uncle Bob," *Scene* (*Dallas Morning News* Sunday Magazine), December 5, 1976.

Pell, Edward Lee. *McKinley and Men of Our Times.* St. Louis: Historical Society of America, 1901.

Porterfield, Bill. "Is the Metroplex Big Enough for Both of Us?" *D Magazine,* June 1976, 46.

Price, Theodore H. "What Texas Has to Advertise and How to Advertise It." *Commerce and Finance,* November 14, 1923, 2107–2109.

Rogers, John W. *The Lusty Texans of Dallas.* New York: Dutton, 1960.

Rose, Billy. *Wine, Women, and Words.* New York: Simon and Schuster, 1948.

Santerre, George Henry. *Dallas' First Hundred Years, 1856–1956.* Dallas: Book Craft, 1956.

Scully, Michael. *Dallas, Texas Centennial Exposition Center, 1936.* Dallas: Turner Company, 1935.

Selle, Ralph A. *The Texas Centennial.* Houston: Carrell Publishing Company, 1934.

Smith, Richard Austin. "How Dallas Failed Business." *Fortune,* July 1964, 137–216.

Stewart, Rick. *Lone Star Regionalism: The Dallas Nine and Their Circle.* Dallas: Dallas Museum of Art, 1985.

Stone, Harold A., Don K. Price, and Kathryn H. Stone. *City Government in Dallas.* Chicago: Public Administration Service, 1939.

Texas Centennial Scrapbook, 1936. Fort Worth: Fort Worth Press, 1936.

Thomas, Jesse O. *Negro Participation in the Texas Centennial Exposition.* Boston: The Christopher Publishing House, 1938.

Thometz, Carol (Estes). *The Decision Makers: The Power Structure of Dallas.* Dallas: Southern Methodist University Press, 1963.

Timmons, Bascom N. *Jesse H. Jones: The Man and the Statesman.* New York: Holt, 1956.

Tinkle, Lon. *The Key to Dallas.* Philadelphia: Lippincott, 1965.

Vickers, Sue Bitner. "HemisFair 1968." Master's thesis, University of Texas at Austin, 1968.

Walker, Stanley. *The Dallas Story.* Dallas: Dallas Times Herald, 1956.

Whiffen, Marcus. *American Architecture Since 1780.* Cambridge, Mass.: M.I.T. Press, 1969.

Whitten, Margaret. "Certain Aspects of the Texas Centennial Celebration." Master's thesis, Southern Methodist University, 1937.

Williams, Mack (compiler). *In Old Fort Worth: The Story of a City and Its People as Published in the News-Tribune in 1976 and 1977.* Fort Worth: Mack Williams, 1977.

Windels, Susan Bean. "The Art of the Texas Centennial Central Exposition of 1936." Master's thesis, Southern Methodist University, 1979.

Wineburgh, Harold H. *The Texas Banker: The Life and Times of Fred Farrel Florence*. Dallas: Harold H. Wineburgh, 1981.

Newspapers and Journals

Art Digest
Boston Herald
D Magazine
The Dallas Downtown News
Dallas Express
Dallas Journal
Dallas Morning News
Dallas Times Herald
Eastland Chronicle
Fort Worth Star-Telegram
Galveston Tribune
Houston Chronicle
Houston Post
New York Sun
St. Louis Globe-Democrat
Southwestern Historical Quarterly
San Antonio Express
Texas Business Review
Texas Centennial News, 1934 Edition
Texas Centennial News, 1935–36 Edition
Texas Centennial Review
The Texas Weekly
Time

INDEX

New York Sun, 149
Nichols, Perry, 182; photograph of, 188
Nicolson, Janice (Holmes), 222
Nicolson, Olive, 222
North, J. M., Jr., 102, 219, 220, 288–89
Northe, Gayle, 231
North Texas State College, 126
North Texas Trust Company, 287
Novy, Louis: photograph of, 137

Ochs, Herman H., 36
Odom, C. H., 42
Old Globe Theater concession, 249
Old Nuremburg Restaurant, 258
Old Stone Fort, 101, 160; photograph of, 162
Olmsted, Harry A., 109, 291
Ort, William, 43
Oumansky, Alexander, 223
Our Catholic Heritage in Texas, 99
Outdoor Poster Association, 24, 39–40
Overbeck, Harry, 93, 95

Pack, Leonard, 150, 153
Panama-California Exposition, 257
Panama-Pacific Exposition, 181
Pan American Airways, 46
Panhandle-Plains Historical Society, 101
Papert, S. W., 23, 42
Paramount Publix Theaters, 40
Parker, Bonnie, 33
Parker, Cynthia Ann, 100
Parmley, Nell, 225
Parr, Archer, 31
Patman, Wright, 107
Patterson, Glennie Vale, 43
Patton, Nat, 31
Peacock Terrace, 228
Pendleton Dudley Advertising Agency, 148
Pennington, Ann, 217
Petroleum Building, 255
Pickford, Mary, 133
Pioneer Palace, 289, 295
Plainview Panhandle-Plains Dairy Show, 160
Pool, Robert, 70
Popeye, 167
Port Aransas Tarpon Rodeo, 160
Portland Cement House exhibit, 256
Powell, Dick, 216
Price, R. N., 41
Price, Theodore, 3, 4, 115, 118, 302–303
Progressive Texans, Inc., 23
prostitution, 287–88

Publicity, Department of (1936): activities of, 119, 120, 121–26, 131, 132, 133, 147–48; objectives of, 117, 118; staff of, 116, 117; Texas myths used by, 142, 143–44, 145
publicity campaign (1934), 38–43
Purl, George C., 64, 67
Pyle, Ernie, 221

Quinn, C. K., 47, 48, 57, 58, 59, 122, 170

Racey, Earl, 23–24, 39–40
radio broadcasts: from expositions, 221, 253–54
Radio City Music Hall, 215
Raft, George, 228
Rainey, Homer Price, 100
Raitt, John, 213
Rand, Sally, 217, 230, 289; photographs of, 278, 279
Rawlins, Frank H., 102
Rayburn, Sam, 107, 146
Raymondville (Texas) Onion Show, 160
Reagan, John H., 103
Reed, W. O., 70
Reeder, R. L., 72
"Rhapsody in Blue," 264
Rice, J. Percival, 106
Robertson, Geraldine, 284
Robertson, Perry S., 57
Rogers, Buddy, 254
Rogers, Dan, 264
Rogers, Edith N., 79
Rogers, Ginger, 132, 212, 216, 254, 284; photograph of, 135
Rogers, Nat D., 109
Rogers, Ted V.: photograph of, 279
Rogers, Mrs. Will, 133
Rogers, Will, 43, 208; photograph of, 269
Rollins, A. P., 90–91
Roosevelt, Eleanor, 246–47; photograph of, 204
Roosevelt, Elliot, 260, 265
Roosevelt, Franklin D., 29–30, 79, 106, 146, 152, 158, 202, 265; at centennial exposition, 128, 246–47; photographs of, 202, 204
Roper, Daniel C., 159, 168, 231–32; photograph of, 192
Rose, Billy, 210, 290; background of, 213; and Fort Worth exposition, 211, 212, 215–18, 221–23, 252, 261; photograph of, 267
Rosenfield, John, 250, 264
Ross, Robert, 93

The Year America Discovered Texas: Centennial '36 was composed into type on a Compugraphic phototypesetter in ten and one-half point Caledonia with two and one-half points of spacing between the lines. Caledonia and Playboy in-line were selected for display. The book was designed by Jim Billingsley, composed by Metricomp, Inc., printed offset by Thomson-Shore, Inc., and bound by John H. Dekker & Sons. The paper on which this book is printed bears acid-free characteristics, for an effective life of at least three hundred years.

TEXAS A&M UNIVERSITY PRESS : COLLEGE STATION